RED HOUSE

RED HOUSE

Being a Mostly Accurate Account
of New England's Oldest
Continuously Lived-In House

Sarah Messer

VIKING

VIKING
Published by the Penguin Group
Penguin Group (USA) Inc., 375 Hudson Street, New York, New York 10014, U.S.A.
Penguin Books Ltd, 80 Strand, London WC2R 0RL, England
Penguin Books Australia Ltd, 250 Camberwell Road, Camberwell, Victoria 3124,
Australia
Penguin Books Canada Ltd, 10 Alcorn Avenue, Toronto, Ontario, Canada M4V 3B2
Penguin Books India (P) Ltd, 11 Community Centre, Panchsheel Park,
New Delhi–110 017, India
Penguin Group (NZ), Cnr Airborne and Rosedale Roads, Albany, Auckland 1310,
New Zealand
Penguin Books (South Africa) (Pty) Ltd, 24 Sturdee Avenue, Rosebank,
Johannesburg 2196, South Africa

Penguin Books Ltd, Registered Offices: 80 Strand, London WC2R 0RL, England

First published in 2004 by Viking Penguin, a member of Penguin Group (USA) Inc.

1   3   5   7   9   10   8   6   4   2

Acknowledgments for permission to reprint copyrighted texts
appear on pages 361–375.
Illustration credits appear on pages 389–390.

LIBRARY OF CONGRESS CATALOGING IN PUBLICATION DATA
Messer, Sarah
    Red House : being a mostly accurate account of New England's oldest
continuously lived-in house / Sarah Messer.
        p.   cm.
    ISBN 0-670-03315-4
    1. Red House (Marshfield, Mass.). 2. Hatch family. 3. Marshfield (Mass. :
Town)—Biography. 4. Marshfield (Mass. : Town)—Buildings, structures, etc.
I. Title.

F74.M4M47 2004
974.4'82—dc22   2003065780

This book is printed on acid-free paper. ∞

Printed in the United States of America • Designed by Nancy Resnick

For my parents—who made everything possible
and
in memory of Richard Warren Hatch,
who gave us the story

Old houses that have sheltered a family for 300 years are forever invisibly inhabited by jealous ghosts, and it is absolutely essential for any dweller therein to get them on his side.

—Richard Warren Hatch, 1966

This earthly house must be dissolved, that is the bodyes of gods children, that theire soules now dwell as in a house, an earthly house the body is. . . .

—Increase Mather, 1687

Of those so close beside me, which are you?

—Theodore Roethke

Contents

CONTENTS

PART ONE

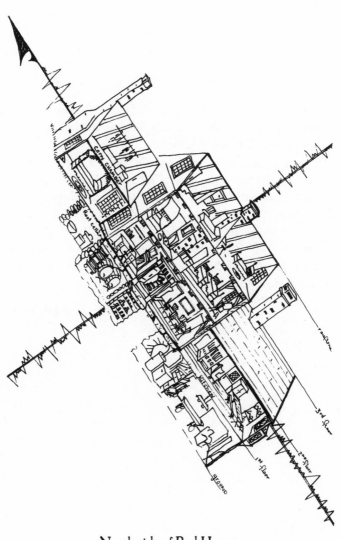

North side of Red House

HATCH: *To keep silence. A hatch before the door.* HATCH *(nautical) A moveable planking forming a kind of deck in ships. Under Hatches = below deck. Over Hatches = overboard. A square or oblong opening in the deck by which cargo is lowered into the hold. Under the Hatches : Down in position or circumstances; in a state of depression, humiliation, subjection or restraint; down out of sight.* HATCH: *A wooden bed frame. A hatchet. A knot. To incubate. To brood.* HATCH: *The action of hatching, incubation; that which is hatched, a brood of young.* HATCH: *To engrave or draw a series of lines, usually parallel.*

—Partial definition, *Oxford English Dictionary*

One

Red House, circa 1900

Before the highway, the oil slick, the outflow pipe; before the blizzard, the sea monster, the Girl Scout camp; before the nudist colony and flower farm; before the tidal wave broke the river's mouth, salting the cedar forest; before the ironworks, tack factory, and shoe-peg mill; before the landing where skinny-dipping white boys jumped through berry bushes; before hayfield, ferry, oyster bed; before Daniel Webster's horses stood buried in their graves; before militiamen's talk of separating; before Unitarians and Quakers, the shipyards and mills, the nineteen barns burned in the Indian raid—even then the Hatches had already built the Red House.

The surname Hatch most commonly means a half-door, or gate, an entrance to a village or manor house. It describes a person who stands by the gate; a person newly born; a person who waits.

My father could not wait. He had made an appointment with a real-estate agent, but when he found himself on a house call in Marshfield, Massachusetts, he decided to see the Red House himself. It was August 1965, and he was a thirty-three-year-old Harvard Medical School graduate with a crew cut and bow tie, married to my mother for just four months. Done with his residency and his army service, he had begun to specialize in radiology—broken bones, mammograms, GI series. The practice of seeing through people. With all the self-consciousness of a latter-day Gatsby, he would eventually raise a herd of kids patchworked together as "New Englanders"—four from his first marriage, four with my mother. But for now he was moonlighting for extra cash and driving his sky-blue VW Beetle down dirt roads, into brambles and dead-ends.

Marshfield, then as now, is a coastal community thirty miles south of Boston, 225 miles north of New York City, whose famous residents over the years have included "The Great Compromiser" Daniel Webster, some Kennedy offspring, and Steve Tyler of Aerosmith. Driving through the north part of town, my father passed seventeenth- and eighteenth-century houses, two ponds where mills had been. The afternoon light lay drowsy, the air motoring with insects. He knew he was getting close to something, and his stomach clenched. He had always loved ancient rooflines and stone walls, half-collapsed barns—templates of what had come before—plain churches, fields rolling down to rivers, shipyards. Yet, within this two-mile stretch, modern houses and gas stations had grown up around their remains like flesh over bone. He was following his intuition, as if, eyes closed in a dream, he felt his way with his hands stretched out. The road began a violent S-curve at the edge of a string of ponds. At the blind part of the curve, my father found the road to the house, and turned there to begin the half-mile drive past yet another pond.

He drove by the dilapidated Hatch Mill, over the narrow bridge, then through a canopy of crab-apple trees, over a stream that ran beneath the road. It was the last few weeks of summer, and the timothy was high at the roadside, the milkweed setting off parachute seeds.

Meanwhile, in the adjacent town of Norwell, in the apartment he was renting, my mother was preparing his four children for a bath. They were: Kim, seven; Kerry, five; Kate, four; and Patrick, three. The children were spending the summer away from their mother in California. They had been to Martha's Vineyard, Benson's Wild Animal Farm; they had spent the day riding bicycles on the blacktop driveway.

Lately a raccoon had been banging the lids of the garbage cans below the second-floor bathroom window each night. "That raccoon with his black mask, that thief," they'd say. My mother was relieved: animal stories were common ground. She said, "It's getting dark; do you think the raccoon is out there?" She squeezed Johnson's baby shampoo into one hand, and then turned the water off. The children shrieked, "Raccoon! Raccoon!" Pale-skinned kids with tan lines: Kim, tall, broad-cheekboned; Kerry and Patrick, a girl-and-boy matched pair with the same androgynous haircut; Kate, a tantrum-throwing tow-head.

My mother, twenty-seven years old and petite, wore her hair long, usually in braids or in a large bun with a thin path of gray twisting through it like a skunk stripe. That day she wore it in a ratty ponytail, having had no time to brush it. Her only cosmetics: an occasional eyebrow-penciling, and lipstick in the evening if she was going out.

It had been almost four years since my mother, a lab technician, had met my father at the cafeteria in Children's Hospital in Boston. As she stood in line, she saw him leave his dirty plate and tray, linger, exit the cafeteria, and then return to the line. He was wearing his signature bow tie. He approached her and asked her to have lunch with him.

"You already ate," she said.

"I'll eat again," he replied.

From the beginning, my father had mentioned his divorce

and his custody of the children for school vacations and three months every summer. Early in the relationship, my father had brought my mother and the children to Cape Cod, where she had her own room in the rented cabin. Nearly every night, Kim had sanded and short-sheeted the bed, leaving seaweed and crabs under the blankets. Besides these incidents, though, the children gave her little indication that she was unwanted. Summer was over, and the next day they were returning to California. The bathtub was by the window, and when they stood at the edge, the children could look down on the dented lids of the three garbage cans. My father had said that the house call would take only an hour at most. Now it was getting late, and my mother had no idea where he was.

He rounded the corner at a large white house, turning sharply to the right at a vine-covered lamppost. He drove through two large stones that made a gate. Then, suddenly, the house was before him, rambling to his left along the crest of a ridge. Below, to his right, a yard fell away into a field of ragweed, bullfrogs.

In architectural terms, the house my father saw would be described as a five-bay, double-pile, center-chimney colonial. It had post-and-beam vertical-board construction, a granite foundation, and small-paned windows. The windows were trimmed with chipped white paint, the body of the house was a deep red—Delicious Apple Red, Long Stem Rose Red, Evening Lip-Stick Red, Miss Scarlett Red, a red that neared maroon. Otherwise, the house was plain and, with its the chimney in the middle of the roof against a backdrop of sky, appeared as simple as a child's drawing of a house: big square and triangle, smaller square on top. The cornice seemed the only detail out of place: attached to the doorway as if to elevate the exterior from utilitarian farmhouse to Victorian estate, it hinted at Greek or Roman Revival, something lofty—like a hood ornament on a Dodge Dart.

The house was large and debauched. Four bushes grown shaggy with tendrils sat beneath the first-floor windows. Lilac trees tangled the farthest ell. The driveway wound around the house to the right, where it climbed a small hill. In the backyard, a man and woman sat in lawn chairs drinking old-fashioneds. It was 5 p.m.

My father, stepping out of the rusted VW, might have appeared to Richard Warren Hatch and his wife, Ruth, to be an affable character—friendly and perhaps a bit too unassuming, with a boyish way of loping when he walked. My father was raised in Polo, Illinois, a small farming town known only for its proximity to Dixon, the birthplace of Ronald Reagan. He was six foot two, with dark hair and bright-blue eyes, size-thirteen feet, crooked teeth, prominent ears, and a nose that had been broken seven times playing football. He was the son of a cattle-feed salesman and a grocery-store clerk. In 1948, he was the captain of his high school's undefeated and untied state-champion football team—a 188-pound fullback once described as a "ripping, slashing ball carrier capable of chewing an opponent's line to shreds." He was from a one-street, one-chicken-fried-steak-restaurant, one-road-leading-out-into-cornfields, one-stand-of-trees, one-historical-marker-from-the-Indian-war, one-railroad-track town. A town with a history of drive-by prairie schooners. More than anything, he had wanted to get out, and probably even now, sixteen years later, he still wore that desire in the face he presented to the unknown, to strangers. Few of my father's ancestors had ever owned anything; his parents still rented the house they'd lived in for twenty years. Harvard had taught him to love tradition and antiquity, and my father was impatient for a life he had only caught glimpses of in the educated accents of professors and the boiled-wool sweaters of his college roommates' parents. He was looking for a piece of history different from the one his own heritage had provided him. He was looking for just this type of New England home.

The older couple did not get up to greet my father when he closed the car door. But they did smile. So he walked up the yard toward the house and their arrangement of chairs. "I've got an appointment to see the house on Monday," he said. It was now Saturday. "Oh yes," Richard Warren Hatch said, "we've heard about you."

———————

Inside, the house was low-ceilinged and dark. Hatch led my father through the honeycomb of rooms, past walls with buckled plaster and wide-paneled boards. Doors slanted in their frames, wind blew out the mouths of small fireplaces. Candleholders extended from mantels like robot arms. Rooms opened into more rooms of boxed and hand-hewn beams. A staircase on the north side of the house unfolded itself like a tight, narrow fan, disappearing to the second floor. The house smelled old, the product of its accumulated history—books and talcum powder, wood, silver polish.

Hatch showed my father old photos in which the paint peeled off the house in ribbons, the sides clapboarded and bowed, the trim gone gray. Hatch had hardly led my father through the inside of the house and already he was revealing its history—the way a parent might present to guests his child's baby pictures, framed drawings, and graduation photos arranged along a hallway before introducing the actual child. The photos depicted several driveways ringed with post, fences long gone, absent gates—the house standing starkly in a nude landscape. They showed a house often in disrepair: sagging roofline, loose shingles. In one photo, a barn loomed larger than the house, extending at a right angle toward the pond. The house and the barn together formed an elongated ell. Windows stacked three stories up the barn's flat red side. The roofs glowed grayish in the photo, and in the foreground, hoed rows of a garden extended toward the bottom of the frame. One photo, circa 1900, showed three small children standing in front of the house in long white shifts that glowed like filament against the dark clapboards.

What the photos did not show, of course, was the beginning— the narrowness of the first structure, the forest behind it, the river a distant smudge, the piles of stumps and roots torn out of the ground, the parts that could not be used for shipbuilding knees burned in bonfires. The photos did not show the stones dug out of the earth for cellars and walls. How the house exterior was first covered with boards, or the roof thatched with reeds, or the windows crosshatched. The photos did not show the close-string stairway replacing a ladder, or someone standing too far in the kitchen's giant hearth when the pot spilled and a skirt hem caught flame, burning lard pouring out over the floor. The photos caught occasional in-between moments, but they implied more, and my father, prodded by Hatch, began to imagine the lives of ancestors—Puritans, shipbuilders, somber Victorians—the blurred wheels of a chaise along the lane in a time before telephone poles.

Hatch led my father, finally, to the root cellar beneath the house. They walked through the tin-backed door from the boiler room into what Hatch called "the passageway." It was more of a tunnel, really, twenty feet long and curving slightly— the stone walls supported by cement and brick. When he extended his arms to the side, my father could touch both walls in the passageway, the stones damp, sweating. My father was fidgeting, talking too much.

"My parents lived in Chicago," he said. "They never finished high school."

The passageway opened into a large underground room where stood part of a chimney, the carved-out kettle drum of the original cellar behind a stairway of half-log beams that led up to a trapdoor in the ceiling, which was the floor of a closet in a room above them. It was the most primitive part of the house. The room smelled of something sweet and dank. Several potatoes grew eyes in the corner. Wires stapled to the underside of boards of the floor above snarled with webs, the mummified bodies of spiders.

"My father played poker with John Dillinger," my father said. "During the Depression, he had a general store that went under."

"These are very old beams," Hatch said, pointing up. "They're part of the original cellar and structure of the old part of the house."

My father stopped, looked up at the beams.

"My mother, you know, she has a heart condition—rheumatoid, arrhythmia."

Hatch nodded, seemed distracted. He was built like a ladder. A bunch of wiry hair grew out of his eyebrows. Whenever he talked, his voice boomed off stone, as if the volume were turned up too loud in the room. My father found himself nodding; the tone of Hatch's voice was one of antiquarian authority.

My father, a storyteller, thought of narratives he could recycle in the appropriate occasion. "One time . . ." Or "I once knew this crazy guy . . ." But he had learned Hatch was a writer; had been the head of the English department at Deerfield Academy from 1925 to 1941; had served aboard the battleship *New Mexico* and the aircraft carrier *Yorktown* in World War II; had been married with kids and divorced; had since 1951 lectured at the Center for International Studies at MIT, researching and writing about U.S. foreign policy. He had more stories to tell than my father.

Earlier, Hatch had told my father that his great-great-great-great-great-grandfather Walter Hatch had built the house in 1647; that it had always been called the "Red House"; that it was one of the first houses built in this area called Two Mile, which was also casually referred to as "Hatchville" thanks to prolific and intermarrying progeny. As a testament to this, Walter Hatch's framed will, dated 1681 and written in legal English, hung on the living-room wall as it always had, stating that the house should be passed on to "heirs begotten of my body forever from generation to generation to the world's end never to be sold or mortgaged from my children and grandchildren forever." While talking to my father, Hatch had traced the lines of the will with his finger. My father was having difficulty absorbing everything. He gazed at the will, the paper the color of a grocery bag trapped under the glass now streaked with Hatch's fingermarks.

"This house has been in my family for eight generations," Hatch repeated, delivering his most subtle sales pitch. "The Oldest Continuously Lived-In House in New England," he said.

On the cement floor beneath my father's feet, Hatch's two sons had carved their names in cement: "Dick and Toph '41." If the house had been in the family for over three hundred years, my father wondered, why was Hatch going against the weight of tradition and selling it? But he kept his mouth shut, fearing that Hatch would suddenly snap out of it, change his mind.

"I need to talk with my wife," my father said.

———

The distance from the Red House to the apartment my parents were renting was five miles. My father turned off the rattling VW motor and coasted into the driveway. Then he rounded the corner of the house and stood under the second-floor window by the garbage cans. He grabbed the lids and smashed them together. Inside, the children rushed to the window—"raccoon, raccoon!"—bare feet across the floor. Instead they saw their father in tan corduroys and bow tie, a lid in each hand. He saw their faces crowding the panes, their hands on the glass. He entered the apartment through the back door, ran up the stairs to the kitchen, and shouted my mother's nickname: "Scout, Scout!" He insisted she and the kids come see the house, dressed as they were in pajamas and slippers. He said, "This house . . . ," standing there with his elbows at his side, hands clenched before him, as if he were holding ski poles, skiing in place, one foot, then the other slaloming the floorboards. "Come now," was all he could say.

Patrick followed his sisters and stepmother downstairs to the driveway, dragging the worn remnant of a stuffed animal behind him. "You've got to see it," my father said.

Then, suddenly, they were bumping along in the crowded VW. My mother had Patrick on her lap with the hairless toy. "Who is this?" she asked.

"Rabbit," said Patrick.

My mother looked at herself in the tiny square mirror on the sun visor and saw behind her the three girls flopped over each other in the back seat. Patrick dropped the rabbit between her knees, where he saw bits of road through the rusted floor-holes. "Uh . . . nope!" my mother said, as she pinched her knees and caught the toy.

My mother never spoke about herself, and when speaking with others was forthright and blunt, often offending listeners unintentionally with her honesty. This habit was derived from her attempt to lose her "Southernness"—the friendly openness, the drawn-out syllables. She would rather say nothing, or say something sharp, because she really believed her Southernness was a cliché, and it reminded her of her childhood, which she preferred to forget.

All my mother ever said about my grandmother was that she divorced my grandfather in order to marry her second cousin, had a thick Southern accent, smoked two packs of Camel no-filters a day, kept a shot glass of whiskey at her side, and died when my mother was twenty-two.

"We were," as she often put it, "a bunch of Georgia crackers."

RED HOUSE

After her parents' divorce, my mother moved with her mother and stepfather to Allapattah, Florida. She was eight years old and spent most of her time weaving through kumquat hedges behind the apartment building, or sitting in the mulberry tree with a neighbor girl who lived in a house with an old stove tossed in the front yard—no toilet or running water. They would sit all day in the tree, pelting fruit at the stove and getting stains on their hands, until one day my mother got head lice and wasn't allowed to see the girl again. "White trash," her stepfather said, and my mother thought about the stove they had just thrown in their yard, which was white enamel. *White trash.* Yet, the next year, they moved to a housing project in North Miami where all the buildings were one-story cinder block built on coral rock and barbed grass. Behind the development, through a thin strand of trees, sat a working slaughterhouse on the edge of a rust-brown river. Bits of hoof and bone chips had been carried off by dogs, scattered on the banks. Her only brother dared her to swing across the "river of blood," as he called it, holding a rope swing tied to a tree. She watched a series of her brother's friends swing out and over to the other side. Then she did and missed, fell up to her knees in slime and viscera, had to bury her stained tennis sneakers in the woods so her mother would not know.

By sixteen, my mother had developed the habit of hanging out with bikers. When her father saw her wearing pink leather pants, she was immediately sent to a girls' school in Virginia, where she learned the correct posture for walking downstairs in pumps, how to get out of a car while wearing a skirt. She graduated from high school, went to junior college, then transferred at nineteen to an elite private college in Vermont.

When she arrived at the college, she possessed seven pairs of elbow-length gloves dyed in pastel colors to match her collection of semiformal dresses, but no one had ever told her about snow. Sometime in late October 1957, seeing snow fall for the first time, she rushed out of the dormitory wearing canvas tennis sneakers, no socks. After a forty-five-minute snowball fight, she was taken to the clinic and diagnosed with frostbite.

She compensated for this naïveté with toughness and non-plussed Southern denial—"I'll just put that out of my mind," she'd say, as if determining, since leaving the South, that nothing was going to bother her anymore. The result was very Yankee-tomboy. She was always Pat—never Patricia, or Patty, or Patsy—and eventually she rejected that for Scout. As in: hunter/tracker; the girl in *To Kill a Mockingbird*, a book my father happened to be reading the day he asked her out. In photos taken before they were married, she sported a boy's haircut and held a rifle at her side. A series of photos shows her taking aim and knocking off rounds of clay pigeons.

Now, three years later, her arm out the window of the Volkswagen, she traced the landscape on the way to the house. Absentmindedly, she aimed. They were passing fields of tall grass, square colonial houses, stone walls. The sky was growing gray; her eye caught the spark of a firefly at the roadside.

"The kids are falling asleep," she said, pulling her arm back in.

———

They arrived at the Red House to find the Hatches exactly where my father had first seen them: sitting in chairs on the lawn, halfway through their drinks, eating cheese and crackers. My mother stood with her hands on someone's small shoulders, introducing herself and the children.

In the yard behind them, two apple trees stretched their umbrellas over a carpet of wormy green-apple windfalls. The children were told to stand by the apple trees. My father and mother disappeared into the house with Mr. Hatch. The kids made little piles of apples. Ruth Hatch stood nearby, clasping her hands, her soft white hair swept up.

Richard Warren Hatch brought my parents through the east

ell to a modern kitchen, and then into the older portion of the house. Stepping over the threshold, my mother noticed crooked doorways and floors. A half-model of a ship pushed out of the fireplace mantel.

When he would talk about that day, my father always said, "You could tell that they really liked us. And we really liked them. I think the fact that he had been married before and then was divorced . . . I think he looked at us with the knowledge that I had been married before, and he was very open-minded."

"We moved all the time when I was a child," my mother heard herself say aloud, though in reality she only had moved three times. Yet this house seemed permanent. On the north side, a stairwell rose, nine curved steps, to the second floor with its bedrooms. She was in the attic, and then, just as suddenly, she was down a staircase and back in the living room, where windows stared out into the backyard. To her back was the dining room, where she had entered; to her left, a desk scattered with papers and several unplugged lamps.

Outside the house the children were silent, wandering between the apple trees and stepping barefoot over mashed apples. Patrick stuck his arm into a hole in the tree and pulled it back out. The air carried the smell of marsh; they walked to the edge of the meadow, looking for ferns.

My mother and father left the house and crossed the lawn, where they talked behind a bush.

"What do you think?" he whispered. "Do you want to buy it?" He grabbed her arm, brought his face close to hers. My mother kept glancing at the children.

Hatch asked Kim to go with them—him and my father—for a walk down into the woods.

"I'll show you the clearing," he said, "and the Indian burial ground."

Kim walked between them past a meadow and into the pines, the carpet of needles. They walked along a stone wall. Hatch described the salt hay that had stretched down to the river and the "rabbit runs": mounds of earth piled up for bridges across marshes, and used for the shipbuilding trade.

"Those rabbits like high ground," Hatch said, looking at Kim and winking. Kim imagined legions of rabbits building small rabbit-ships.

They traveled down a hill, where the road curved and the wall broke open, and found another gate. They walked through trees and into a large clearing. Here clumps of soft grass and moss grew around fieldstones and overturned granite posts.

"This is an Indian burial ground," Hatch said. "Go and play." He was talking to my father in serious tones, occasionally looking toward Kim and shouting, "You might find an arrowhead! Go ahead and look." Kim walked on top of a few of the sidelined slabs of granite. She dug her hand down into a clump of grass, where she felt roots, a rock.

The rock was pink with white veins running through it like pork fat. "You mean like this one?" she asked, holding it up in her hand. Upside down, it could have been a heart. They were talking about the house, she realized, about money. "I found an arrowhead!"

"Well, I'll be darned," said Hatch. "Nobody has found an arrowhead down here for twenty years."

My mother wished that she could brush her hair. She excused herself from Ruth and went into the bathroom off the kitchen. There she found a blue plastic comb on the sink, picked it up, put it back down. It was getting dark outside, all the light seeping out. She took the elastic band out of her hair, ran her fingers through it, and put the elastic back in.

Outside, she heard Hatch's deep voice. He was telling Ruth and the children about Kim's arrowhead. Kim held out her palm to them but did not let anyone touch it. It was night now; the bats were out, swooping as if pulled by strings. My father was at my mother's side again, asking her the same question about the house: "Should we get it?"

That summer, they had been discussing moving to Berkeley, California, to be closer to his children. In fact, they had been sure of it. My father had already accepted a position at a San Francisco hospital, and was scheduled to begin in October. Now, in one night, in a few hours of walking through a house, he was changing his mind. She looked at him, studying his face. She knew he was impulsive, but he'd never done anything like this before.

"Decide where you want to live," she said. There were houses, she knew, that you bought simply to inhabit—apartments or houses like those she had grown up in—nothing special. And then there were houses that could change your life: the rooms, the walls, the roof, the land, and view from its windows could reshape you, mold you. This house was older than most of New England; it wasn't the kind of house you just bought and sold. If they bought this house, my mother was certain they'd have to live in it for the rest of their lives.

Across the lawn she saw the glow of the children's pajamas against the dark shape of trees and the roofline.

"It's your decision," she said, finally.

"This is where I want to live," he answered.

The Land
1614–1647

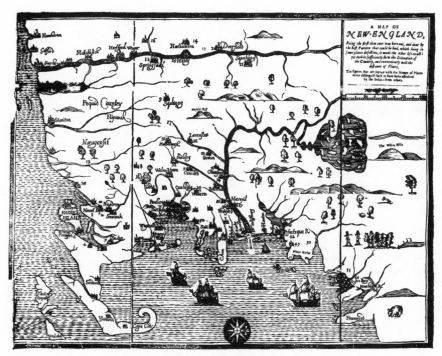

New England, 1677

Seip *or* **sepu:** *The Algonquin word for "river," derived from a root that means "stretched out," "extended," or "became long."*

Peske-tuk: *The division of a river by some obstacle, near its mouth, which makes it a "double river," or a "split river" divided forcibly or abruptly.*

—J. Hammond Trumbull, "Algonquin Indians—Place Names," collection of Connecticut Historical Society, vol. 2, p. 7

In the early seventeenth century, the North River zagged through the New England landscape the way lightning appeared in the night sky. Fed by more than forty kettle ponds and lakes, the river split itself between fresh and salt water. The fresh water upstream curved its way through glacial deposits and granite; the salt water downstream, with its rise and fall of tide, entered and left the mouth every six hours. The river reflected a sky flocked with swans and folded itself until it split in an area called "the crotch" at Indian Head and Herring Brook. From there, each deep channel and switchback would later be called a "no-gain" by the English settlers, a bend that doubles back on itself like a trick or a sleight-of-hand. In the inlet, the North River joined its twin, the South River. The two rivers would stay locked this way until, centuries later, a violent storm would pull their mouths apart.

One of the earliest recordings of interaction between the European and Algonquin people was written in 1614 by Captain John Smith, who, along with a small party of men, was exploring an inlet in the northeasternmost tip of what would later become Plymouth Colony. From some distance, Smith observed three men in an open canoe moving quickly across the water toward an outcropping of rocks. The inlet was a wide skirt of water fanning from the ocean over marshland and into the North River. At the time, the Algonquin Nation stretched down the entire East Coast, including Manhattan and the Hudson River Valley, a confederacy of tribes. Governor Bradford and his band of Pilgrims, searching for their own promised land farther south, in the curved arm of Cape Cod, would not arrive until ten years later.

In the inlet, the men who disappeared behind the outcropping of rock shot arrows at Captain Smith. Smith and his party responded with gunfire, killing one man and shooting another in the thigh. So this was one beginning: no sharing of corn and blankets, just a whiz of arrow shafts and gunpowder, an anonymous volley across water that ended in balls of lead pushing through flesh. And then Smith pushed his pen, a carved goose-feather, across paper made of torn rags. He took this back to England with him as some sort of record or discovery. He dragged ink across the paper landscape the same way that land grants were drawn up only twenty years later, and the inlet, the river, and the lands surrounding them became the property of the English.

The inlet would eventually become the town of Scituate, Plymouth Colony's largest port, and the rocky outcropping would sport a lighthouse and later a mansion called the Glades, the summer retreat house of U.S. presidents John and John Quincy Adams.

But in 1614, this inlet had not yet appeared on any English map. Scituate, which takes its name from the Algonquin word for "cold brook," was the second settlement established within the Plymouth Colony patent, after Plymouth itself.

When the English returned to New England in 1623, they discovered that smallpox, introduced by European fishermen, had destroyed more than 90 percent of the native population. William Bradford and scouts from the *Mayflower* found abandoned fields, unused storehouses of corn and grain buried in shallow hills. The cultivated lands and the villages were empty or filled with dead, and those who survived were too weak to fight. It was as if the English walked right into an abandoned house—filled with furniture and stores of food—finding the owners gone.

———

When William Wood published *New England's Prospect* in London in 1634, he included Scituate as a jagged outline running along the ocean, made up of four cliffs: First, Second, Third, and Fourth. The cliffs rose from the beach—steep and stacked behind each other like cards. Barren, slapped by wind and rain, they were void of fresh running water. The land along the North River was deeded to Scituate Planters in a grant called Two Mile, two miles long and one mile wide—a direct response to the complaint that the land in the town was "too narrow and straight" to farm.

The Two Mile settlers used the river, not the highways, for transportation and trade, and generally did what they wanted. The grant, though only three square miles, included "all woods, trees & rocks ponds rivers swamps meadows," and the settlers quickly used all of them, flushing the swamps of wolves, enforcing various animal taxes, felling the giant trees. Isolated and unpoliced by either Plymouth or Boston, they were fiercely autonomous river-people who continually split their churches, argued over baptism rites and land boundaries, built houses, and set about defending them against natives, other immigrants, and natural and supernatural disasters.

Walter Hatch was born in Kent, England, in 1623, two years after the Pilgrims celebrated the first Thanksgiving in Plymouth. In 1634, he immigrated to Scituate with his father, William Hatch, his mother, and five siblings on a ship called the *Hercules*. William Hatch was a wealthy wool merchant, descendant of a line of farmers hailing from County Kent (the village of

Selling), where they named their land parcels Horselife, Pierce Gardyn, Stone Regg, and Sandpytts. By the time William left with his family for America, he was tired of squabbling over tiny patches of English soil, arguing about the corrupt church, the shifting ideas of the soul, good deeds versus grace.

When the Hatch family arrived, Scituate wasn't much better—just a narrow row of house lots bordering large cleared areas of land called "the commons." By 1642, approximately twenty-four thousand people had settled in New England. Puritans, with an already high sense of the symbolic, were living, worshipping, and drinking in a new and wild landscape. Householders were required to bring six blackbird heads into the town hall each season as a tax. Eels were dug out of the riverbanks, skinned, and thrown in stews or pottages. The air smelled like gunpowder and roasting meat. Eventually, a woman in Scituate accused her neighbor of turning into a bear; a brother and sister were caught embracing in the same bed; in Plymouth there was an unfortunate incident involving a young man and a pony. Walter's brother-in-law died from burns he received when, during a routine check of his artillery, the powder house exploded in a giant fireball. At sixteen, Walter was old enough to bear arms and become a freeman with voting power; at twenty-four in 1647, he bought some land in Two Mile, separated from the main town by the river, salt-hay fields, and forest. Compared with Kent, England, or even Scituate proper, it was an outpost of an outpost.

———•———

In order to define what was his, Walter walked the land and carved his initials into the trunks of trees. Starting at the southeast corner of the lot, near the marsh and the old cartway, he walked 160 paces to a tree where he cut a mark with his knife. Then he moved west sixty rods to a heap of stones—walking, swinging his arms around white oak, pine. Turning to the northeast and the first marked tree, Walter created a circle around ten acres of swamp and swampy meadow. Boundaries were set at the cartway, the heap of rocks, and his marked trees carved with the letters "W.H." and three notched lines.

Walter had purchased the land from Thomas and Elizabeth Ensign, who had purchased it years earlier from Timothy Hatherly, a partner in a large land deal called the Conihasset Grant established with native leader Josiah Wampatuck. The grant—containing vast tracts of land in six separate townships—ended with the inscription:

This is the marke of
X
Josiah Wampatucke

The "X" represented ownership, relinquishment. Josiah Wampatuck was the son and heir of Sachem (or Chief) Chickotaubutt, a name the settlers translated to mean "House-on-fire." Walter Hatch would build a house on this land that would embody the meaning of that name, and be inherited by Hatches for more than three hundred years. But before the house, there was the idea of the house. Perhaps it had been in Walter's mind for years—in his passage from England, smelling a month of salt water and ship, and then, slowly, something more solid, leafy, the inkling of a horizon. Now Walter was the stranger who walked into Two Mile, the way the idea of the house had walked into his mind, into his crowded forest of thoughts. As he walked, perhaps he placed his hands on the trunks of trees as he moved among them, as if they were the waists of dancers in a reel. Circling the trees, perhaps he realized that he owned them now—the native sachem, the earlier settlers had relinquished, and he had stepped in. Their loss was his gain, and so it had begun—swinging his arms around the trunks of trees, his future walls and roof.

Two

"Scout" Messer with her gun

When my parents next returned to the Red House, Richard Warren Hatch gave them a pair of yellowed whale's teeth. It had been three days since my father had walked up to the Hatches and said, "OK, we'll take it," and Richard Warren had stuck out his hand, grinning. They had invited my parents over for old-fashioneds—in Hatch's words, to "talk things over, to get to know one another."

My parents had been back in the Red House just two minutes when Hatch handed over the teeth—five inches long and decorated with faint scrimshaw. He said that they had been given by a returning whaleman to one of his ancestors. Each tooth had a figure carved on its front and back—four in total, one man and three women.

The carving looked faint, as if penciled or simply scratched. My father tilted a tooth in the light to see the rendering clearly. The portrait certainly looked like a sailor: a bearded man leaning against a stool and holding a telescope, his body a thin outline. The other side depicted a woman in profile sitting on a bucket. The second tooth showed a barefoot woman nursing a baby, and another dressed for travel with a hat and fan. Richard Warren said that he had found the teeth under a board in the attic, the same place he had discovered many of the family documents. The teeth felt heavy and smooth; they fit in my father's palm like the butt of a pistol. "At least a hundred years old." Hatch nodded.

That evening, my parents returned to the apartment and sat on the only good piece of furniture they owned—a large four-poster bed. They talked it out. Thirty-five acres and an old house. When my father talked, he looked at his hands, which were heavy and square. They needed twelve thousand dollars for a down payment. My father's children were spending the school year in California with their mother. They had been giddy, chatty on the way to the airport, asking, "Did you buy it? Are we going to live here now?" They had fought over the arrowhead in the back seat. Now, my mother sat on the bed with her feet tucked beneath her, pushing her hair behind her ears, a nervous habit. She said that her father might be able to cosign a note, as she held a pad of paper in her lap and touched the end of a pencil occasionally to her lips.

My father's name, Messer, means "knife"; my mother's, Watrouse, means "water house." Together they were a blade sliding through water, a knife tossed in a lake, sinking fast, or a jackknife found in an outhouse. Or maybe they were a way to get things done quickly, cutting through the waste or bullshit of a moment. But with the Red House, it certainly didn't feel that way. When asked by friends why he wasn't moving to California to be near his children, my father shifted agency—"The house made the decision for us," he would say. Although relatives had come through with money in the first few weeks, it wasn't enough. The closing date was set for October, and as it grew closer, my parents' finances grew tighter, my father's stories about the house more overblown: "Scout and I looked at her, fell in love, and decided to get married. We're marrying the house," he'd joke. "It was love at first sight."

Meanwhile, the cocktails with the Hatches became a nightly ritual. The drinks outside on the lawn moved inside with the colder weather, then turned into dinner, and soon my mother and Ruth were cooking together while my father and Richard Warren built fires in the fireplaces and hauled various pieces of furniture in and out. Ruth was what my mother called "artsy." Sometimes after dinner she would take my mother up into her "studio," one of the bedrooms on the second floor of the Red House. The room was scattered with oil paints and brushes. Ruth practiced tole—elaborate painting on tin trays popular in the late nineteenth century. She gave my mother copies of her patterns and some extra brushes, encouraging her to paint. "A good hobby," Ruth said, "for people who are living at least a hundred years in the past."

After dinner, the four of them would sit on the camel-backed couch in the living room in front of the fire. Most of their conversations fixated on the Red House of Richard Warren's youth, when his grandfather Israel H. still lived there with no electricity or plumbing. Hatch also talked of the restoration he did in the late 1930s. After his father and grandfather died, the house was finally his. But for years, when he was raising his own family, Richard Warren could only spend summers and long weekends at the Old Farm, as he called it.

My parents had their own histories to tell, but they didn't divulge much. My mother talked of Georgia and Florida—the kumquat hedges, the slaughterhouse river, spinning in circles on the lawn while her mother, leaning on the porch rail in a red kerchief, played the same Dominos 45 over and over again and smoked. My father talked about Chicago—how his father drove a lettuce truck and his mother worked in a German deli; how they lived in a one-room flat where my grandfather would host John Dillinger and his poker games; how my grandfather, too poor to own a gun, always left the laces of one shoe untied so he could slip it off quickly and throw it at someone. "Wham, like that," my father pantomimed, imitating my grandfather's shoe-fling.

"Charming," Hatch would say. "Simply charming." And he seemed to believe this.

———————

My parents moved into the Red House at the end of October—miraculously, the money had come through. The last two thousand of it came through the auspices of Mrs. Berini, Italian immigrant and owner of Berini's Meats in Cambridge, who, when told about the house by my father, her favorite customer, replied, "So you still need two thousand? So you really love this house?" And then she reached under the counter and pulled out a crumpled paper bag, counted out two thousand in twenties right there, a line of customers looking on. "Just invite me down sometime," she said, "and pay me back when you can, no interest." Now the key, less than twenty-four hours old in my father's hand, turned the lock at the back door of the kitchen ell. My parents were giggling, walking across the kitchen linoleum, feeling the echo of absence—Ruth and Richard Warren were gone. The empty walls and rooms were quiet except for the hum and tick of appliances. It seemed that the Hatches should still be there, that at any minute Richard or Ruth would float down the stairs and greet them, confused that their belongings were gone. My parents walked down the narrow hallway past clusters of boxes, then lifted the latch that let them into the old part of the house, which felt even more empty, as if the walls were made of paper. Gone were Ruth's curtains with the pompom fringe; gone were Richard's framed prints of schooners and carved decoys. In the living room, my parents' brown secondhand couch slumped across from Hatches' dignified camel-back in a furniture face-off, the scattered boxes like witnesses circling the beginning of a street fight.

But the house didn't feel lonely, my mother said, describing that first night they walked through the hallways and parlors. Not threatening either, as they climbed the staircase to the second floor. Their four-poster still dismantled, they spent the night in the one old Hatch bed left behind. Nothing else save the camel-back remained—the walls, floors, and fireplaces swept clean. They set the whale's teeth upright on the empty mantel like sturdy, unlit candles.

———

That first winter, when my father was working late, my mother sat alone by the kitchen fireplace balancing a cup of tea on her pregnant belly. One night she heard, in a distant room upstairs, the crying of a baby—a soft wail that disappeared whenever she began to climb the stairs. She thought it was the wind, the house creaking. But the noise sounded like a baby, fussy, as if it had just been woken up. Another evening, the teacup balanced, she heard the crying again. But before she could get up to search for the sound, the teacup was punted across the room. She stared at the overturned cup five feet away—a plain china cup, now with a broken handle, a small string of tea across the wooden floor as if it had crawled from the ocean. She held her hands before her, still holding the space of the cup, feeling how the cup had suddenly been pulled from her, its broken handle a parenthesis, a small letter "c."

"A baby ghost," Richard Warren Hatch said when she called him to ask because she just couldn't stop thinking about it. "Lots of children have been born and died in the house," he said. "It has something to cry about." One day a woman from the *Boston Globe* called—while preparing an article on old homes and ghosts, she had received my mother's name from someone on the planning board and heard of their recent purchase of the old Hatch place. Had my mother seen any ghosts? "I think there is a ghost of a baby in this house," my mother said. But could she prove it? the newspaper woman wanted to know.

The sound only came to my mother when she was alone. She said she didn't believe in ghosts. Trying out Yankee domesticity, she would concern herself with the recipe for crown roast of pork, the correct pigment for colonial wall paint. But a few years later, during a blizzard, she would be seen out in the snow shooting rats as they ran toward the house for shelter. She would lie awake all night with her gun by the bed, having found rat droppings under the crib of her new baby. What did she know about being domestic? She whose most vivid memory, besides that of the slaughterhouse, was of spinning on the coral rocks in back of the North Miami housing development while the drunk neighbor kicked his wife down the stairs into the backyard. Years later, when a neighbor's Great Dane wandered into the Red House yard and ripped the throat out of a poodle sitting a foot away from her children, my mother would pick up the telephone, warn the neighbor, and then shoot rock salt up the Great Dane's ass. But in the beginning, alone and pregnant in the house, she felt defenseless. She was swinging out over the slaughterhouse river, missing the bank. She had left part of herself there in Florida, with her shoes in woods. She imagined the white rubber soles of her tennis sneakers glowing underground. She wondered if they were still there—how long something could stay buried before it became something else, became dirt, disappeared. At the Red House she would hear the baby upstairs, crying from a bedroom, twice a week for six months. She knew that someone somewhere was unhappy—she just didn't know who, or where, or in what century. She would start up the stairs and the crying would stop. She would walk outside and it would be dead calm.

One evening in early spring, Richard Warren Hatch Jr. appeared on the lawn. He was a tall man with dark eyes and thick eyebrows like his father. He stood on the north side, staring up at the house his father had just sold out of the family. My parents had met him before, informally, at a dinner the month when they had visited the Hatches at the Red House. "What does he want?" my mother was asking; she was seven months pregnant and trying to struggle out of a chair.

Even though they had only been in the house six months, my parents had heard many stories from neighbors and people in town. Richard Jr. was an artist, an inventor—some said genius, some said eccentric, some said an eccentric genius and meant it as a compliment. He was the son who was supposed to own the house, but something had happened and Richard Warren Hatch Sr. sold the house to our father instead—this was one rumor. In another version, Richard Sr. offered to sell the house to his son, but, being an inventor, Richard Jr. couldn't afford it.

Richard Jr. knocked on the front door, the one my parents never used anymore. They unbolted the door and stood in its outline, an early-spring evening shining past the man who stood outside. He said he had the money now, had sold some of his inventions which were 0's and 1's arranged in specific orders, the earliest versions of computer code. But at the time few people had even heard the word "computer." Certainly not my parents.

Richard Jr. said something about his father's being temperamental. He said that the town of Marshfield had tried to raise money to help keep the house in the family. It apparently wasn't supposed to leave the family, so here was Richard Jr. determined to rectify the situation.

"I'm sorry," my father said, "but you can't buy the house back. We live here now."

Over the years my mother would tell this story and change

the details—that Richard Jr. was alone; that his wife was with him; that the wife had taught her how to cook crown roast of pork; that they were all friends. But why have we never met them? we would ask. They existed only in her words. She would tell the story sitting at our bedside, before sleep. It was, in a strange sense, a story about being born—my parents to the house, me and Suzy to the world. We, as yet unborn but listening, behind the wall of our mother as she struggled out of the chair and stood in the doorway, putting her hand to the small of her back. Told this way—so watery, so close to the edge of sleep—Richard Jr. became a ghost. The ghost at my bedside, the ghost who once stood on the lawn, waiting like a midwife. For years I would look out my window for him and see only cold moonlight—this man from the story, the person who brought us here. Years later, when asked about it, my father would say, "Don't be silly, that never happened."

Yet all the versions of the story had one element in common: *it was a mistake*—we weren't supposed to have the house. This is what my older sisters and brother were told, and what they would pass on to me, and what I would pass on to my younger sisters, the same way we would tell and retell ghost stories, urban legends—the one about the dog in the suitcase, the story of the campers and the serial killer, the lady with a velvet string around her neck, the story of the Hatch who tried to get the house back. *He stood on our lawn and said, "There has been a terrible mistake." Like some sort of omen. Then he left.*

In June 1966, I was born with my legs bowed around my twin sister, Suzy, her legs pinched inward like a fin. At first they thought she would not live. My mother was having "complications." I imagine Suzy was swimming somewhere below my vision, her curved legs like a fishtail flashing. "Mrs. Messer, you have another baby in there," the doctors said. Until we were born, nobody—neither my mother nor the doctors—knew that she was pregnant with twins. The only person who guessed was Kim, who, since a young child, had always been witchy. At the age of eight, she whittled divining rods out of willow branches, collected pond snakes and bullfrogs, let them go in the house; she dangled my mother's wedding ring by a string over her pregnant belly and watched its revolutions. That spring, nature mirrored twins—twinned clovers, cattails, yolks in breakfast eggs. Kim observed all that doubling in the natural world. *Twins*, she had said, but nobody listened. When they pulled Suzy out, they thought she was dead. Then she coughed. Suzy had to stay in the hospital incubator for a month, and I was taken back to the Red House.

My father wrote Richard Warren Hatch, telling him of Kim's prophecy, our births, and the mysterious twinned vegetables and flowers they had found around the house. Hatch responded:

> We have researched the available records and find that although the Hatches did their duty of not letting the line die out, they do not seem to have produced any twins. . . . It would seem that the guardian haunting spirits of the place have accepted the Messers as one of the family—this being a subtle matter of the spirits' evaluation of the Messers' character and, most especially, of the Messers' sentiment towards the place. It was obvious of course when the Messers produced twins that they were putting their mark upon the place; so what could be more natural than that, in order to show approval and acceptance, everything else should emulate the Messers? It all adds up—not to jinxes—but to a favorable omen and a very important one.

Richard Warren Hatch's Puritan ancestors would have believed in omens; no matter how "good" a person was, he or she still might not be "elect," or saved. Only God knew, and believers were left with a collection of oblique and deeply metaphoric symbols to interpret. Hatch's ancestors, in other words (like Kim), would have been looking for signs. My parents, however, were only looking to belong—their own kind of "election"—hoping that Richard Warren Hatch and the house would accept them.

Eventually, Hatch began referring to my father as his "caretaker" and "personal physician . . . on whom [his] fate and Ruth's depends." He sent my parents a series of letters he called "Red House Notes," detailing the restoration he had done to the property and what, if anything, my parents might want to continue fixing. "Don't let any restorer lead you to forget that the object is not to recreate a mid-17th century house—a museum," he wrote early on. "A house grows and changes. Restorers are too often obsessed with what they conceive to be the 'original'— but no family continued living in an 'original' unless they were bankrupt—which the Hatch land-owners and mill-owners certainly were not." This letter detailed ten suggestions having to do with windows, fireplaces, fuses, circuits, and heat. He also suggested a plumber and an oil service the way a householder might direct a house sitter, *Cellar under study: Windows should be kept open during summer months but closed in winter.* One such letter described each room of the house and Hatch's impressions. Dining room: "no change." Front parlor: "no change." Front hall: "no change."

Slowly objects began to return to the Red House. My father would visit Richard Warren Hatch, and Hatch would give him a book, a document, or a piece of furniture, saying, "Take this back to the house." Most of the documents were receipts and daybooks that Hatch had found in the attic when he inherited the house. A receipt for a church pew, six cords of wood, twenty-one bushels of salt, fifteen bushels of Indian corn; receipts for medicine, eight doctor visits, bloodletting; a petition to build a bridge across the North River; tax receipts for 1790 and 1796; a bill of sale for a quarter-interest in the "good sloupe" *Sally Board*; receipt for the boarding of a school teacher, eighteen dollars; a contract to build a church.

And he continued to hand my father things: a stack of books that had belonged to his great-grandfather, Stiegel glass, a broken wooden plate, a pewter plate and fork, a carved plover, an alphabet sampler, four old bottles, a half-model of a ship, twin beds, a drop-leaf table, one twenty-gauge double-barrel shotgun, a Fox Sterling rifle.

Finally, Hatch gave my father Walter's will from 1681, the probate records of Walter's inheritance from his father, and family diaries and letters. According to my father, Hatch emphasized that these documents had always been with the house and that they "belonged there," as if the house were the rightful owner.

My father hung the framed wills and documents exactly where they had always been; he put the rest of the documents in the parlor closet and shut the door.

Walter
1647–1699

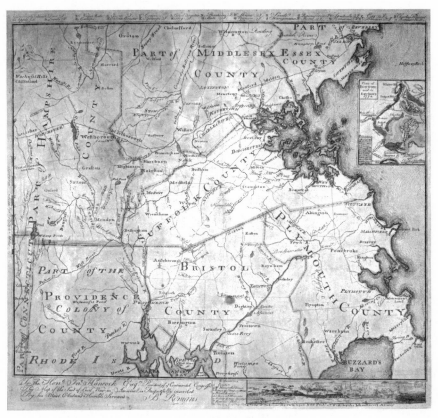

Southeast Massachusetts, 1775

I, Walter Hatch have two cows "Cari" and "Paci" and one heifer that's called Gentle and one steer calf, and a sword and a belt and in consideration of this William Hatch has one pair of oxen called Spark and Golden—

I, Walter Hatch have one black coat, two black doublets, one red waist coat, one broad axe and one hatchet, in consideration thereof William Hatch has one (stuff) suit, one pair of breeches, three tables, two axes and the hoe—

I, Walter Hatch have the iron mortar and pestle and the wheat sieve and the spade and dungfork and instead thereof, William Hatch has one pail, one spit, one pair of shears, and a rake and a hayfork and a shufell (shovel).

> —Probate agreement between Walter Hatch and his brother, William, dividing the estate of their father, Elder William Hatch, November 1651

When Walter returned to Two Mile, he carried his belong-ings up the North River on a long, flat barge called a gundalow. Family history speculates that four years probably passed between Walter's marking the land and his completion of the Red House. When his father died suddenly in November 1651, Walter had been married to Elizabeth Holbrook for a year and a half, and the house would have been nearly finished.

At the funeral, gloves, scarves, and rings had been given to mourners, the body washed and "laid out," wrapped in a linen cape dipped in beeswax, tied at the feet. The coffin: a red or black body-box with the date of William Sr.'s death—1651—stamped in nails on the top. In this, Walter's father was carried aloft in the arms of the pallbearers, his friends and sons, out of the crepe-strewn parlor to the back of a wagon drawn by horses harnessed with black ribbons and death's-heads fixed on their forelocks. Or carried to the burial ground by foot through the snow, the line of mourners balancing the coffin on shoulders or with straps, some bearing black arm bands, fans and bonnets, gloves or hats, or black ribbons tied to canes. There was gunfire along the way—a salute to such a decent freeman, a merchant, church elder—and rum and cider were passed around to those who stood at the grave.

After the funeral, Walter had drawn up an inventory dividing the household items with his younger brother, William Jr.— the cows, the sword, the red waistcoat, the oxen, the breeches, the shovel. But when William Jr. died suddenly a few months later, the inventory became moot; Walter got everything except his father's house, which went to William Jr.'s daughter.

So Walter was setting up housekeeping now, gundalowing up the river with a few items he'd acquired himself: a wooden document-chest marked "W.H.," a silver tooth- and ear-pick shaped like a sea monster. And everything living he'd inherited— four cows, two oxen, one horse, one pig, two piglets—and everything inert—rugs, curtains, nails, trundle bed, door lock, cow bell, ladders, spoons. All of it traveling with the river's tide, or pushed along by wind, the small sail on the bow, Walter guiding with long poles pushed off the banks.

It would have taken several trips. The center of Scituate, the rows of house lots along the harbor where Walter had spent his teenage years, was north of the river's original mouth. By bird flight, the diagonal southwest trajectory to Walter's land spanned only eight miles. But Walter had to carry his belongings in an oxcart along an ill-graded road to Bisbee's ferry, then pole it all up the river. The bird, flying from the harbor, would have passed over farms and houses of South Scituate, a corner of Norwell; it would have passed over the river that wound north from the ocean, then west, then south. From the air the river would have looked like a piece of string thrown down from a loom, squiggled and contrary on the floor. Two Mile lay where the river turned sharply from west to south, narrow and curved slightly like an arm extending to pick up the string.

Elizabeth, Walter's new wife, would have made one of these trips, sitting square in the middle of the gundalow on a trunk that held her belongings from her old life and what she would need for her new—a "marriage portion," as they called it. Unlike most of the Scituate population (who hailed from County Kent, England), Elizabeth was the daughter of a Welshman; she had a mother named Hopestill and a grandmother named Experience. When Elizabeth married Walter, she was nineteen years old; she was perhaps twenty now, when the gundalow reached the edge of the Two Mile land.

All but the swath of meadow and some salt hay by the river was covered with forest. Walter and Elizabeth would have wheeled the oxcart into the woods. Walter's land abutted the sunken "ancient" road that had been used by native trappers. The road wound by the marsh and followed the river toward Pembroke and Hanover, eventually connecting to the Plymouth Coast Road to Boston. Walter built the Red House some distance back from this road, sitting half a mile east of the river, near Two Mile Brook.

—•—

Because there was no brickyard, Walter would have built his first chimney out of clay and wattle and daub, the way birds spit and fit nests together. Walter must have framed the house with the help of others, fitting the posts and beams together, then pushing them vertically into slots in the groundsill. The largest framing member, the summer beam, would have extended out of the top of the chimney and across the ceiling of the chamber. The men would have fitted smaller beams into the summer, perpendicular, like ribs along the backbone of a whale. Then they'd hoist story posts, prick posts, side-bearers, and girts, fitted into notches as they built upon each other, and raised up as if out of sleep, the skeleton of the house against the tree line. Then the men climbed on the back of the house and laid on rafters, thatched the roof with reeds from the river. Below, others sliced Two Mile timber vertically into wide boards and then planked the walls with it, edge to edge. Floorboards were fitted on, and clapboards or shingles, a few windows of oiled paper or leaded glass brought over from England.

For all this Walter would have used a ripping chisel, a draw knife, a jack plane, a hatchet, the hands of other men.

The words they spoke: "tusk," "tenon," "beveled shoulder."

"Freeman," they said, "neighbor." Slot and groove, the house went up.

———•———

A householder now, Walter carried the heads of squirrels and birds, light as shoemakers' awls, from his land in Two Mile to the meetinghouse; he carried hinges, door clates, nails back from the ironworks—and with these he fastened doors. The squirrels traveled above him in the trees, migrating in huge chattering herds. A flock of pigeons flew by, blackening the sky with their bodies.

When finished, the Red House would have been quiet inside, insulated against wind, and smelling of dirt and new wood. It was half a house at first—just one room or two. Most settlers constructed houses with a one-room plan—fireplace at one end, door at the other, summer beam like a giant minus sign stretching between the two. Houses started this way—a cellar scraped in earth, a parlor and hall, a lean-to kitchen, perhaps a second-floor loft chamber at the top of a ladder. If Walter had money enough, he would have fitted the space above the door with two round bull's-eyes of greenish glass, letting a little more light shine in.

Elizabeth would have busied herself making soap from lye and tallow, or cooking over the fireplace hearth, which was big enough to walk into and strung with iron pots. Light from the fire would have cast shadows over the long-handled pans, the flax wheel, a row of apples strung from the ceiling. Elizabeth cooked meat on spits or in rounded tin reflector ovens. She used a clamshell in a split stick for a large spoon, cupped another shell in her hand as a skimmer in the milk pail. Gourds became bowls, dippers, bottles. A turkey wing became a hearth brush, a hemlock branch, a broom. The fork had not yet been invented. Walter ate the meat with his hands off a wooden plate. His left hand held the meat while his right hand cut with the knife; he used the pointed end of the knife to convey the food from the plate to his mouth. Because the meat was flavored with saffron, Walter's left hand would have been stained bright orange.

The meat, butchered in large chunks, was carved away from the bones, which were thrown with other refuse outside the kitchen door. Broken plates lay a few feet outside the door, picked over by pigs and chickens, walked over and crushed by boots entering and exiting. Dogs, or children with sticks, dug shallow pits in the dirt.

In winter, vast geographies of heat and cold shifted from one side of a room to another, an aesthetic of extremes. The family stood scorch-faced before the fire, while the rest of the room to their backs filled with frost, clouds of breath. Pies and meats froze in the corner a few feet away, stayed that way all winter. The Hatches stoked the fire, built it high with logs and walked out of the house to travel to the meetinghouse, riding together on a horse or in the oxcart, or walking with blankets thrown over their heads. They arrived at the meetinghouse, which was never heated, the floors covered with sand; they stood and witnessed a baptism where the minister broke the ice in the christening bowl, and the child, just a few days old, wearing only a bearing cloth, was held up by the women who had assisted the birth.

Only women would have helped with childbearing, the midwife if she could be fetched in time. Certainly there was no doctor yet, and no one would have known the mother's condition—one or more babies, a boy or a girl. They could have done divinations, as was popular, the way some young women carved the skin off an apple in one long tail and flipped it over their shoulder to see what letter it fell into on the floor behind them, the initial of their future love. They may have watched the shape of an egg yolk dropped into a drinking cup. A monster birth, of course, would have prophesized something horrible about the mother—that she was ungraced or, worse, a witch. And many infants were born dead, or "died of baptism," perhaps from being exposed to the cold or the ice water; they were carried home and then buried a few days later. If they survived, they were placed in hooded cradles by the fire, or carried up ladders to second-floor lofts clutching gold or silver in their hands as was the ritual for wealth, with a scrap of scarlet cloth draped on their heads for luck. These same women may have continued the folk rituals with the older children, tying deer's and wolf's teeth around their necks for strength, rubbing an osprey bone over their gums to ease teething. In the morning and evening, they would make the children stand before the fire hearth, naked except for their long shifts, anoint their joints with snail water, and place snails on their legs and elbows to cure rickets.

Elizabeth had eight children in eighteen years: Hannah, Samuel, Jane, Antipas, Bethia, John, Israel, and Joseph. All but Hannah lived into adulthood. Each slept with its parents until another baby came, and then was placed with siblings in the trundle beside the larger bed, later in rooms off the kitchen, or on the second floor, or in the kitchen itself in fold-down beds or pallets. Until the age of six or seven, male and female children wore the same clothing—long gowns, resembling their mother's dress, that tied at the neck and wrists, with caps on their heads trailing ribbons.

By the time all of Walter's children were born, there were still only six stagecoaches in England, one private coach in Boston; paper money would not be used for another twenty years. Elizabeth died before her youngest child was four years old. She had lived to hear about the plague in England, the London fire; she had survived Scituate's own smallpox epidemic, and there had yet to be an Indian War. She barely made it to forty.

The shipyard at the base of Bell House Neck, where Walter worked with his cousin Jeremiah, had no work house, only a series of flat rocks set into the bank of the North River that supported the building of a hull. Behind the landing, a hill rose to a cleared crest where a large iron bell hung between two posts. The bell acted as an alarm; during hostile Indian attacks, the shipwrights, or a neighboring farmer, would run to the top of the hill and ring the bell, which could be heard over the entire valley.

Later, Walter would build mills along the Two Mile Brook, creating a string of four ponds. These mills would support the shipbuilding industry and provide work and goods for many others. Yet the men who worked for Walter and Jeremiah were paid in food—bushels of corn, candles, butter, sugar, cheese. The first ships launched out of the shipyards on the North River were named *Swallow, Desire,* and *Industry.*

From his arrival in Scituate until his death sixty-five years later, Walter remained essentially British. Having spent his entire childhood in England, he spoke like an Englishman, used the crown's money, and dressed in a doublet, waistcoat, and breeches. He came into adulthood in a town racked by weather and disease; Quakers were beginning to preach and be persecuted; Harvard College was chartered; and, in England, Charles I was beheaded.

As town constable, Walter was responsible for errant animals and misguided people—public drunkenness, predator bounties, entries in the "Animal Book." He was the town cop, appointed by law to walk the dirty streets carrying a six-foot brass-tipped staff, calling out the time of night and the weather: *7 o'clock and cloudy skies; two o'clock and fair winds.*

In town, the animal tax increased and householders were expected to bring six more blackbird heads into the meetinghouse at the beginning of planting season. Here townspeople recorded the description of their animals that ran in the large common herd. The animals were known also by their earmarks, the specific notch an owner had carved in their ears. The earmarks always resembled something else: a swallow's tail, a half-moon, a penny. For example, on February 29, 1659, Walter listed his horse in the Animal Book, a bay gelding. His descriptions joined the town's already lengthy list of horses: mouse-colored, blackish, roan, bay, red; horses with stars, stripes, a white ring just above the hoof, feathers in the forehead. For a marking, Walter chose a short horizontal line curving into a vertical cut that lopped off the bottom third of the ear. His earmark looked like this:

One can imagine that Walter helped others earmark—someone held the horse or cow, while another placed a hand at the base of the ear, working the knife. Still another man may have held the animal by the neck, his hand over the muzzle to keep it from throwing its head back. Then the knife would be turned sharply, bringing a short perpendicular cut to the edge of the ear; the piece of flesh would fall to the ground as the wound was cauterized with a hot iron stake. When Walter found a sheep or cow with its throat ripped out by wolves, he would check the earmark first to see if he knew the owner.

While Walter walked the streets, wolf packs patrolled the swamp, alone or in pairs at the edge of timber, jogging in their lanky, side-winding way. Colonists identified these scruffy, golden-eyed creatures by their markings—*black wolf, gray wolf, she-wolf with pup.*

Cattle and sheep running in large herds together through low fields and on "the commons" were easy prey for wolves. The ground was marked up with hoofprints as if a giant patterned carpet had been laid down. Seen at one end of town and then the other, the herd animals grouped beneath trees, or at the river-bank. The patterned carpet shifted over itself across the commons, as if it were its own entity, hundreds of invisible hooves. The only animals, it seemed, that could defend themselves against wolves were goats and hogs. They traveled in smaller groups, and stuck to the thick underbrush in the woods.

Many people believed that the wolves were not merely predatory animals but familiars—shape-shifting imps that acted out the devil's whims. Familiars, the devil's helpmates, usually took the form of animals, Indians, or women. Accusations of witchcraft also included the human ability to change into an animal—a bird, a pig, a black dog, a wolf. A traveler walking along Walton's Creek heard the sounds of hoofbeats behind him, but when he turned, nothing was there. Some heard laughing at the edge of a glade, or the sound of musket fire and the stampede of many ghost horses.

Drunkenness, it was believed, started everything—bred hoodlums, swindlers, rogues. Scituate had passed its first sumptuary law in 1633, which allowed "wine, strong water, or beire" to be sold only in taverns or inns. But people brewed alcohol in private. Those who "could not follow their calling" stumbled through the shadow-boxed semblance of town. They passed out on the commons or slumped by the swine pen, behind the house of a neighbor, to be found later in the evening in ill health, taken in, and reported the following morning for public intoxication, then brought up on charges and fined. In order to avoid fines, residents began wearing masks when searching out or buying alcohol, fornicating, skipping church service, or engaging in other dubious activity performed while drunk. One can imagine groups of drunken revelers yelling behind the false grins or scowls of masks, hoods thrown over their heads.

Given the town's high consumption of alcohol, Walter was often drawn into drunken fisticuffs and other conflict. In 1652,

George Russell was fined three pounds for abusing "the Constable of Scituate in the execution of his office." Three pounds was
not a small sum—Walter had bought his 260-acre home site in
Two Mile for five pounds, and forty years later Russell would
leave five pounds a year to his widow as her yearly income from
his estate. In 1654, William and Elizabeth Randall were brought
to court for attacking Walter in the line of duty and drawing
blood. "When [Walter] strained for the magistrates table, [the]
wife tore the detresse out of his hand, and hurt his hand soe as
blood was sheed."

Eventually, Scituate's wolf problem became so bad that bounties were posted and hunting parties appointed to flush the
wolves out of swamps. With the increased bounties came independent bounty hunters—freemen from other townships, or
native trappers. Most of them were wandering hunters who ma-
nipulated townspeople by bringing heads to the constable, receiving the bounty, then burying the carcasses, only to return at
night to unearth them and sell the heads the next day to another
town.

In order to prevent wolf-head swindling, Walter, in his position as town constable, began cutting the ears off bounty
wolves. But bounty hunters dug up the ears as well. Eventually, the town began nailing the skinned wolf heads and half-
dried skulls to the side of the meetinghouse, which became the
clearinghouse for animal head-taxes, earmark records, notices
of town meetings, the sale of livestock, and other announcements. The meetinghouse, with its oiled-paper windows and
gray and moss-covered clapboards, fluttered with paper ordi-
nances, a list of nos and don'ts: *No adultery, no theft. No selling
or lending boats, gear or guns to the Indians. No profane swearing
or cursing. No removing or defacing landmarks. No burning fences.
No embezzlement or forging deeds. No reproaching the Marshal.
No lying. No playing cards or dice. No denying the scriptures. No*

skipping public worship, making seditious speeches against the government. No smoking tobacco. No failure to ring swine.

It was here, more than twenty years after Elizabeth died, that Walter may have seen a paper scrap on the meetinghouse wall announcing that his son Israel was intending to marry Elizabeth Hatch, his mother's namesake, a second cousin. Israel still lived with Walter, and now, after so much had changed—the oldest son, Samuel, gone to work in the mills and the second son, Antipas, now crippled—the Red House would fall to him, the intended soon-to-be-married. Israel had asked her, and she had said yes. The wolf heads, some earless, some bleached, dried on the side of the meetinghouse among the many flapping declarations. When the skin pulled away from the skull, the heads, with their blank eye sockets, resembled masks—the exposed teeth forming a snarl and a grin at the same time.

Three

Sarah and Suzy Messer

The waiting room in my father's radiology office was antiseptic. Women staring at magazines sat in beige chairs surrounded by framed prints of flowers. They sat and waited for mammograms, for the technicians who passed behind the small window that looked like a window in a taxicab or a drivethrough bank; they waited for the technician to call their names and take them to back rooms, where the lighting was dimmer and there were more flower prints. They were asked to slip out of their clothes and into robes that wrapped around, tied in the front. They were smiled at, led into examining rooms—the high vinyl tables, the steel drawers, unending sheets of white paper. Asked to lie back, then to sit up again and raise one arm, the other, while hands were circling, armpits patted, pinched. Then they would be led to other rooms, where they would be asked to place their feet inside the outline of feet drawn on the floor. They would stand and open their robes. First one breast and then the other would be placed between two frames of glass and photographed, X-rays passing through from the bent hood of the machine that looked like a robot from a space thriller. The technician would apologize if the machinery, her hands, were cold. The plates of glass pressed down from the top and up from the bottom, pressed in from the left and right. Then the procedure would be over, the technician would say "That's it," and smile broadly, sliding something out of the machine, and they would be led back to the waiting room, where other women raised their eyes and sat stiff in their robes. It took ninety seconds to develop a film.

All my father had dreamed of, he said, was this house and his establishment as a doctor in New England. Every day, he sat in a room illuminated by two light boxes that slanted back toward the wall like a cellar door. The clinic was in a basement. To his right, below the curtained rectangular window, sat the shelf where the technicians placed the films under his name and a smiley face that someone had drawn there, with a crooked grin and blank circle eyes. To the left, more shelves thick with books—*Cancer Manual, Diagnosis of Diseases of the Chest, Roentgen's Clinical Diagnosis*—and other items: Fanta cans, a model of an X-ray tube, a joke baseball cap with foam breasts.

Somewhere, in other rooms, were examples of Kim's and Kerry's artwork—a snail, a circus pony. Somewhere too were his collection of antique medical tools and early glass X-rays that showed paired images—two broken arms, two rib cages, two fractured hips, two copies of the heart's aorta.

My father sat facing the light wearing a headband with magnifying goggles that swung down over his eyes. He was molelike in the cave of the room, his eyes blank and round behind the goggles, as he shuffled films up onto the light box and looked at the insides of women's breasts.

The breasts were a row of moons, the milk ducts fanned like

white knotted thread. He looked for black pockets, moving his eyes slowly over the hazy images, which were nippleless and seemed less like breasts than maps of rivers seen from the air.

My father took the films down from the light box and talked into a tape recorder—"INDICATION," *describing the film,* then, "IMPRESSION," *a diagnosis.* Later, a typist would transcribe his words into the patient's chart and file it back on one of the long shelves that were in the hallways of the medical office, but now my father would rise and go to meet the woman, who had been led to yet another small room to wait for him, and tell her that everything was clear, that nothing had been found.

But sometimes this was not the case; sometimes, at least two or three times a day, my father had to tell a woman that she might be dying of breast cancer, and this task sometimes made him feel connected to others—that what he had done with his life was important, that he helped people—but other times it made him feel like a ruined man.

Next to his chair, on top of the light box, a coffee mug said, "I'm a Virgin . . . Islander." And on the other side:

ST. THOMAS
ST. THOMAS
ST. THOMAS
ST. THOMAS

But he had yet to go there. At the end of the day, he would telephone women—the ones for whom he had especially bad news—and if they were not there he would leave a message with his phone number, saying, "Call me at home."

The designation "X" in "X-ray" stands for "Unknown," because in the beginning Wilhelm Roentgen, the scientist who discovered them, was uncertain of their nature. The X-ray is an easy metaphor for history—where history leaves gaps, the imagination fills in.

Outside the office, my father's X-rays were ghost bodies sliding on the back seat of the car, stored on shelves in the barn, invading the house, stacked in the corner of the kitchen. They were illuminated strangers—transpierced and articulated by my father, a cowboy of the invisible with stethoscope lariat. Four years after he began his private practice, my father had established Mobile X-ray, a portable X-ray unit for the South Shore—twenty-four-hour X-rays in the back of a van. This way, he figured, doctors could save time with diagnosis—when someone slipped and broke a hip at 3 a.m., the staff of the nursing home could call Mobile X-ray and get a film taken immediately. The X-ray would be developed on the way to the on-call doctor's house, the doctor would read the film and give a diagnosis, and then treatment could proceed promptly. He volunteered himself for the graveyard shift.

X-ray technicians entered and exited the house at all hours of the night, standing and shifting in parkas in the corner of the room as my father plugged in his light box and placed it on top of a table. I would sit on the edge of the staircase, looking through the open door of the north parlor. In the light box's pale and bluish glow, my father's body was outlined through his flannel nightshirt as he held each X-ray up and murmured into a small handheld tape recorder. He would pass the X-rays back to the technician, click off the tape recorder, and hand over the tape. Then I would know to run upstairs, although sometimes he would catch me, my hands pawing the stairs above me.

"Hey," he would say, grabbing my foot, "what are you doing up?"

My father had explained that X-rays were pictures of what people looked like on the inside. In medical school, his professor had confronted him with a "question of a foreign body" in the abdomen of a three-year-old child, showing him the X-ray. "A choo-choo train," my father said, "was going across the transverse colon. The engine was at the splenic flexor, the caboose at the hepatic flexor." The swallowed toy train was seven cars long, and the X-ray showed it clearly, winding beneath the boy's tiny ribs.

Some nights, my father would let me watch him read the films—the broken femur set with pins; the woman who, by chewing her hair, had amassed a hairball the size of a softball in her stomach. The hair caught pear seeds and bits of food as if she had swallowed it in order to create a net, as if she were fishing inside herself.

"That's what you get when you suck your braids," my father said as he held the X-ray up to the light.

———

As a child, I spent most of my days wandering out of the house into the fields and collapsing. From my hiding place in the grass, I could look back at the house: a smear of red on the hillside. Where I came from and where I was going began at its red center—a red that used to be redder, the way that blood is red when it first leaves the body. As I lay still in the field, the house moved like the reflection of sky in water, contracting and expanding in the landscape. My eyes traversed the house—forehead, nose, mouth. Each windowpane was a way of looking through the people who had once lived there. Above the door: four panes in a row below the cornice. The door was a torso with four chests, four stomach panels, carved wood. A latch, a wrist. The chimney with its thick four-sided neck.

Rooms collar the central chimney of the house, and as a child I walked through them like fluid moving through the arteries of a huge heart. At night I would wander the dark house, touching lampshade, nightstand, the bed's rounded footboard. There were spots rubbed smooth on the door moldings from three hundred years of touching and moving through rooms without light. Within the rooms were hidden rooms—beneath the stairs, behind the chimney, or in the backs of closets whose walls were doors that led elsewhere. And I'd move through the house and put my hands on all these places, imagining a time when my family and I did not live there.

———

The bedroom I shared with Suzy was called the Borning Room, where people were born and died. Unlike other rooms in the house, it had no fireplace, probably because people didn't stay there long enough. Our twin beds sat three feet apart, headboards against the wall.

"Don't go to sleep yet," we'd whisper to each other in the dark. I'd tell stories, anything to keep her awake—horses rescued from slaughterhouses, the tale of a ladybug village, our mother as a shipbuilder down by the river hoisting sails.

Our mother had wallpapered a neon floral print between the gunstock beams. It was the era of Pop Art and giant cartoon flowers—orange, fuchsia, lime green—everything outlined in metallic, as if to make a psychedelic point.

Darkness, therefore, was a relief. The house came back to itself like a beautiful body disrobed of an unfortunate outfit. In the dark it was just soft murmurs, the smell of wood and ash. I knew the wallpaper was there—it had just stopped yelling.

On the other side of the room, a music box sat on top of a dresser. After the hand crank was turned, the rows of tiny drums and bells played themselves through twelve songs.

"Are you asleep?" Suzy would whisper, her hand reaching across the empty space when the music box wound itself down. Sometimes I thought I could see her face, glowing pale in the other bed. I stretched my arm out and our fingers brushed. I had to lie at the edge of my bed and she on the edge of hers to have our hands clasp fully together.

"Yeah," I'd whisper back. Then, "No." It was like talking to myself.

Sometimes the voices of our parents' friends, the smell of cigarettes would drift up from the dining room. Our beds creaked as we stretched out of them toward each other. The bed-runner dug into my rib cage. When our arms got tired, we would lean our cheeks against the wooden runners and chew on them, leaving soft dents with our teeth.

Fifteen minutes between my birth and Suzy's had been enough to give me a head start, if not older-sibling authority. Rebekah was born only a year later, making us near triplets. My parents decided to name her after Rebekah Hatch—sister to Israel H., Richard Warren Hatch's grandfather—taking the traditional spelling. Jessica was born three years after Bekah.

As far as looks went, Bekah was more of my twin than Suzy. We were both blonde and somewhat sturdy. Bekah's hair was nearly platinum, and she was born with a slight sway in her back that made her hips swing when she walked, even at the early age of three. "A blonde bombshell," my parents called her because of her habit of stripping her clothes off slowly throughout the day. "She's deciduous," they'd say as Bekah danced around the kitchen singing "Rock the Boat," her behind wagging.

I had been born bowlegged; Suzy, the inverse twin, was skinny and pigeon-toed, tripping over her feet. Starting with her setback in the incubator, she racked up infirmities: two pneumonias, three ear infections, measles, a bitten-off (then reattached) tongue, two broken hands, a sprained ankle, and a near self-blinding with a stick. All before the age of five. She kept her hair cut short like a boy's; it grew thicker and thicker, like an over-trimmed bush. Suzy, though sickly, worked her waif status: she could touch her tongue to the tip of her nose, and do a back bend so her hands touched her feet, creating a complete circle. She grew increasingly elflike. Jess, also delicate, squished her face and cried a lot. Kerry called her "my little red ant."

It was like this with both generations of kids: the robust and the frail. In the earlier group, Kim and Kerry were certainly the strongest. Tall, with long, thick brown hair, they were the Amazon role models for Bekah and me. In a copycat move, Bekah and I both grew our hair long, even though it was blond and stringy. Summers, Bekah and I were covered with scrapes and mosquito bites, baking soda and calamine lotion spotting our shoulders and ankles. On the other side were the fairy people, the beauties: Kate and Patrick. Cream-pale skin, heart-shaped faces. Kate had a curtain of thick hair like Kerry and Kim, except hers was gold and fell so far down her back that she often sat on it at the dinner table. "You're pretty now," Kim joked to Kate, "but just you wait. It's like a reverse ugly-duckling syndrome. You'll be ugly later."

Kim spent summers outside the Red House, stomping trails through marshes, marking nests of marsh wrens or red-winged blackbirds. Local bird-watchers employed her. In the marshes she found the remains of bridges, catwalks that led out to the old shipyards. She tried to redefine the paths, the grasses already two feet over her head, mashing down reeds with her tennis shoes. She stuck a red flag on a pole at each nest she found so she could find it again.

Sometimes she would try to lose herself, slog so far out among the reeds that she couldn't find her way back—shaking along the edge of the river, or circling around the beaver pond or an old bottle dump; digging with a stick for someone else's ancient broken plate.

Summer nights were hot, and she didn't like being contained indoors, even though she was allowed to sleep in the old canopy bed. She would sneak jars of fireflies into the room and let them go. They'd flash in the embroidered canopy above where she lay sweating. No wind. No sheet thrown over her. It was as if all the breath had been sucked out of the house as she stared up at the canopy, the darkness lit by an occasional blink of her smuggled fireflies.

Each summer she lived inside a historical play, a stage set that often seemed fake. A mockingbird sat on the scrim of the chimney and called out a series of stolen songs. It rattled them off quickly—blue jay, red-winged blackbird, bobwhite, mourning dove—in various orders. It imitated the telephone's party-line rings; it imitated Jess's high wails. The calls echoed down the chimney and through the old part of the house, so that often, if you were walking through rooms, it sounded like a flock of birds, an entire population perched on the roof. In August, when Kim returned to California, all that history, the mockingbird, the red-flagged marshes, slowly disappeared as the plane scrolled over the Midwest—the river and the world east of the plane were slowly erased, her memory of us, of the Red House, becoming a transparent film.

The First Israel
1667–1740

Hearth scene engraving from *The Visit*, a chapbook

Remember souls, Christ and grace cannot be overvalued.
Is not the duty clear?
And dare you neglect so direct a command?
Are the souls of your children of no value?
Are you willing that they should be brands of hell?
Shall the devil run away with them without control?

—Cotton Mather, from his introduction to
  A Token for the Children of New England (Boston, 1700)

L *isten to me.*

Perhaps the whole family was against Israel Hatch and his second cousin Elizabeth as they sat in the kitchen of the Red House at the end of the seventeenth century. A hollow tube, six feet long, stretched across the room between them, a room that was filled with people. Israel put his mouth against the flared edge of the courting tube, and on the other side Elizabeth placed her ear. This way they could whisper without being heard. Israel knew that he would inherit the house and land from his father, Walter, so he waited, continuing to live with his family—the stepmother, the younger brother Joseph, and Antipas, whose mind had disappeared, head dull as a wooden bowl against the chimney jamb.

In 1681 Antipas had been willed the house and all of Walter's land; he must have been successful and well loved in order to inspire Walter to break his family's tradition of equal inheritance. But a few years later, in 1697, Walter revised his will, changing everything. Elizabeth must have asked at some point, and maybe Israel whispered back, *"Non compos mentis"*—not mentally capable. Not there, you know, in the head. Antipas had been incapacitated somehow—by a capsized boat, or a falling beam. Or kicked by a horse, knocked off a wagon, dragged by an ox. Or crushed in the mill, a shirt snatched up in gears, winched into the waterwheel. Or caught fire and burned, or nearly froze. He could have been shot—accidentally or on purpose, by himself or someone else. He could have had cancer, or a brain tumor. He could have simply lost his mind.

He had been a freeman and witness on many of the town's legal documents, could once sign his name, a well-slanted script from the quill, but now his signature was just a shaky "X." In the revised will, Walter instructed Israel and John to support and shelter Antipas for the rest of his days. In short, whoever got the house also got Antipas.

So Israel and Elizabeth waited, whispering in front of the fire grate. At night, their courting included a fold-down bed, a gown that tied at the neck, an iron coil around a candle that was a way of counting the hours they spent without touching. In the kitchen, a bed would have been folded down from the wall and a board placed between them so they could talk late into the night without wasting firewood. Elizabeth would have taken off her accordion bonnet, her pumpkin hood, her petticoats and heavy stays, slipped into the bundling gown and onto the mattress of straw ticking. The only light would have been the bundling candle, the dying fire, or the moon reflected off snow, shining cold through windows. In the dark, Israel placed his cheek against the bundling board as if along the belly of a schooner's hull, imagining an ocean. Breath like waves on the other side. Hands smoothed wood, wishing for skin instead, feeling that each grain, each feather of rough pine was a scar along the belly, an ache that the finger traced down. Each time, she had to wear that gown bound at the neck and feet. All they could do was talk and listen to each other breathing. They spent years this way, it seemed, beneath the same blanket, each feeling the heat of the other, the wooden board between them. In the morning, after the candle burned down all its coils, the bed would be folded up. This was how they survived together, or suffered. Half sleepers. With the stepmother, the father, and the siblings always watching. Years of not touching, or touching in secret ways around a wall of wood, until they were both over thirty years old and tired of waiting.

Israel didn't marry Elizabeth until he was thirty-two years old; three months after their wedding, a child, Lydia, was born. Though many couples were fined for fornication as evidenced by an early birth, Israel and Elizabeth, for some reason, were not.

———

In May 1699, the same month that Israel and Elizabeth most likely realized they were pregnant, Walter was struck by lightning and died instantly.

At least we can assume he died instantly—when someone is struck by lightning, electric current can bolt through tissue at ninety thousand miles per second. It follows no predictable path through the body, leaving burns on the skin where it enters and exits. The body itself becomes a conduit for an exchange of power and force, the electric jolt paralyzing the respiratory center of the brain, which controls breathing and heartbeat.

One would like to think that, struck by lightning, Walter died both unexpectedly and instantly. That, in his last moment on earth, his body was filled with light, and that the force of it exploded his heart like a time-lapse-photography rose. But when lightning strikes a person, every muscle in the body contracts, which is why people are thrown off their feet and bones splinter. Which is why, finally, Walter died. Not because his heart burst open, but because, growing tighter and tighter, it spiraled in on itself.

———

After the funeral and the settling of the estate, Israel and Elizabeth's wedding began with the firing of guns—although even in Elizabeth's advanced state this would have nothing to do with what later became known as a "shotgun wedding." The groom and his friends would have walked from the Red House toward the bride's house "saluting," or firing shots at every house they passed. Inhabitants of those houses would have answered with their own gun blasts. Halfway to the bride's house, someone probably ran for a bottle of rum. The group continued on, drinking and shooting.

During the ceremony, the couple would have placed their right hands behind their backs. At the end of the ceremony, the bridesmaid and the best man would pull the wedding gloves off the couple at the same moment so that Israel and Elizabeth could grasp their suddenly naked hands together.

Lydia, the unveiled product of Israel and Elizabeth's bundling, would grow up to marry into the Rogers family, which would become one of the most powerful shipbuilding families on the North River, and a family that the Hatches, like others in Two Mile, would marry into again and again. It was just like the fingers of their parents and their parents' parents folded together behind their backs—despite themselves, increasingly linked.

———

The Hatches were members of the Second Church of Scituate—where William Hatch Sr. had been an elder—since the mid-seventeenth century. In the beginning, all churches went unpainted and unheated, the rafters left exposed in the large open room. Parishioners paid for a family pew, built like a box with wooden seats that folded up on hinges or banged down loudly when dropped for sitting. Some had wolf- or beaver-skin bags nailed beneath the seat, in which people could warm their feet. The services were often two to three hours long. Churchgoers brought foot stoves, metal boxes filled with hot coals, or their dogs. The dogs lay in the family pew on their masters' feet—unless they barked and became unruly and were thrown-out by the "dog-whipper," one of the many church officers.

The Puritan Church was organized around five main officers of various ranks and duties: pastor, teacher, elder, deacon, and deaconess (sometimes called the "church widow"). Seating charts were drawn, a map of pews; anyone who strayed from his assigned seat was fined. All fines were handled by the deacon, who sat at the front of the church, near the pulpit, in a "deacon's pue." A "deacon's box" was fastened to the front of his pew, and after services, parishioners lined up to contribute money, goods, or promises of money for the congregation's upkeep and the pastor's salary.

Most churches were independent from the Church of England, self-governing. Psalms were "lined" (or read aloud) by the deacon, then sung by the congregation, a call and response that might continue uninterrupted for two hours. Some people folded up their seats and stood leaning against the high back of the pew box. Children fidgeted and sat on small footstools near the dogs, or on the gallery stairs that led to the loft where the in-dentured servants, slaves, and Indians sat.

The Hatches were Anabaptists, baptized twice—once in infancy, and again on a confirmation of faith at an age of reason. One reason for baptizing the children may have been the high child-mortality rate coupled with the very real Puritan fear of damnation. In 1700, Cotton Mather published a New England version of James Janeway's book *A Token for Children: An Exact Account of the Conversion, Holy and Exemplary Lives and Joyful Deaths of Several Young Children*, which included as a first example the pious death of John Clap of Scituate, who was fortunately twice baptized before his sudden death from lockjaw. This "children's book" existed to scare children and parents into baptism before it was too late to be saved.

In response, the population of Two Mile asked for religious house calls. Over a period of forty-five years (1711–57), the minister of the Second Church of Scituate baptized over ninety infants and children "in their homes[s]" who were ill and "not expected to live long."

The Red House, lasting still, must have been awkward nearing its hundredth birthday, having grown and rambled on fitfully as different generations cohabited through adulthood and old age. Israel and Elizabeth eventually had five children, built more rooms onto the house, and divided it in half—half for them, and half for dowager residents, Antipas and Israel's stepmother. It wasn't until later, until it had survived so much history, that the Hatches might have begun to view the house as something more than just a shelter for bodies—as a vessel for memory and family history that could transcend and withstand time. But in the mid-eighteenth century, they had only begun to think of their own bodies in this way—as souls separate from the body, as spirits that could leave the earth. Janeway's dead-baby books were accompanied by New England primers, then Evangelical primers—books that begged questions about life before and after the moment at hand.

———

Listen to me.

Israel, reading aloud to his children, would have asked, *Who made you?*

God.

What else did God make?

He made the stones and hills, the brooks and trees, all living creatures, the sun, the moon, the stars.

Four

South side of Red House, 1971

M y father did not believe in Providence, he believed in Prevention. When he wasn't reading X-rays, he made maps
of the house, showing stairways, doors, and windows. He traced
the blueprint and drew escape routes. He installed an elaborate
heat-and-smoke alarm system with loud clapper-horns. "There
are two deaths that are completely preventable: drowning and
fire," he'd say at the end of every drill, and then he'd look over at
Suzy and me.

At the age of five, I had already saved Suzy from drowning. The incident had occurred the summer before, at Duxbury
Beach. By the time Suzy and I waded into the water, Kerry,
Patrick, Kate, and our father had made it to the sandbar and
were walking back and forth as if across it, their feet below the
surface of the waves.

We decided to swim to them. It was as easy as stepping off,
sliding horizontal, dog-paddling and kicking, as we had been

taught so many times in the North River. But the current in the channel was strong, the sand beneath our feet suddenly gone. Water slapped my face. My father, brother, and sisters waved from the sandbar—distant, like sails tacking down the horizon. On the beach behind us, our mother dropped Jessica to a blanket, then ran fast across the sand. They were yelling at us, trying to get to us, mouthing something I couldn't hear as the water slipped over my head. My father was in the water now, his arms thrashing. "Suzy!" I heard him yell.

She had been beside me, but then, just as suddenly, she was not. I sank below the surface, reached down with my hand. I felt the soft brush of her hair and grabbed and pulled, held on to her head, which seemed smaller and colder, grabbing it from above with my hands. All this I did simply and without thought, the way I reached out for her hand across the space between our beds each night.

Then our father was with us, then our mother. We had drifted far down the channel between the sandbar and the beach. We moved inside the circle of our parents' arms, our chins lifted above the water. When we got to the beach, my father laid Suzy down and pressed on her chest, breathed into her mouth. She coughed, turned her head to the side, and threw up water, then began to cry.

Fire or drowning. Preventable, he said. Perhaps because of the near drowning, or the number of children in the house—six at that time—our father began to worry that something was likely to go wrong. By December 1971, when Patrick (ten) and Kate (eleven) had returned to live with us and Jess was a year old, my father was springing regular surprise fire drills in the middle of the night.

He would trip the alarm at 1, 2, or 3 a.m. without warning, jolting us from our beds. A rope ladder with wooden rungs sat coiled below the window in Patrick's room. Kate would hold the sash open while Patrick drew the storm window up and threw the ladder out; then they would climb across the roof of the kitchen and down to the lawn on the north side of the house. Our mother would be at our door in her nightgown saying, "Hurry, kids, hurry," but we could hardly hear her: she was just a mouth moving as we descended to the bottom of the stairs. My father then instructed everyone to pull the bolt that ran the entire width of the door. "Everyone has to show me they can do it. Everyone has to pull the bolt," he'd yell. Patrick, Kate, Suzy, Bekah, and I would be standing beside the door in our pajamas, our bare feet twisting; my mother held Jessica in her arms. The alarm was foghorn-loud, an overwhelming ring of panic, the sound pressing down on our heads as we would each pull the bolt on the door, push it open, and run out of the house. Then my father would bolt it again for the next one of us in line to step up and prove that we knew how to get out.

On December 7, my mother hung rags drenched in turpentine and linseed oil on the branches of a cherry tree outside the Red House. She had spent the majority of the afternoon and evening crawling backward along baseboards with a can of stain and a rag. Newspapers scattered the floor of the east ell. Despite what Richard Warren Hatch had written in his notes about the futility of perfect restoration, my mother had researched colonial paint and was trying her hand.

It had all started with the Save the Hatch Mill Committee; every time my mother drove down the lane past the shabby mill, she was reminded of historic preservation and the importance of "authenticity."

The committee, in conjunction with the Marshfield Historical Society, was selling "Save the Mill" bumper stickers, and holding potlucks and other fund-raisers. To help the cause, my parents had included the Red House on the "Harvest Home Tour of Old Two Mile, Marshfield." The local paper had advertised the event in advance, running a photo of a horse and carriage driving along the mill lane, "along the time-worn road from the Hatch homestead, now the home of Dr. and Mrs. Ronald Messer."

Local historian Cynthia Hagar Krusell had also published a poem titled "Old Two Mile" in the same edition of the paper:

> . . . *The river wound beneath the hills*
> *Amongst the marshes wide.*
> *Salt hay was cut and carried out*
> *All down the riverside.*
>
> *'Twas once the scene of busy days*
> *For along old Two Mile Way*
> *Dwelt farmers and millers and sawyers*
> *The Hatch family had their day.*
>
> *There were Walter and Israel and Ichabod,*
> *Samuel, Benjamin and John*
> *Luther, Charles and Joel*
> *The list goes on and on . . .*
>
> . . . *Today along old Two Mile Way*
> *The Hatches still remain*
> *And ghost of those departed*
> *Haunt yet the old domain.*

Now involved with the local historical movement, my father built a large reproduction fireplace in the kitchen with antique bricks and a Dutch oven—an undertaking that required an entirely new chimney. In order to get used to baking without a thermostat, my mother would set the conventional oven at various temperatures, stick her arm in and out of it, then walk across the room and do the same in the Dutch oven. When she wasn't singeing hairs off her arm, she cut colonial stencils and stripped the wood floors in the east-ell bedroom. My father added an enclosed entryway and a mudroom off the kitchen. A metalsmith down the street made eighteenth-century pewter lamps and candleholders, and plumbers installed a half-bath.

All the work, save for the staining my mother was doing herself, had recently been completed—the plumbers, the electricians, the masons who had been there for months, all gone.

That night, Kate and Patrick sat at the kitchen table doing their homework. Later, Patrick played with his hockey stick, rolling a tennis ball across the slanted floors, bouncing it off chair legs, the grate at the bottom of the refrigerator. Upstairs, I had been put to bed, with Suzy in the other twin bed, and Jessica in a crib. Bekah slept in the adjacent bedroom by herself.

Sometime after this, our mother walked out the kitchen door, through the narrow entryway, and into the dark backyard. She lifted each rag off the tree and smelled it, then took it from the limb.

She remembers distinctly the worry—how she put the rags in an empty cardboard box; how she placed the box in the new entryway, opened the windows. The entryway extended five feet from the back of the kitchen. My mother remembers folding the rags loosely. Then she walked back into the kitchen and told Kate and Patrick to go to bed.

In her room in the attic, Kate had a dollhouse made from a wooden box turned on its side. The dollhouse was cut in half lengthwise, revealing all three floors. There were scraps of wallpaper and carpet, a Coppertone suntan-lotion-box refrigerator, beds with toothpick posts, a fireplace made of cardboard with real chips of brick glued onto it. At Ben Franklin's 5&10, Kate had picked out more dollhouse items—a tiny fry pan with two eggs, a toaster, a fake-fruit bowl. Every night, as she placed each doll safely in its bed, she thought about her mother and sisters in California, the younger children sleeping on the floor below her, and her father and stepmother—all in their beds.

At midnight, our father returned from an office Christmas party. He was driving the first new car he had purchased in his life, a tribute to his success with his private practice. He tooled around the back of the house, up over the lawn, and parked close to the back door and the new entryway. Perhaps he was slightly drunk. Perhaps he slammed the car door, stepping out into a night that was getting colder, a sky filling with clouds. In the entryway, he saw the box under the open window. He smelled a tinge of turpentine and put his hands in the box to check the rags. They were cold.

———•———

In the beginning, it's chemistry—conditions that coincide, causing an event to spark. An event that causes a different future or outcome from what is planned or expected. In the beginning, it's about a seemingly small thing overlooked, the ignition point—oxygen, heat, fuel—the air, the chemical, the rag. Linseed oil, especially mixed with turpentine, is an extremely volatile chemical. A soaked rag folded on itself can heat up, explode. These explosions seem sudden or "spontaneous," as if they have volition of their own. They seem this way to the people whom they impact, leading them to revise circumstance as "God's will," or "a tragedy" when they become victims of the event. But in the beginning, it is just science.

Sometime around one or two in the morning, it began to rain. The rain came in the open window in the entryway of the Red House and fell onto the box of rags. The temperature dropped drastically, causing a thin layer of ice to form, hardening over everything—the hood of the new car, the stone steps winding up to the kitchen, the thin branches of the cherry tree, the open windowsill, the box of rags. The ice created just the right amount of oxygen to mix with chemicals in the linseed oil for the folded rags to become fuel. Perhaps the ice created a seal, holding the heat down. The center of each rag was a crumpled seam, a layer of folds like the fist of a peony before it opens, glowing hot from the inside. There might have been a string of smoke, a smoldering warning, the ice melting, but by then the chemicals would have already been working. Even without the temperature inversion and the ice, they could have reached an ignition point.

Sometime before 3 a.m., the box burst into flame. It burned quickly, and because the entryway was new wood, the fire spread to the walls and the ceiling. A few cans of paint in the entryway exploded. The fire licked up the walls, running across the edges of windows to the wiring, the overhead light dangling from the ceiling. The fire burned through the roof and out the door to the backyard. When the fire ate through the door, air rushed in, punching the fire backward into the kitchen.

The fire entered the kitchen with a tremendous amount of smoke, tripping the alarm. The clock on my mother's bedside read 3:07 a.m. She felt my father's body next to hers. *He is here. This is not a drill.* Then she smelled the smoke—bitter, burning her nose and throat. In the kitchen, the fire lit across the new linoleum floor, the base of which was made of glue and oil. The floor buckled, melting into a liquid that burned instantly. The fire burned hotter and sent off large amounts of black, oily smoke.

My father was out of the bed, his bare feet hitting the floor. Six kids and a fire in the house. In the attic, the horn positioned between Kate's and Patrick's rooms blared. Patrick thought: *Drill.* Thought: *Rope ladder, window.* But when he reached the window, he saw orange light, a wall of flames rising from the windows below him.

Beneath the loud wail of the alarm, Kate heard the house embroidered with voices. She heard people yelling to each other, their voices weaving up through the three floors. She heard footsteps running and doors slamming two flights down. She heard the urgency of her father's voice below her, beneath the alarm's metallic roar.

"*Patrick,*" she said.

The room was filled with smoke, and she could not find his door. She found him in the corner of his room near the rope ladder. She had looked down the stairwell, and it was filled with smoke but clear; she took Patrick by the hand, leading him. And there was our father suddenly at the bottom of the stairs.

"It's a fire," he yelled.

They felt their way through the warren of second-floor bedrooms and down the north staircase, where one of them pulled the bolt on the door.

Meanwhile, Suzy, at the instant of the alarm, set off running out of our room and down the stairs. My mother followed, turning the corner at the stairwell's landing just in time to see Suzy— blonde five-year-old in baggy flannel pajamas—run down the hallway to the kitchen, and into a wall of flame and smoke, and disappear.

My mother stopped for a second before the hallway, her hands over her mouth. She took her hands away, yelled. She couldn't even hear herself. Then she covered her mouth again and ran through the doorway, which felt like a storm of hot wind. Ran toward the fire after her child.

Upstairs, I was banging on the walls. Suddenly Bekah was next to me and we were yelling. We could not find the door. I could not see my hands before my face, but I knew Bekah was there with me in the room. The smoke burned my eyes and throat. I knew where the door was, but all I felt were the walls, the windowpanes, banging with the palms of my hands. I heard the voices of my parents, but they were thin threads of sound.

A door opened, and my mother stood there, a light from behind her transpiercing her nightgown, the outline of her body.

She had just watched one daughter run the wrong way into the fire, and then, like a miracle, run back out. She had just passed in and out of the hallway leading to smoke and flame, turning her back on the fire, with Suzy now in her arms, to hear a loud crash, the sound of the refrigerator exploding. And now she was upstairs again, in this doorway, saying, "This way, this way," and we were dragged by our arms down the stairs and out onto the lawn, where I was told not to move, standing with my bare feet on the frozen grass.

My father was counting heads. *Six, six, six.* There were only five. Suzy, Bekah, and I held on to each other's fingers or nightgowns. Somebody yelled, "The baby," and my parents were now rushing back toward the house, my mother stopping in the doorway, my father running up the stairs, back into my room, the house swallowing him. At the top of the stairs, he fell to his stomach and crawled on his elbows across the floor, finding Jessica still asleep in the crib, an inch beneath the smoke.

I stood in front of the open doorway and watched my father toss Jessica, a perfect bundle, over the banister and into my mother's arms, who accepted her so easily, as if they were one person, as if that gesture had been choreographed and rehearsed a hundred times before, the way action can be in a crisis—without thought, with only faith that the action is the right one.

———

There are many versions of what happened next—my father's story, my mother's, my siblings', my story.

In one version, my father did not leave the burning house right away but ran to his office on the first floor to try to call the fire department, finding the phone disconnected. Or my father, after throwing Jessica over the staircase, ran back into my room, where, disoriented, he grabbed the music box and carried it down the stairs and out the door. In yet another version, my father left the

house but then returned one last time to try to telephone the fire department and save the music box, couldn't accomplish either task, and quickly ran out again.

Then we all ran, in nightgowns, across the frozen lawn. The air was cold, painful to breathe. We tore through the bushes to the neighbors', where my father (a) yelled and kicked the door in, (b) threw rocks at the bedroom windows, (c) used swear words. Then the neighbor, Mr. M, appeared in the doorway—some say stark naked, some say using swear words, some say both.

We were, it is agreed, a huddled mass on the lawn, our backs to a burning house. Mr. M was ghostly and pale in the doorway—legs, arms, torso—his skin purplish white. He stood looking out at us, looking at the shards of glass from the storm door my father had smashed with his foot. My father's foot was bleeding. Mr. M was a thin, angry, naked man. Sometime after this, we were let into the house and somebody called the fire department.

The firemen took a long time to arrive, because the Union Street Bridge was out and they had to hook up their hoses to the fire hydrant a half-mile down the street. Also, they couldn't get their trucks around the stone wall and the apple tree.

My father blamed Mr. M for not waking up sooner, for being a bad neighbor. While we were waiting for the fire department, my father took us back over to our yard, where we sat on the lawn staring at the house. The house seemed to pulsate with heat, the slate roof like a cap screwed down tight against the flames. Glass in the windowpanes melted or burst. Black smoke streamed from the seam of each window, through every crack in the shingles.

In yet another version, my father did not blame Mr. M for not waking up sooner, for being a bad neighbor; he understood that things were chaotic and that we were lucky to have escaped with our lives. While we were waiting for the firemen to arrive, Mrs. M put us in chairs around the kitchen table and we drank milk. We talked about when the firefighters would come. She said that Patrick was in shock and gave him a blanket; he was shivering and rocking and would not talk to anyone.

Suzy was crying about her guinea pig. I was crying about the kittens. Bekah was crying about the mother cat, the dog. Kate was crying about her dolls. Jessica was crying as a chain reaction. This is the way it happened with us: a suddenly whipped-up fury of anxiety at 5 a.m. at the neighbor's table, with our mother saying, "Hold it together, kids; everything will be all right."

The firemen were working next door. A few of them had come in, checking, rechecking: "Are you sure there is no one else in the house?"

By daylight, the firemen were back, large men dragging ash behind them into Mr. and Mrs. M's kitchen of blue cupboards. Their yellow rubber jackets and hats had turned black. Slick with water from the hoses, they smelled acrid and burned. The skin on their hands and faces was beaded soot, like rain on an asphalt road. One fireman had something squirming in his coat.

"Does this belong to somebody?" he asked, as he opened his coat and held out the guinea pig to Suzy.

Outside the kitchen, in the hallway, I heard my father talking to the firemen. He was still in his nightshirt. His feet were bare, and blood had dried on his foot. They were talking about the slate roof. How the fire couldn't burn through. They were saying that slate was denser than wood or asphalt, that it trapped the heat. They were saying that if they had come five minutes later the entire house would have exploded. Exploded to pieces, sky-high, they were saying; there would have been nothing left.

It is called a "flashover," the technical term for how a room or a house explodes. Heat rises. During a fire, the temperature always increases more dramatically at the top of a room; there is sometimes a difference of five hundred degrees between the floor and the ceiling. If the room temperature reaches more than a thousand degrees, the buildup of carbon dioxide will ignite into flames that travel six feet per second. The slate roof trapped the heat, but the house did not explode.

Eight o'clock in the morning, the house was still smoldering. Ash swirled in the air, whipped up in tiny tornadoes of wind. My father's car was half collapsed, as if it had been melted with a blowtorch, the driver's side gone. The entryway was a pile of rubble; the kitchen wing, a fifteen-foot hole out of which black ribbons of smoke wound into the sky. The firemen had stayed for hours with hoses fixed on the beams.

"This is an old house," the firemen were saying, implying that the wood was more burnable. At 6 a.m., one of the sills had ignited again.

Now the fire was out, they said. My father, my mother, Kate, and Patrick went back into the old part of the house, the part that was not burned. They went in to find clothes, to see if there was anything left. They borrowed flashlights from the firemen who were standing around the one remaining truck.

Kate borrowed tennis sneakers from Mrs. M; they were slightly large, and she tied the laces tight. Everyone was still in pajamas as they entered the south side of the house.

Smoke from the burning vinyl floor had dripped over everything. The windows were covered with soot, and it was impossible to see except for the narrow scope of the flashlight's path through the dark. The house was hot and wet; the firemen had come through spraying the surfaces of every room with water. Water kept dripping; rivulets ran down the walls.

Everything in the old part of the house was coated with black, as if spray-painted—the Hatch wills, the record player, the pencil on the desk, the toothbrushes lined up by the sink, the halved dollhouse in the attic, the faces of the dolls in their beds.

Door handles were still hot. My mother led Kate and Patrick

up the back staircase and told them to go into the attic and take any clothes that did not seem ruined. She then entered the bedrooms on the second floor. She wrapped the bottom of her flannel nightgown around her hand as she pulled open a drawer. Inside the drawer she found rows of neatly folded children's T-shirts, corduroy pants, and sweaters. The clothes had turned a dull gray. She placed her hands inside the drawer and found that the clothes were warm, almost hot, to the touch. She kept her hands there for a moment, feeling the heat from the neatly folded clothes, as if they were the curved backs of sleeping children.

Kate picked a ring off the dresser in her room and turned it over, surprised to see that the other side was still silver. She began to turn everything over, looking for the parts the smoke had not touched. The insides of books, the circle the lamp left on the table. In the toy chest in Patrick's room, they pulled out a stack of board games, reading the names Sorry and Monopoly between the smoky layers.

Everywhere Kate walked, her borrowed tennis sneakers scuffed the floor, leaving a silvery trail. Her hands were black and her white nightgown was smudged as she knelt before the dollhouse, which looked nothing like itself—all definition and pattern lost. She shone the flashlight into the tiny blackened rooms as she heard my mother at the bottom of the attic stairs saying, "We're taking nothing. Nothing can be saved. Leave everything here."

Kate reached into the dollhouse living room, the hand of a giant, invading. She left all of her dolls in their beds but took the cardboard fireplace. She carried it with her downstairs, through the larger house, and out the door.

On the lawn, it was a brilliant morning. Our father then appeared from the gaping hole in the kitchen. His face was covered with soot. He was holding a box.

This box had always been kept in the kitchen, on the counter beside the sink. "Somer's Brother's Fine Metal Boxes, Brooklyn, NY. Patented April 29, 1878"—we had all memorized it, memorized the etching on the top of the palm, five fingers spread. On the tip of each finger was a pig: one with a basket in its mouth, one beneath a roof, one with a plate of meat and a carving knife, one crying, one running. *This little piggy went to market. This little piggy stayed home.*

But now the box was completely black. Our father held it wrapped in a towel, moving the terry cloth beneath his hand as he opened the lid.

Kate still carried the fireplace. She thought she knew everything that was in the box—a pack of matches, a bent corkscrew, a slide of Patrick on the USS *Constitution*, a rubber toy policeman, spare change, keys. But our father removed a fifty-dollar bill.

Did they want to save it? This was the question that the insurance agent would pose only eight hours later—after we had been sent to relatives, after my parents had borrowed clothes from friends and rented a room at the Clipper Ship in Scituate Harbor. *Did they want to restore the house, or put it up for auction, emergency sale?*

"We want to try," they would say, "to keep it."

But that morning, when they stood on the lawn, they knew nothing except that they had escaped, and that our family's survival was entirely due to the false alarms, to my father's madcap exit maps. As if someone had whispered a warning in his ear.

"Take this money and buy the kids some clothes," our father said to our mother.

One side of the bill was completely black; the other side was green and readable. He held the money out to her across the bright-blue day.

The Second Israel
1701–1767

Marshfield Meadows, by Martin Johnson Heade

I give and bequeath to my son Israel Hatch all that part of my farme whereon I now dwell which my father Walter Hatch gave me by his last will and testament. . . . I doe also give my son Israel Hatch all my horseflesh; the bed he usually layeth on with furniture belonging to it; half my greater scales and great leaden weights; meat and meat tubbs; a chest I keep my writings in; a small cupboard marked W.H.; two Come chests; my biggest iron pot; tongues; tramell and fishingline; all my Come English and Indian . . .

—Will of Israel Hatch to Israel Hatch Jr., 1733

At some point in the eighteenth century Israel Hatch Jr., born two years after his grandfather was struck by lightning, decided to paint the inside of the Red House like leopard skin.

The pattern was actually common at the time, made with a round, bristled brush, a spot of black with a half-circle swept over it:

The design covered every surface of the whitewashed kitchen—walls, ceiling, beams, doors. Then he painted the outside of the house red. Leopard on the inside, blood on the outside, like an animal turned inside out.

Red, because it was the cheapest of pigments, was traditionally the first color laid down by the housepainter, used as a primer under white and other, more expensive pigments. Israel probably mixed his own color—grinding with a stone on a slab or in a paint mill, rolling the stone up and down a trough, following recipes:

Sarah Messer

Red Color
May be made with either 1. Vermilion; 2. Red Lead; 3. Rose Pink; 4. Dutch Pink, ground in oil. Venetian red, Spanish Brown and red ochre are coarser paints.

Red Cedar Color
Prime with red lead and white lead, equal quantities. For the second coat use the same. For the third coat, to four pounds of white lead add two ounces Vermillion well ground and mixed, and immediately while the third coat is green, shade with Indian red in imitation of the grains and knots of cedar. For shading, the Indian red should be well ground and mixed.

Israel Jr. was second in the succession of three Israels (born in 1667, 1701, and 1730) who would inherit the newly "red" house. Centuries later, historians would speculate that some houses were painted red solely for economic reasons, or because the owners intended to paint the house white but never got past the primer. Perhaps this was the case with Israel and his sons. The house was left red, primed year after year in anticipation of a windfall, a wash of white that would never arrive.

———

Red as it was, the house must have been visible from the river, glowing at the edge of a shrinking tree line. And perhaps visible too from the shipyards. By now, Two Mile was already reconfiguring itself, sparked by the four ponds that had been dammed for mills on the Two Mile Brook. In the eighteenth century, every business in Two Mile orbited around the shipping industry, a solar system of closer and more distant mills, iron forges, nail factories.

Before daybreak, the sound of industry would have echoed over the river. Men called to oxen that pulled against a load, geeing and hawing. The men called to each other and set the keel, caulked, joined, scraped, applied tallow and pitch. Every day at 11 a.m. and 4 p.m., someone would yell and the men would break for rum. And in the evening, the children or wives of shipbuilders would carry dinner out over the frozen or tide-strewn marsh.

Millworkers felled trees in the woods, dragged them out with oxen, and sliced them down in the mills to be sold to shipbuilding contractors, who hired out shipwrights from the various yards.

Ships were usually contracted by several different owners—slips and brigantines, sixteen or thirty-five tons. When they were finished, shipwrights pushed the boats out into the river. But because the river was so narrow and the ships were so large, the prows often shot into the soft mud of the bank on the opposite side. Sometimes it took two or three days to dig out the boats and turn them downstream. Six men on each side with ropes flung over their backs pulled the ship down to the river's mouth, the ocean. The vessels were guided by a hired pilot, an expert negotiator of the bends in the banks, the rise and fall of water. The pilot would carry a gun and fire it off in the air to mark passage, or would shoot sharks that swam into the mouth from the ocean.

In 1752, Israel Jr. built a gristmill on the third pond on Two Mile Brook, a quarter-mile from the Red House. The exterior of the mill was simple, resembling a barn with a few double-hung windows and shingled sides. It sat facing the pond, on the opposite side of the cart path, the water running through a sluice gate under the road. At one end, the ridge of the roof extended out so that large bags of grain could be hoisted up from wagons. The mill was sturdily constructed to withstand the weather and the vibration of the waterwheel and the grinding stones.

Gristmills like this one needed two grinding stones—an upper stone called a "runner," which turned against a stationary lower "bed stone." The stones ranged from four to six feet in diameter, each with a hole in the center called "the eye." The stones' surfaces were cut with deep sickle-shaped grooves. The furrows and the bed stone worked against each other, serving as shears that tore away chaff from the grain.

The part of the stone that was not grooved was called "the land," the area that actually crushed the grain to powder. The upper stone rotated above the stationary stone below, like two faces perpetually about to kiss.

The mill could not run itself; it required Israel Jr.'s presence, standing and watching the revolving stones. The stones themselves could never touch. If they did, a spark could fly and ignite the dry flour, causing everything to explode. So Israel Jr. stood and watched the revolving stones, maintaining a minute space between them with hair-fine adjustments. The mill was stark, and infested with birds and mice. Flour dust drifted in corners like a snowstorm pushing its way out, dusting everything, drifting into Israel Jr.'s lungs. He wore his own hole in the floor from all that standing and watching.

———

At the base of the Red House meadows, the fourth pond edged up to a long shed. This structure, or a mutation of it, would eventually be photographed at the end of the nineteenth century, a slanted one-story building with a sagging roofline.

This fulling mill, even in the first Israel's time, was used for cleaning and shrinking wool cloth, preparing it to be dyed. The mill primarily fulled cloth for men's and boy's clothes. Eventually, an undershot wheel would be installed in the mill, adding enough power to card wool as well.

Even though the Hatches owned a fulling mill, linen still had to be made by hand from flax grown in fields around Two Mile.

In August, after the flax had been harvested and a stench of rotting plants hung in the air, traveling flax "hacklers" (or "hetchlers") arrived in Two Mile looking for work. With flax grime on their faces, fiber dust on their clothes, they'd inquire at houses, walking into kitchen yards that were filled with the clunking crush of the wooden flax brake, the clank of swingling knifes separating bark from fiber, the whir of spinning wheels, the tick of the clock reel counting skeins. Hackling was the delicate final step in transforming flax from a plant into fiber ready to be spun into thread. The hackler dragged the stems through a series of increasingly smaller iron-toothed combs, the tough barky pieces falling to the ground at his feet. Children scooped up this tow, took it into the backyard, and used it to build little bonfires. If it was done right, the hackled flax resembled handfuls of limp, fine hair.

After the hacklers left, the women would dismantle their flax wheels and carry them on horseback to a neighbor's to hold spinning parties. Towns all over New England established spinning schools, and contests were held on commons for the quickest, most efficient spinner. In 1749, the Boston Society for Promoting Industry and Frugality celebrated their fourth anniversary by organizing three hundred young women to set up their spinning wheels and spin on Boston Commons.

Even after the copious spinning and the weaving, a housewife might end up with just a yard of cloth, the raw gray color of an autumn sky. Bleaching took place in "bleach yards," set some distance from the kitchen door and squared off by a fence to prevent geese, dogs, and children from running over the drying cloth. The process took about one month to complete:

1. soak linen 36 to 40 hours in warm water, rinse and dry.
2. soak in lye and cow dung 48 hours.
3. stretch cloth over the grass in a bleach yard.
4. wash off the cow dung.

5. beat cloth for 2 to 3 hours.
6. place cloth into boiling lye; then removed and soak 24 hours.
7. wash cloth; stretch it over the bleach-green 24 hours.
8. beat with bat staffs.
9. repeat the last three steps for 8 to 10 days.
10. place cloth in buttermilk for 1 to 2 days.
11. wash and beat the cloth again, then stretch it over the bleach-green.
12. sour it again in buttermilk.
13. repeat the process for another week, until the cloth is white enough.

———

In the eighteenth century, Two Mile's population became increasingly tangled and inbred. In typical Hatch fashion, Israel Jr. had married his first cousin once removed and fathered nine children. The Hatches, living in cramped quarters, had begun fighting—brothers not speaking to each other, a Yankee freeze-out. One brother who owned a mill on the upper pond would secure the dam so that only a trickle wound down to the next pond and his brother's mill below. Then, eventually, he would release the water so it flowed in full force, flooding the lower pond and forcing his brother to scramble to use power. But the brother on the lower pond had his own tricks—draining his pond when the dam was down on the upper pond, causing all the ponds to go slack as the water was released to the river.

Day and night, the levels of ponds would rise and fall dramatically depending on the mood of the brothers who never spoke to each other because of an impassable dispute, the origin of which was never written down and which no one seemed to remember. Israel Jr. and his wife, Bethia, all their nine children grown, dealt with the conflict in their own way:

They left.

Then died abroad, leaving no graves, no death records to speak of. Yet, even after their mysterious exit, the ponds continued to roar with the sound of pent-up force released over the thin boards of the sluice gate. Each pond, when full, was flush with the level of the path beside it, the rocks supporting its banks submerged, the surface smooth as a piece of oiled cloth. Israel and Bethia were just two Hatches; by now Two Mile was full of them—each with his or her own genealogical link to Walter, each with his or her own elaborate agenda. Some days, the mill ponds were silent. Other days, their sound could drown out the thoughts in a person's head, could become the argument itself.

Five

Bekah, Ronald, Sarah, Scout, Suzy, and Jessica Messer,
Plimoth Plantation

In his mid-seventies, restoration carpenter Edgar Wentworth had the air of someone who had seen houses like this before—New England homes that had been badly burned, some of them salvageable and some not, depending on how deeply the smoke had sunk into the walls, how much the fire had destroyed. He knew how the house would look: the walls melted and blistered, wood braided, charred table backs, a pantry of exploded bottles—jam, syrup, flour, vinegar—run over surfaces onto the floor, plastic melted over bread, lumps of copper and liquefied electronics. There would be puddles of candles in rooms the fire did not reach, frozen in cascades over the edges of things. Knots of melted wires, scorched hinges. Light switches with arched backs. The blackened faces of clocks. Iron latches would be turned red from the heat, the impurities rising to the surface of the metal; solder in the seams of lanterns flowed to liquid, the pieces strewn where they had fallen clanking to the floor.

The window glass would be almost gone—melted or black-ened—the panes that remained run with cracks—blond hairs on a chalkboard. And light would come through faintly in these places, glowing amber. Fire made even an old house age life-times, made it seem desperate and abandoned. Smoke pulled across walls, across ceilings, and through rooms, tracing the lathing, every crossbeam and nail head visible. Sometimes the smoke-crossed lathing intersected with vertical drips of water left from the firemen's hoses, creating a perverse gingham pat-tern. In the heat of fire, nails pushed out of doorframes, pushed to the surface of plaster, prying their way out.

Wentworth knew that fire burned in a V, heating the highest parts of the room first, leaping through open doors toward the ceiling of the next room, licking up wallpaper, rolling back paint, a rash blooming before the path of the flames.

Entering a burned house was like entering a dream mind—some elements were missing entirely or moved to other loca-tions, the rooms the same but clouded, slightly off. Everything was itself and not itself—like walking through the mind into the shadow parts—the bed the firemen had hauled away from a window now posed in the middle of the room. Fire desires and consumes; it is filled with impatient wanting, the roar of needing more. Wentworth had seen how fire pressed its back against a closed door and moved past it, pushing through every crack.

Outside, trees bent away from the structure, the leaves and branches blackened. The exterior paint dissolved into gobs of crusted tar—the spots where the water in the wood cells boiled and escaped, causing the paint to crater like a peeled sunburn.

Wentworth expected all of this, and he entered the house carrying a yellow No. 2 pencil, stopping at each door molding, each wall and wainscoting, lightly removing a dot of soot with the pencil's eraser.

Three days after she had run out of the burning house, my

mother was back with a flashlight, following Wentworth and his precise, aquatic movements through the gloom, the bright pencil held out before him like a feeler, a neon lure. The flashlight beam passed over rubble, dark shapes, as he tried to determine, from a professional standpoint, whether the house could be saved. The fire had burned the entire west kitchen wing—eating away through the ceiling to the eaves above, stopping at the slate roof. Water had flooded the lower rooms and the basement garage, leaving wires and plaster hanging from the ceiling in coughed-out chunks. The appliances were disgorged, melted. We had lost everything that had been in those rooms—the kitchen, porch, hallways, and bathroom—pots, toys, clothing, a closet-full of wrapped Christmas presents, a player piano, bookshelves.

In what remained of the screened-in porch, they found the bodies of the two kittens, curled around each other in a make-shift bed of towels; the dog and the mother cat had found their way out.

But the fire had not spread to the rest of the house, thanks in part to two firemen who had spent the night monitoring it, wan-dering through rooms up and down the stairs thinking, *So many beds—whom have we missed?*

During the first few days after the fire, neighbors and mem-bers of the local church had come to help sift through the wreckage; they had carried ash out in wheelbarrows, then dug through it, lifting out a door hinge or a nail, a spoon or a cup.

Now Wentworth stopped and bent down near the corner of the fireplace in the living room, touched the eraser to a molding.

"Ya, we can do that," he said, and then, standing, ran the eraser along the mantel. "Ya, that'll come down."

My mother's flashlight beam fixed on Wentworth like a leash, glancing off his shoulder or to the wall or the floor or the window casing where he was tapping the pencil, erasing. Went-worth, after all the silence and wandering, turned to her sud-denly and said that his crew could start the next week.

While we were safe with relatives, my mother and father spent their days in the cold shell of the house, their nights in Scituate Harbor, at seafood restaurants, or in the aqua-blue room at the Clipper Ship, with is faint smell of chlorine and mothballs, sanitary soap. And during this time, my mother tells me as if it were an addendum, she cried constantly. Not necessarily sobbing, although sometimes it was that, but more of a constant stream of tears, like a slow-leaking faucet. It was her fault, she feared—although the workmen all claimed it was their mistake—bad wiring or construction, a faulty appliance. But she knew otherwise. How to explain those rags? She had almost killed her entire family.

"It's not your fault," my father said again and again. Still, her tears made streaks down her sooty face; her nose was red and raw, her face striped.

An elderly neighbor who wintered in Florida was on his way to Logan Airport when he heard about the fire on a local radio station. He made a call from the terminal, telling us we could stay in his house until he returned in May.

His house was a large Victorian filled with long hallways and bathrooms with worn tile. There was a mudroom off the kitchen, and every day my mother would spend mornings in the Red House carting out our burned and smoke-stained belongings, boxing them, and bringing them to a pile in the Victorian mudroom. In the afternoon and evening, sometimes late at night, I would find her standing by the two stainless-steel sinks in the kitchen, up to her elbows in rubber gloves, washing smoked objects.

There is a photograph from that time of my father sitting in the living room of that house holding me on his lap. I am squirming in the photo, perhaps tired, perhaps bored, trying to wrench free of his grasp; I appear as a blonde blur in a mustard-colored turtleneck. My father stares straight ahead at the camera, and his face is one of direct surrender—the kind of look that only comes from extreme exhaustion, or the mental clarity that occurs after surviving severe trauma. It was evening when the photo was taken; a lamp had been clicked on in the background, next to a radiator and the corner of a table piled with books. My father's brown hair is styled in a long bob with bangs brushed across his forehead, and sideburns. He wears a pink-and-brown-striped cotton dress-shirt open at the neck. The photo captured the tension between us—I am a whirl of motion, waving a small stuffed bear that I had sewn from a kit of acrylic fur, foam rubber, and glass eyes; my father is extremely still, his eyes boring a hole through the camera lens and beyond to the eyes of the photographer, who is my mother. He is saying something with his eyes—he is saying that he feels defeated but is trying not to look defeated at the moment because of her, because of the children. *We could have all died*, his eyes are saying.

My mother had left her post in underwater salvage to come out and take a few pictures. They had six kids and a burned historic home between them. At Christmas, there had been few presents—Patrick had received a hockey game with metal players moved by levers and rods; Jess had received a wooden pony with yellow wheels that made a clicking gallop sound when she pulled it across the room by a string; I had received the Sew Your Own Bear kit. In photos, the smell of smoke seemed to permeate us, even in this temporary house. It had seeped into our hair and teeth, into stuffed animals, mattresses, and pillows, so that it seemed our bodies carried the musky odor of our burned belongings—it hung over us like a glower, a depression, a bad mood. The burned house was a ship that went down with all its passengers, my father thought, but somehow no one had drowned. It was a miracle he didn't quite understand.

The year of the fire, I was enrolled in a private kindergarten called Steeple School, in the same classroom as Suzy. The school was housed in a white, steepled Congregational church, a product of the continual church-mitosis that had been happening in Marshfield since the seventeenth century. The church had long since been without a parish, but ran a thriving kindergarten and nursery school, boasting a large staff, good resources, new playground equipment. Our activities involved a lot of pipe cleaners and Styrofoam balls, milkweed-pod parrots and construction paper, or felt animals stuck onto the wall behind bars of a "zoo."

In the classroom I spent little time with Suzy, fixing my attention instead on my newly acquired best friend, Maryanne McGuire. On Halloween, Maryanne had dressed as a witch and approached me in her pointed hat, with black smudge on her face, carrying a broom. "I don't have a best friend yet," she said, "do you?"

I was dressed as a bride, in a truncated, hemmed-in version of one of my mother's cotillion dresses.

"No," I said. "Not yet."

Maryanne was a precocious reader, outgoing and funny. Her favorite book was titled *Ann Likes Red*, which included lines like "Ann likes red. Red, red, red. A blue dress Ann? I like red, said Ann. Red! Red! Red!" One might assume that the book concludes with Ann getting her monochromatic comeuppance and seeing the benefit of other colors of the rainbow. But I'm not sure whether this happened, and even if it did, we never focused on this message. We ran up and down the scrappy dirt hill behind school yelling "red, red, red." These lines became Maryanne's mantra, her code of living. It seemed that Maryanne (who also had red hair) wore, more often than not, the color red. Maryanne was cast in the school play, *The Little Red Hen*, playing, of course, the Red Hen. When asked her name, she would say "Mary-ANNE," emphasizing the *Ann* at the end.

At our borrowed house, my mother continued to line up the blackened items on a dingy towel spread on the left side of the sink. If the object to be washed was a toy, she would hold it up in the air without turning from her position at the sink and say, "Yes or no?" Whoever belonged to the toy would then decide its fate—if we said no, she would throw it in the dump pile, in the far corner of the garage; if we said yes, she would try to wash it. She would dunk the toy in water and begin scrubbing, occasionally rinsing it in the second basin. Then, when it seemed she had cleaned it as best she could, she would place it in a dish drainer, take it out to a different corner of the garage, beyond the mudroom, and put the clean object in a plastic laundry basket.

As a part of her biology major in college, my mother had worked banding small brown bats. The mouths of the caves were very narrow, and my mother, the only woman in the group, was the only person with shoulders small enough to fit through the openings. The caves were halfway up a hill—a series of crevasses that dropped straight down through rock. Her professor gave her a banding gun, strapped her in a harness, and lowered her down by rope. Inside, the cave was narrow and the walls were thick with sleeping bats. Every wall was alive with them, their bodies shitting and crawling over each other in their sleep, elbowing, blind. She dangled in the middle of the cave, headlamp strapped over a knit ski mask. She barely had room to swivel, to bring her arms up to her sides. Her legs felt loose and weak in the harness; darkness fell below her into the sound of dripping water.

She told me how she grabbed the soft body of each bat and clamped it with the gun. She wore heavy leather gloves, so there was no chance of being bitten. The bats barely woke up, and when they did, they screeched and peed on her. After she let them go, they fell a bit, a dark flutter below her where they landed farther down the wall and clung. The biology professor and the other students were above her, in the circle of daylight. Down in the cave, she heard nothing but the rustle and shriek of bats, and the occasional echo of a voice from the surface, followed by a jerk, a lowering of the rope.

With the dim yellowish glow of her headlamp, she was

trapped in a dark jar. When she described this experience years later, she used the same words as she did about those months entering and leaving the burned house. She lived inside the smell of soot, the same way that she had lived among the bodies of the bats, within the vertical hive of bodies.

———

The Red House, having survived the fire, was restored—better than before, some people said. Wentworth, ripping down the damaged ceiling and wall plaster, had found something remarkable: a ceiling panel that resembled leopard skin. The boards were painted with swirls of black over a wash of tan milk-paint. All over the house, in fact, on the first and second floors, Wentworth found hidden ceilings beneath the lower, ruined ones. When he ripped the wet plaster down, there they were, perfect beams. Richard Warren Hatch had found a pile of similarly painted boards in a trash heap during his restoration of the house in 1959. At the time, Hatch was not living in the Red House and thus could only oversee the restoration on weekends. He had salvaged what he could of the boards and fitted them into the ceiling of a bedroom upstairs, but he always felt that he had let this historical aspect of the house be destroyed by ignorant workmen.

The restoration discoveries brought Richard Warren Hatch into our lives again. When he sold my parents the house, he had made it clear that he would never return. But the spring after the fire, he wrote my father a letter:

> *Dear Ron,*
> *If you can stand a surprise—when your old red house is ready, Ruth and I will come and inspect it. No week-end, no night driving, but a morning or early afternoon visit. Just send us a proper signal.*
>
> *Yours, Dick*

And he did return. Our devotion and restoration brought him back, and, as if on cue, when he saw the painted beams he thought had been lost, he fell to his knees and wept.

"He's no small man," my mother said. "Down on his knees in the living room weeping."

Hatch wrote my parents again immediately following the visit, the letter dated only "the day after."

Dear Pat and Ron,

I know that I have never been quite able to express my feelings about the Red House, I suppose because they were a combination that escapes definition. You see, it was not only the love of the house itself with its setting, its long history of family ownership, its every physical inch, so to speak, but something more than that . . . the fact that always there was love inside the house, love not made evident by overt signs simply but recognized by intuition and the heart, and that has been a resource on which I have drawn all my life. A combination, as I say, quite beyond words, but which perhaps explains why, when I had to leave the house I felt that I could never go back—

Anyway I have to write to tell you both that Ruth and I came away yesterday feeling above all that there is the same combination in your house—your home—something transcending the skill and work and perfection of what you have done with the physical house. And so you both have done something immeasurable for my spirit.

"It doesn't look like our house," Kim said when she returned for a visit that summer, "it looks like a museum." She was referring to the new blankness of the low-ceilinged rooms, the walls stripped of wallpaper, the sixties neon gone from the bedrooms upstairs, as if the house had traveled back in time. Though householders of my parents' generation might have tried to keep some historical feel, they also might have put up a contemporary painting or two—a Georgia O'Keeffe print, a Pollock—or at least reserved a wall for pictures of their own children and parents, other relatives. I had seen such a wall of family photos extending the length of the second-floor hallway in Maryanne McGuire's house. The photos documented every year of Maryanne's childhood: her red hair growing longer, then banged, then ponytailed; a sister, then a baby brother joined her. There was no such hallway in our house; in fact, there were no hallways, just a series of rooms, branching off each other like rabbit dens. There were eight kids in the family, but still my parents hung no family photos—no baby pictures, no wedding photos, no grandparents sitting in funny old cars, or in boats, or leaning on cannons or monuments. Nothing. Perhaps they thought it was all too modern.

After the fire, my parents carefully rehung candleholders, secured a brass bed-warmer on the wall near the fireplace, scattered the mantels with hurricane lamps. Silvery daguerreotypes were propped on parlor moldings, Richard Warren Hatch's grandparents and other former inhabitants of the house—a reminder of the house's true lineage. The walls held a ledger from a Hatch Bible, a needlepoint sampler, and a series of wooden butter-molds secured with tiny hooks. The discovered beams remained exposed, and the floor too, the wide boards sanded and stained, strewn with faded hooked rugs. Rooms contained hard, straight-backed chairs and a clock reel used for counting and winding flax, a Victorian rocking horse missing its hair and saddle.

The reframed Hatch wills sat on the dining-room table for about a week after we moved back in. They stared at me every time I walked by—six documents framed in double-sided glass so that both front and back could be read. They were enclosed in thin wood bands, with picture-framing wire, and eye hooks screwed to the top. The paper behind the glass seemed fragile, the handwriting and ink tentative. In the shifting light of the window, I saw the reflection of my face moving over the field of writing and the cloud that seemed to crawl up each document, a stain from smoke or water, a stain I knew was because of the fire, because of us.

Meanwhile, our old smoke-stained and burned belongings, those prefire items that were not salvageable—furniture, carpets, doors, and appliances—had been tossed in a huge pile in the woods along the road to the North River and buried. Another dump was eventually established for smaller smoke-stained objects that could not be cleaned—lamps, clothing, ruined board games, toys. This became known as the Toy Dump, the charnel ground of items from our childhood that did not survive. Grass, a few baby oak trees, and scrub pines eventually grew over the mound that had been buried beneath a pile of dirt by a backhoe, yet, after particularly heavy rains, the matted hair of a stuffed creature would be left exposed, the wheel of a melted truck. We pretended that the charred refrigerator, the plastic chair, the stained dolls or sled or stuffed rabbit had gone away, but we had buried it all so close to us, in our backyard, in the woods behind our house, and for years the earth kept churning things up.

The Third Israel
1730–1809

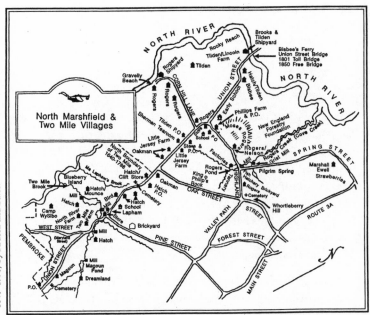

Map by Cynthia Hagar Krusell. Courtesy of Cynthia Hagar Krusell and Betty Magoun Bates. Originally published in *Marshfield: A Town of Villages, 1640–1990*, by Krusell and Bates.

North Marshfield and Two Mile

The inhabitants were awakened in the night by a very loud noise, the houses shaking. They believed it to be an earthquake. The noise was a loud cracking of the earth, heard several times by many people. Some residents rose immediately and found outside their houses that the ground itself had cracked in many places, the fissures several yards in length. It was thought that severe frost had ripped the earth apart, the cracks—like a rift, a small chasm—being wide enough in several places for a man to place his whole arm down into it.

—Lysander Richards, *History of Marshfield* (Plymouth, Mass: Memorial Press, 1901), discussing the event of March 21, 1773

In 1768, a comet dragged its tail across the sky like a wedding gown, a runaway bride. Below it, families in Two Mile split their allegiance to England, to Scituate, to each other. The land, instead of being willed to the eldest son, was continually divided and overfarmed, the parcels growing smaller and smaller.

The Red House, like other houses in Two Mile, probably sheltered boarders, dowager residents, many generations at once—stepchildren, step-grandparents, single men, older unmarried sisters and aunts, schoolteachers, apprentices, hired men and girls, orphans, the sick, the feeble-minded, the bedridden, the elderly, infants.

In winter, the house got even smaller. The Hatches would have "banked" in, piling up reeds from the river, straw, and sand around the sills (or base) of the house to keep the floors and root cellar insulated. Wind blew snow through the cracks in the second-floor chambers. At the time there were no hairbrushes, no toothbrushes, no thermometers to measure how cold it was, no washstands or washbowls. The three buckets of water the Hatches kept by the cooking area froze just a few feet from the fire. Even the well froze. Snow drifted over the banking, built a mountain against the northeast side of the house. The Hatches shut the inner and outer shutters, nailed blankets over the doors.

By spring, the house would have been filthy, smelling of bodies and fermented apples, half-spoiled food. The banking around the house would have started to rot, and clothing, towels, blankets, diapers that hung all winter drying before the fire would have been smoke-stained and pocked with singe marks from stray sparks. Everything in the house needed to be aired out, scrubbed, whitewashed, the fireplace swept of its ashes, the sheets bleached in the yard.

Yet outside the kitchen door, where the Hatches tossed the dirty water, pansies would have begun to bloom, named for the mood that ran high in spring: *fancy-flamy, kiss me, kiss me ere I rise, jump up and kiss me, bird's eye, garden gate, none-so-pretty.*

Israel Three was twenty-five years old when he married his second cousin, Mary Doty, the great-great-granddaughter of rowdy *Mayflower* passenger Edward Doty, who had fought the first duel in Plymouth Colony. They had two children, Amos and Mary, within the first three years of their marriage. Israel was thirty-three years old when he bought the mills from his father, and thirty-eight years old when he purchased half of the Red House, in which he was living. During that time, four of Israel's children died young. His last and youngest, Joel, who would eventually inherit the Red House, was born in 1771.

By then, Two Mile residents would have built their own school and maintained it for fifteen years; they would have twice petitioned for succession from Scituate, a town that taxed them on common land, beaches, and mowing fields they never used. Even though a bridge over the North River had replaced the ferry, the residents of Two Mile rarely needed to go to Scituate Harbor.

In 1773, they drew up a petition asking to be joined to Marshfield. At the time, Marshfield was a motley confederacy of villages—Green Harbor, Ocean Bluff, Marshfield Village, Sea View, Marshfield Hills, Standish Village, Littletown, and Brant Rock. It was also the home of several wealthy Tory families, a cause of much conflict in the surrounding villages. Roiling up to the Revolution, a colonial militia was placed at the mouth of the North River, and several Hatches enlisted in Captain Lothrop's army. "How I long to see those lobster-backs driven off this continent!" one young man wrote. But he wasn't a Hatch.

Neither Israel Jr., Israel Three, nor any other Red House Hatches fought in the Revolutionary War. Marshfield, the town Two Mile wanted to join, was heavily Tory. By 1773, the prominent Tory, Nathaniel Ray Thomas, had already asked for British protection of 240 "loyally disposed people."

The Hatches, it seemed, were divided between Patriot and loyalist. The British troops had come into town looking for information on militiamen who had publicly condemned the crown. Some were squealers, turning their neighbors in. Those who couldn't write gave oral confessions and then signed their names with an "X"; those who were ratted out began sneaking into Tory cellars and, finding bags of British tea, hauled them out, carried them to the top of hills, and set them on fire.

In 1774, when a loyalist merchant of Marshfield made the mistake of admitting that he was selling Tory cattle at town auction, he was attacked by an angry mob. The crowd butchered a cow, threw the carcass into a two-wheeled oxcart, and tarred and feathered the merchant. They then shoved him inside the animal's body cavity and wheeled it to the Duxbury Line, where another mob took over. Occasionally, the crowd would stop, pull the man out of the oxcart and the cow's body, and beat him about the head with the animal's tripe, or intestine. Eventually, they deposited the merchant, half dead and covered in blood, tar, and feathers, in front of a Tory house.

On April 20, 1775, three shots were fired that signaled the beginning of the Revolutionary War, and Marshfield patriots marched over Black Mount carrying a coffin intended for a local Tory leader. By the time they arrived at his house, however, they found only his wife, who claimed her husband had fled for Boston over the marshes.

During the war, resources in Two Mile grew scarce but there was plenty of flax, rye, and beef. Wood could be sold for twenty dollars a cord in Boston, cider eight dollars a barrel. People exchanged flax seed for salt. Some men were drafted, but, reluctant to leave their farms, they paid others to enlist in their place.

Things were going well—crops booming, babies born—or going terribly—inclement weather, inflation, leaking roofs, and no men around to repair them. Family members wrote to each other about clothes and money, about a drowning off a sandbar in the mouth of the river, a woman thrown from a horse, a tree falling on a neighbor who was cutting wood. British soldiers occupied some houses in Marshfield as residents continued to get sick with fever and ague, or cancers that swelled their arms and legs, weeping in running sores. Theses subjects persisted in letters until the end of the war.

In the parlor of the Red House, the standing clock Israel had purchased in 1785 kept perfect time, the clockmaker's name, John Bailey, written across its face. Inside the door of the body of the clock, where the chains and weights hung, the third Israel wrote his name. Whoever inherited the Red House, he decided, would also inherit the clock—each Hatch after writing his name beneath Israel Three's on the paper tacked to the inside of the door.

Perhaps the third Israel was thinking of legacy because only Joel, the youngest of his four sons, had survived into adulthood. And Israel himself had always been a sickly man—he had been sick as far back as 1758, receiving two doctor visits during which an abscess was opened and drained and six dressings were applied.

From 1781 to 1785, Israel had at least nine doctor visits with Dr. Isaac Winslow, who would have arrived carrying treacle water, crocus-mellorium vomits, and glisters in his saddlebag. If Israel had a fever, the doctor would have applied blister plasters to his ankles, neck, and wrists, or given him barley water boiled with anise. If Israel had a pain in his side, the doctor might press hardened horse-dung to his skin to draw out poison; then he would soak more dung in white wine or cider and give it as a drink with salt water. He might ferment strawberry leaves or violets in water and pack them in Israel's mouth.

Mostly, the doctor was called to let blood. He would take from his bag a series of knives that unfolded like a fan of small-toothed hatchets. The arms of the hinged instrument had blades that varied from the size of an infant's thumbnail to that of a grown man's. The blades were flat and pointed like teeth, and fit together like a spike in the doctor's palm when closed. Along with the knives, he brought a pewter bowl that was ringed from the middle down to the bottom in numbered circles, a way of measuring the amount of blood drained. Israel would lie on a bed with his arm extended, his shirtsleeve rolled above the elbow, and the doctor would make a small, clean cut with the knife, holding the bowl under the wound to catch the blood. Over a period of years, the doctor was called to bleed Israel eight times.

In 1790, the Red House kitchen hearth and chimney caught fire. Perhaps a spark flew out of the fire and onto the wood floor, or caught a spinning wheel laced with flax, or someone's skirt hem. Perhaps rendered fat spilled and ignited, poured over the floor.

The fire destroyed the entire cooking hearth and burned up through the second-floor bedchamber into the attic. Records indicate that no one was injured, but it is clear from the extent of the damage that the Hatches must have lived with the ruin for a while, or moved somewhere else temporarily. The kitchen—all the pots and swing arms, the fire grate—was reconstructed in a new ell on the east side of the house, a Dutch oven added for baking. The central chimney in the old part of the house was remodeled with three smaller fireplaces, and, depending on the extent of the ceiling damage, the roof may have been repaired as well. The Hatches boxed the rough-hewn beams, added hearths and mantels to the second-floor chambers. A series of sheds formed the west wing, connecting the main body of the house to the large barn.

———

Israel Three's wife died in 1802, at the age of seventy-one. Two years later, Israel, at the age of seventy-four, married his third cousin. Within the year, he sold "all my homestead with the building thereon . . ." to his son Joel Hatch for two thousand dollars, leaving dower rights to his second wife until she died or was remarried. In his will, written a few months later, he mentions no house or land, but leaves two of his sons a one-eighth part of his "money and securities for money." Joel received all of his father's cattle, horseflesh, swine, clothing, farm tools, bedroom furniture, and the clock. Israel Three left his second wife a hundred dollars and a desk.

Israel's son Joel was the executor of his father's estate, drafting an inventory of effects left in the Red House on April 20, 1809: "two silver spoons, twelve teaspoons, one eight-day clock, a looking glass, a desk, hoops, spinning wheels, ironware, glassware, farming tools, one chaise, livestock, horse and cattle, hay in the barn, sheep and lambs, Indian corn, salt pork, cheese and hog fat, three bushels of potatoes."

When Israel died, he was probably sharing the Red House with Joel, who had taken over the mills and was prominent in the church, known by many as Deacon Joel. On a small scrap of paper, the gravestone carver wrote him a receipt:

A pair of gravestones for your father's grave	$11.82
Eight lines of verse	2.00
Coffin and trimmings	3.00
Digging a grave	.50

Six

Kerry, Jessica, Kate, Bekah, Patrick, Suzy, Kim,
and Sarah Messer, 1976

T hough my father had gone to great pains after the fire to restore all of the items that Richard Warren Hatch had given
him, we were also a family of kids with modern kid needs. Next
to the cupboard of breakfast cereal hung a Betty lamp, a wick-
snipper, a cherry-pitter. The more my father collected and replaced, the more extreme the juxtaposition became: Shaker
sewing box and Snoopy doll; glass-bottomed pewter mugs and
plastic Goofy Grape cup; Civil War musket and abandoned
Slinky; a cobbler's bench, awls, and shoe pegs, and Hoppity
Horse, a row of muddy Keds.

If there was any doubt about the heritage we inhabited, it
was gone now. My father repainted the sign at the end of the
driveway: "The Red House: 1647."

16-47, 16-47, 16-40-se-huh-ven. The date burned in my
brain. I said to the house: You are a ship. Your bones are made of

wood. You have floated in this field for over three hundred years, and the men who built you have all drowned.

My father, meanwhile, had begun using the house and its history as coercion. The walls of the house were extremely thin, and whenever one of my siblings complained about the cold, the dampness, or the frost on the *inside* of the windows, my father always sighed and said, "Think of all those years when people lived here without electricity!"

Questions like "Why do windowpanes clatter or crossbeams creak?" were always answered with: "It's an old house!" A common phrase became, "We're roughing it like they did in the old days." This led to an ideology of sorts, one of sanctity with the past—not our genealogical past, but the house's. Of course we adapted. Since I was born there, I had no choice but to live with the house. I knew nothing different except the increasing and vague recognition that other places—like schools and grocery stores and doctors' offices—were bright and warm in the winter and our house wasn't.

The only structure that resembled our house in the slightest was the Unitarian Church in Duxbury, where my family went every Sunday. For me, at age seven, the church was merely a starkness filled with rows of hard white benches. A highway of maroon carpeting ran from the heavy front doors to the pulpit that looked over the congregation.

There I spent my time either in the sanctuary or at Sunday school, sitting in the linoleum basement on a plastic chair, gluing pieces of construction paper onto empty milk cartons. The Unitarians were always promoting civic or left-wing events, especially, it seemed, those that had to do with either New England preservation or El Salvador. That year, the project was to send a chicken, pig, or cow to Africa to help save a village. I had signed up for a cow, so the milk carton became the receptacle for my money for a year—saved up, I imagined, to buy that cow a plane ticket.

In the sanctuary, the backs of pews held hymnals bound in leather with gold-embossed letters. This, I realized, was what we were worshipping in this place of no icons—no crosses, no references to Jesus or Mary or God or the Holy Spirit—just words. In the second grade, I had been diagnosed with the worst case of "mirror-writing" the Marshfield School System had ever seen. "Mirror-writing" was a fancy term for writing backward. I didn't just write backward, I wrote perfectly backward. So perfectly that you could hold it up to a mirror and read it the correct way. My letters were well formed, my sentences complete. If pressed, I could also write normally, yet sometimes I would switch in mid-sentence to the reflection of the sentence I had just written. Patrick called me "spawn of the devil"; the guidance counselors at the school enrolled me in a special class for a month, told me to stop writing left-handed; and then I was cured.

Still, when I flipped through the hymnal, the notes on the page resembled a cloud of insects moving back and forth, the pages making a soft *plat-plat-plat* sound, a wave of air against my face. Words sped by—GLORY, HIM, SPRING, MORNING, HIM, GLORY, JERICHO, HIM, *plat-plat-plat*, until my mother finally whispered, pinching my arm, "Sarah, please."

But my mother's grip on me was fleeting—she had three of us and a toddler on her lap. A large woman in the choir opened her mouth wide, three times larger than anyone else. The choir began to sing, and this lady's mouth took over, and my sisters and I stood on our footstools and tried to get a look. I could sense that my mother liked church, and I sat next to her to make it clear that I liked it too. But mostly I wanted to sit next to her because I loved the way she smelled, lipstick and Chanel No. 5. I loved the fact that she was dressed up in a gold turtleneck and wraparound Indian-print skirt, knee-high boots, her hair piled on her head; I loved the pendant watch that swung against her chest as she stood holding the book and singing very softly with the rest of the church, who unfolded from their seats when the minister said, "Please rise."

"I make all their clothes in order to save money," she said to the women at the postservice cookie-and-punch reception. "We just restored a very old home. A colonial." The other women nodded their heads. *A colonial.*

My father always stood some distance away from my mother, talking with a group of men who held their punch cups before their wide-striped ties, their chests bursting with Old Spice.

——·——

In the field near the river road, my father built a barn. In it he stored an ever-increasing collection of X-rays, an overflow from the Scituate office. Each thin manila envelope contained a film, a square silver image of the inside of some unknown person, and these were lined along shelves at the far length of the barn. He told me that when he had enough he would sell them for their silver content—the images, the blurry thigh bones and rib cages, melted down to earrings, a necklace, a dime.

In the meantime, he tied hundreds of tinfoil bows to the branches of the fruit trees in order to scare away birds. The sun hit the silver bows and cast spots on the sides of the house, till the whole yard shook with the soft tinkling of the bows and spots of light, the way mirrored balls fanned spots of light out across the floors of discos in distant cities.

There was something magical about our very existence in the house then, an elation, a second chance. Weekends, my father would drive a rusted pickup back and forth across the disco yard, hauling canoes, a pile of weeds, boards to build a dock on the river. He was always hauling some kid over his shoulder and running for the marsh, yelling, "Into the swamp, into the pond, into the river." Throwing us, lighting bottle rockets and firecrackers. Kerry and Kate laced Jacob's ladders between their fingers and sang all the verses to "Bad, Bad Leroy Brown." My father's friends dug a hole in the backyard and spit-roasted a lamb or a goat, standing around all day drinking Ballantine ale. Kate rolled an unending sheet of butcher paper across the lawn and began to sing and illustrate "Bad, Bad Leroy Brown."

My father also drove a battered GMC Suburban that he had nicknamed "the White Whale." The White Whale was losing its ceiling felt, which hung like a billowing sail above where we'd sit, four in a row on the cracked blue seats wrapped in the waft of old vinyl and a slow oil leak. Most of the older children lived with us at the Red House now, and often the White Whale carried as many as ten people, the smaller children sleeping on pillows thrown on the floor between the back seats.

Our large family bred an even larger solar system of friends, honorary siblings, adopted uncles and grandparents. Betty Hatch had lived on the hill above the Red House when my parents had moved in. After her husband died in 1960, she had sold the White House, torn down the hunting cabin on the hill, and built a small modern house, where she lived with her youngest daughter. Betty was Richard Warren Hatch's sister-in-law, wife of his beloved younger brother Tracy, but the two disliked each other vehemently. Betty had introduced herself to my parents at the river, where she often had cocktails with friends. She was a large woman, nearly six feet tall, whose long hair was streaked with gray. By the time she met my parents, she was in her late sixties. She would visit often, bearing a bottle of Absolut vodka, which she drank on the rocks as she smoked and told bawdy jokes, a small tremor in her hand causing the ice in the glass to clink like a tambourine.

Besides the Hatches, my father cultivated several parental figures who would visit and pat us on the head, send birthday and Easter cards. Mrs. Berini, as promised, was invited down, bringing several varieties of salami. "Uncle Max," who wasn't related to us in any way, came and went with my dad, as did Sven Drageset, who set up a bird-watching tent in the back field.

And during the summer and school holidays, Stacy Scott, a boy from inner-city Boston, would live with us as an adopted brother. My father had thought Stacy would be a companion for Patrick, but Stacy quickly established himself as a ladies' man and a crooner, writing poetry and singing pop songs with Kerry and Kate as the White Whale bumped along to the beach or the mountains, or wherever we were going. On particularly long trips, Kate and Stacy would sing from Cat Stevens's *Tea for the Tillerman*, switching parts on the duet "Father and Son," leaning over the back seat.

But inside the Red House, nothing colorful or contemporary was ever placed on the walls. Suzy tried to hang a Bambi poster on her door, but the masking tape kept unsticking and the poster would continually ruffle to the floor. Having seen the movie *Sleeping Beauty*, I developed the habit of wrapping myself in an old velvet curtain and lying in the middle of the living-room floor, my hair spread out like a fan. Whenever anyone asked what I was doing, I'd say, "I'm sleeping for a hundred years." But not many people asked. The older kids had begun to step over me; Suzy and Bekah got tired of my mattress-commercial imitation and went outside.

"Oh, good, she's dead," Kim said finally, and nudged me with her toe, which I pretended not to feel.

"I'm sleeping for a hundred years," I said. And, indeed, the living room contained an eighteenth-century spinning wheel, the cause, according to the movie, of Sleeping Beauty's instant coma. My hands remained perfectly still, crossed over my chest.

In a hundred years, would the house fall down around me? Would my family still own it? Would we be ghosts? All I knew was that in a hundred years I would still be sleeping on the floor, beautiful and unmoved.

"And then?" Kim asked. "And then what?"

"Then a prince will come," I said.

"You're in a *living room*," Kim sighed. "Go outside. Get out of that curtain."

———

There was the house's history, and there was our growing misin- . terpretation of it. For my part, I hardly remembered Richard Warren Hatch, the original Red House storyteller. My parents had taken me to see him on the Cape a number of times, and I did know that he had written two novels about the house and the people, his ancestors, who had lived there. I did not remember the day he returned to the Red House after the fire, breaking his self-imposed vow to stay away. At night, before bed, my mother read us the two children's novels Hatch had written, *The Curious Lobster* and *The Curious Lobster's Island*. The books were set in Two Mile, on the North River, and chronicled the adventures of an old but adventurous Mr. Lobster, who through his wit and intelligence had evaded capture and thus grew to a very large size. As a child, I associated Richard Warren Hatch more keenly with his characters the bear, the badger, and the ancient lobster than with the shadowy image of a tall man weeping in our living room.

The fire had left the lobster books black along their spines, the front covers so worn they nearly separated from the pages as my mother opened them. Inside each was Richard Warren Hatch's bookplate—a line drawing of the Red House with a schooner behind it sailing up the river. On the next page, the inscription: "This copy being especially for Ron and Pat Messer who are the inheritors of Mr. Lobster's private domain in the year 1965—Richard Warren Hatch." The book's first illustration plate, facing the inscription, showed a partridge backed up against a tree in the dark woods and surrounded by the lobster, bear, and badger. " 'It is a good thing I came along,' said the Permanent Partridge."

In the first book, Mr. Lobster confronts an older (and he assumes wiser) lobster in a slatted "house" at the bottom of the ocean. They begin talking about the delicious fish left in the house, but the conversation is cut short when the house is lifted on end and ascends from the ocean floor up out of sight. In a few minutes, the house returns without the old lobster. It is then that Mr. Lobster realizes that he should not go into one of those houses unless he "wanted to be gone." "All his life he had never gone into those houses, which he saw quite frequently at the bottom of the ocean. That was how he lived to be sixty-eight years old and was not gone yet," my mother read aloud. The smoke-damaged music box sat high on a dresser; like the lobster and the house, it represented what survived, what was permanent. Its song became the song of triumph, twisting its off-key tones over our sleeping heads.

Kim, now a teenager, had been sent east from California to finish high school, joining Kerry and Patrick to live in the Red House year-round. Upon returning, she immediately took over the old bunkhouse as her "room." The bunkhouse was nothing more than a dilapidated shed with several ten-by-ten-foot rooms about twenty yards from the back door of the main house, a storehouse for old paint cans and my father's broken-down antique truck. In one of the rooms, Kim installed a wood-burning stove, set a mattress on the floor, hung Chinese paper lanterns from the ceiling, strung beads across the door. Tapestries and velvet swaths stretched across the walls. The whole place smelled strongly of mildew and incense.

Kim came during these years of restoration and recovery, and everyone was trying to make the best of it. When I wasn't sleeping for a hundred years on the living-room floor, I wore the same striped shorts for weeks, and kept my hair in braids that hung down like dirty-blond ropes beneath a floppy cloth hat that Kim had given me from her California wardrobe.

My remodeled second-floor bedroom on the west side of the house still had its narrow twin beds, but Suzy now had a room of her own. Every night, I would hear Kerry practicing the piano in the living room below. I would lie down and peer through the crack in the floorboards where I could see her hands moving over the keys, feeling only the thin space, the board, between me and the room below, where her fingers moved. Her feet pedaled out dirges, processionals, her head nodding, her straight brown hair falling neatly halved down the sides of her face past her octagonal silver-rimmed glasses. I moved my own arms out across the floor like airplane wings. My sister, somewhere in the landscape below me, playing a piano. She played Chopin's nocturnes, music that always sounded like falling wings, a flock of birds circling.

Kim wore the same pair of Levi's and dirty parka to high school every day. She bought an air compressor and a few oxygen tanks and began airbrushing unicorns and rock-band insignias on her friends' T-shirts for extra money. Soon vans with small tinted portals would rumble up the curved driveway, and Kim would haul out her tanks, colored bottles and brass screwtips. She'd spend the day standing in the gravel driveway in her cutoffs, talking to skinny long-haired boys while she painted landscapes on the vast metal sides of the vans.

————

By the age of nine, I had stopped writing backward, but I never learned to spell. My best friend, Maryanne McGuire, taught me tricks. "Want to know how to spell 'eight'?" she asked. "Not 'ate,' think 'e' for 'egg,'" she said. "Egg-ch-t. Eight."

On the school playground, we gave each other new names, developed our own herd of horse-girls—practicing gaits and snorting around the playground, past the kickball fields and tetherball poles.

Maryanne borrowed horses from a nearby investment barn and boarding stable called Rocky Reach. Real-estate developers owned it. Rocky Reach was also the name of Maryanne's street, situated at the other end of Two Mile, above the old shipyard. At Rocky Reach, Maryanne rode horses named Baja and Oh-My-Dassie, all tax write-offs.

When Kerry got a horse for her fifteenth birthday, I got one too as an elderly equine companion. Mine cost nothing and was twenty-five years old. Looking in his mouth, I could see long yellow teeth. He gummed his hay and then spit it out. He came with the name Rusty, already an old thing. My fantasies: pretending that he could eat like normal horses, that his lip didn't droop when he slept. Fantasies included Maryanne. A photograph shows us leading the horse pulling a toboggan filled with wood; we were pretending to be "colonial."

Inevitably, my horse got colic—survived—then got it again and died. The day my horse died, my parents and I had spent hours walking him in circles in the paddock behind the barn. Jess, Bekah, and Suzy shadowed us, tightroping carefully around the top rail of the paddock fence in their pajamas, arms outstretched for balance, saying nothing. Night became day became night again. Finally, at midnight on the third night, my father drove to his office, returned, and shot the horse up with Demerol. For the next four hours, I watched my horse sweat and shake in the middle of the paddock, while the dogs circled, whimpering. The horse seemed oblivious to anything around him, his eyes rolled back, his body tense. When his fit stopped, he walked to the other side of the paddock and lay down and slept. The drugs actually bought him a few more days, the vet said when my father confessed his transgression. Inevitably, the horse got sick again, and the decision was made that he needed to be put down. So this time the vet took out a needle, and the horse put his head on the ground, and I watched the breath go in and out of his nostrils and then just stop. Maryanne was not there—nor were any of my older sisters.

There was a backhoe, a large hole, and a funeral with yellow roses. I held a rose while dirt was packed down with a shovel. A rock stolen from an old stone wall became a headstone. Already I was imagining how a body turned to bone and earth; already I was spinning a story, a great myth to tell Maryanne about his heroic death. So I left the grave and walked back into the house.

———

Throughout the 1970s, the town was caught up in its own myth-making—beginning with a "sea monster" washed on ashore, and ending with a local land-developer's discovery of hundred-year-old horse skeletons buried standing in their graves, fully tacked with bridles and saddles, as if ready to ride off down some colonial highway.

The back of the Scituate Town Report described the day a "monster" washed on shore:

> After the tide receded a long body lay in full view. As news of a "sea serpent" spread, great numbers of people rushed to the beach, and by the next day thousands had seen the awesome sight.
>
> Many were the conjectures made as to the identity of the species—possibly a shark, perhaps a serpent, or some denizen of the deep. Experts disagreed, and a future determination was made possible only by the removal of the carcass from the sand where it had been carried to the New England Aquarium in Boston. There, in about a year, it will be mounted and a decision made as to its identity.
>
> We are pleased to present a picture taken twenty minutes after the creature landed on the shore.

The "creature" turned out to be some sort of narwhal—a whale with a unicorn horn, Kim told me. And the buried horses had belonged to Daniel Webster, the man who, the story goes, argued with the devil himself and won.

The Bicentennial came and went. Banners, "1776–1976," swagged across Route 3A, Duca's 5 & 10, and Famous Pizza. The revolutionary drum-and-fife song was piped into the air-conditioned aisles of Angelo's Supermarket, advertisements on local radio, school hallways.

As part of the Massachusetts Bicentennial celebration, Bob Dylan, Joan Baez, Allen Ginsberg, and Sam Shepard breezed through Plymouth with the Rolling Thunder Review. According to James Deetz, former head of Plimoth Plantation, none of the counterculture icons were very impressed with the Pilgrim town's attempts at preservation. "Plymouth is a Donut of a town," Sam Shepard wrote in the *Rolling Thunder Log Book*. "The kind of place you aspire to get out of the second you discover you've had the misfortune of having been raised there. Old women dress up in Pilgrim outfits . . . and complain about the damn Pilgrim hat, little white bonnets that keep slipping down their necks."

The people he was mocking—the people who were trying desperately to re-create history—were people like my parents. One November, they had even had the brilliant idea to partici-pate in a "First Thanksgiving" re-enactment at the Plantation. "Bringing the 17th Century to Life," a brochure claimed. "Liv-ing History" had evolved in the sixties as a response by anthro-pological historians to antiquarianism—the idea that history could be better learned through interaction with objects and three-dimensional space than with primary documents in archives or summarized textual histories based on those docu-ments. Plimoth Plantation grew out of a desire to "put the visi-tor back in time," "to see what it was really like," "to be a Pilgrim." Plimoth Plantation's self-concept revolved around the choice of "third-person versus first-person history"; whereas the antiquarian would say, "Back then, in the olden days, *they* did such-and-such," and the popular historian would say, "Back then, in the olden days, *we* did such-and-such," the "Living Historians" at Plimoth Plantation took it one step further and said, "Now, in 1627, we do such-and-such."

At first, my sisters and I had loved the idea. We were enamored of the costumes, especially my father's buckle shoes and top hat. There were boxes of child-sized Pilgrim shoes, undergarments, smocks, and a pile of white cotton caps, the dresses slightly scratchy and smelling of hay. For some reason, my mother dressed Jessica like a boy in a stocking cap and tiny leather pants.

The rest of the afternoon had passed with cold regularity and the endless churning of the butter in a wooden tub. Suzy and Bekah and I took turns with the butter, and when we weren't churning, we were allowed to run around the village. But pretty soon I exhausted the boundaries—I'd seen the pony behind the fence, seen the pigpen, seen the geese, the blacksmith shop. I was bored and cold. Jessica had been screaming all day, and I began to live inside the sound of her wails, my skin a halo of needles.

"She is mad that she's a boy," I eventually offered as a solution, thinking maybe we could change her clothes.

"No, she just has an ear infection," my mother had said, moving Jessica across her hip as she struggled with something on the fire, some sort of water with cranberries floating in it. We had no idea where our father was; he had spent the whole day outside, in the distance, from where we could hear the firing of guns.

"Mom, can I have some gum?" one of us asked.

"Gum? What do you mean, gum?" A pause. A blank stare.

"You know, gum."

"Gum . . . Well, I've never heard that word before." She was standing in the middle of the tiny room, the dress, slightly too big for her, a giant bell around the clapper of her body.

One of us started to cry. "I can't feel my feet!" someone was shouting. My hands were raw little pieces of meat. I remember slapping them against the rungs of a chair.

"Silly, gum isn't going to be invented for two hundred years! We live here now. This is what it's like. We're having *fun*," she said, and then we all had a doomed feeling.

———

Back home, we were beginning to realize that our house wasn't that different from the Pilgrim shacks. Sometimes this was a good thing, other times not. The Blizzard of 1978—which clobbered the East Coast, left hundreds stranded, and knocked out power for nearly two weeks—made little difference to us. Expanding the Plimoth Plantation experience, we lit the rush lamps, the kerosene; we cooked a turkey on a spit in the reflector oven placed close to the giant hearth; we used the bed-warmers; we made toast in antique cast-iron toast-holders, and popcorn in a wire basket with long handles that we dangled over the flames. Suddenly there was a use for all the contraptions that had cluttered the shelves and corners of the house for years. During the blizzard, my doomed feeling about the house transformed into a pride that bordered on arrogance. "Our house is older than the Revolution!" I'd tell anyone who'd listen.

But the renewal was brief. The house was becoming, in my opinion, a site of growing embarrassment. During the height of the seventies energy crisis, my father sealed off the old part of the house, covered the windows in plastic, and kept the heat only high enough to prevent the pipes from bursting. The kitchen became the only livable room, and we huddled around a Sunbeam kerosene space-heater that looked like R2D2. But we still had to sleep in the old part of the house. Often I would wake up to find frost on the inside of the windows, frost on my upper lip. Kim and Kerry, it seemed, responded to this by moving out—to Maine, to college. To compensate, my father bought the rest of us flannel nightgowns, long underwear, down slipper-booties, and electric blankets, told us to do the best we could, that we'd get used to it.

Like someone from another country, like a fish thrown out of water and onto the bottom of a boat, I'd walk into other people's houses wide-eyed and confused. Shag carpeting amazed me. An overstuffed chair. Anything new with the plastic still on it. Anything chrome. People said, "Isn't it neat that you grew up in an old house?" But I had no answer for this. After the fire, every last detail in the Red House was meant to be "historic." Did we have toothbrushes? Yes. Did the faucets work in a timely or straightforward fashion? No. There were no wall light-switches or carpeting, only the faulty TV in a dank basement. At first the world outside the Red House seemed backward. Then I did.

I began to sleep over at Maryanne's house, at the other end of Two Mile. Maryanne's father, a lobsterman, kept his traps and his boat in their driveway, and their gray-shingled house was often surrounded by a fortress of wooden pots—with their see-through slats and webbing, the final home of hungry, unintelligent shellfish. Maryanne's father stacked the traps five feet high in places, a makeshift wall. Near the traps lay brightly colored buoys. Big plastic waders hung on the side of the garage like a drowned man's legs.

Inside, the kitchen floor was covered with bright, clean linoleum; Maryanne had posters (posters!) on her bedroom walls, and long flat closets with doors that slid. The bathroom had wide white surfaces, the mirrors ringed with light bulbs like the makeup room of a movie star. They had a "den" with a color TV and comfortable couches. Even the word "den" seemed to imply something both modern and instinctual. I imaged a room filled with very well-behaved bears. Maryanne's mother made us tuna sandwiches, and we spent most of our time in Maryanne's room, eating, curling our hair, and listening to Marshfield's new radio station, WATD—shorthand, we knew, for "We're at the Dump."

Meanwhile, down the road from the Red House, the efforts of the Marshfield Historical Society and the Save the Mill Committee sputtered and failed. They had farmed out the restoration to "Project Enterprise," an ill-fated program designed to give high-school burnouts something to do after school besides vandalizing the Dumpsters behind Tedeschi's Quick Mart. Shaggy-haired in their rock-concert T-shirts, they mostly sat around on sawhorses and smoked, revving the occasional skill saw for kicks. After the blizzard, the teenage boys never came back to the mill. And while contemporary houses all over town blazed back on like power plants and were light and warm again, the Red House remained drafty and cold.

Deacon Joel
1771–1849

1752
Israel Hatch Mill
Marshfield, Massachusetts
George Richardson.

The Hatch mill, by George Richardson

Instantly plunge the part in cold water. If the parts are not blistered, wrap in cotton bats, or wash in alum, whey or vinegar . . .

If fungus or proud flesh arise, sprinkle with powdered chalk . . .

Give opium internally to allay pain and irritation. If the part is absolutely destroyed, apply emollient poultice until it sloughs. See mortification.

—William Hand, "The Care of Burns and Scalds,"
from *House Surgeon and Physician* (Hartford, Conn., 1818)

Under the care of Deacon Joel, the Red House progressed from a patchwork duplex to a formal farmhouse, with north and south parlors and sleeping chambers on the second floor. He planted two apple trees in the yard behind the Red House, planted a wisteria vine over an archway near the back door of the kitchen ell. Deacon Joel Hatch was prominent in town affairs, and, because of his attention to the mills, a one-man institution in Two Mile. He grew up during the Revolutionary War—through the surrender of Cornwallis and the ratification of the Constitution. He was eighteen years old when George Washington became president. At twenty-five, he married Huldah Trouant, and had seven children with her, all of whom lived into adulthood. A daguerreotype taken in old age shows a long, broad face and a mouth pulled downward, slightly sunken from loss of teeth. He exhibits the high forehead, whiskery eyebrows, and full head of hair that would be passed on to his progeny into the twentieth century.

A magnetic family-man and purveyor of church activity, Deacon spent his evenings in the Red House parlor reading the

Bible or one of his many books on religious controversy. His library included the following titles:

1. *Christianity Against Infidelity*
2. *Winchester's Dialogues on the Universal Restoration*
3. *An Inquiry into the Scriptural Import of the Words Sheol, Hades, Tartarus, and Gehenna; all translated "Hell" in the Common English Version*
4. *An Inquiry into the Scriptural Doctrine Concerning the Devil and Satan; and into the extent of the duration expressed by the terms Olim, Aion, and Aionios, rendered Everlasting, Forever, etc., in the Common Version, and especially when applied to punishment*

An anti-lounging book titled *The Duty and Advantage of Early Rising As It Is Favorable to Health, Business and Devotion* began with the following paragraph:

> *Lying longer in bed than the necessities of life require is a habit, which can be distinguished by no milder term than that of* sensual indulgence. *It is not merely a sin of gross omission; it is one of actual commission. It is not merely spending the most precious part of the day in a way that is useless; it is spending it in a way that is prejudicial to the mind and destructive to health. It weakens and pampers the body. It unmans the faculties, enervates and enfeebles the mind, and debilitates the whole intellectual system. It sows the seeds of hurtful and foolish desires.*

The book's frontispiece depicted a young man in a nightcap reclining in an elegant four-poster while sunlight streamed in the window. His friend is caught rushing in the room exclaiming, "I am now come to solemnly inform you, Paley, that if you persist in your indolence, I must renounce your society!"

Deacon Joel took the book's philosophy seriously—he rose every day at 4:30 a.m., milked the cows, made his fire, cut wood, and cleaned out the ditches in the dyke meadows along the salt-hay fields of the North River. After breakfast, he worked a twelve-hour day felling trees, driving his oxen, and running the mills.

One can assume that when he bought the Red House in 1805 Joel and his growing family lived with his father, Israel Three, and Israel's second wife, Jane. At the time, Deacon Joel's oldest son, Joel Jr., was eight years old and learning to write in school, learning to be a gentleman—bowing and taking off his hat if he happened to be wearing one. He was learning grammar and the correct pronunciation of words. His grandfather Israel Three would have spoken differently from the schoolteacher—he would have said, "I sot down," whereas the schoolteacher would have said, "I sat down." He would have described the "pint of a knife" instead of the "point of a knife"; said "yaller" instead of "yellow," "ile" instead of "oil," "jine" instead of "join," "spile" instead of "spoil." Israel Three wore old-style fashions—pantaloons that came down below the knee, the bottoms buckled over the tops of long stockings; his hair growing long, tied at the nape of his neck in a queue.

Leaving for school, Joel Jr. would throw a blanket over his head and wear splatter boots made of his father's old cut-up stockings over his shoes. Sometimes he'd bring a firebrand, a glowing stick from the hearth, to light the school stove. In winter, the schoolhouse never warmed up. Clouds of breath hung around the bent heads of students as they wrote on paper the teacher had ruled for them with a plummet. Often Joel Jr. found the ink frozen in his well when he dipped the pen.

On Sundays, the entire family made the journey to the meetinghouse in an oxcart, riding double on horseback, or setting off early by foot. If they walked to church, they'd stop at least at one neighbor's, maybe two, along the way, to thaw out and continue in a larger group. The meetinghouse still wasn't heated, and wind whipped in through the clapboards; worshippers kept their blankets folded over their laps. Some women brought hot stones or bricks to the meetinghouse and wrapped them in a blanket on the floor, leaving a lake of melted snow beneath their skirts, running under the pews.

In November 1811, the presiding pastor, William M. Shaw, delivered a sermon entitled "The Folly and Danger of Presuming a Time to Come." Six drowned and shipwrecked sailors had washed up on the shore in Marshfield; the bodies of the anonymous men were carried to the meetinghouse, where they were laid out before the congregation.

"Here we have no continuing city. The world is not our abiding place," the sermon instructed. "Life is but a vapour, which appeareth a very little time, and then vanishes away. All sublunary things are liable to change, and man himself, the lord of this lower world, to the greatest change of all."

By 1811, the landscape had changed radically; much of New England had been deforested, and Two Mile consisted of long views of rolling farmland stretching to the river. Earlier that year, a forest fire had destroyed nearly two thousand cords of wood, burning across fields and farmland for nearly a week.

On the other side of Marshfield, eleven-year-old Samuel Parris, impressed with the fires (which were all apparently started by human error), wrote poems about them in his daybook:

> There was a man, a rich old sire
> He carried coals all full of fire
> This man we see was not so smart
> So he upset his apple cart.
> There was a man whom fate did spare
> He tried to make good earthen ware
> But lifting up his head much higher
> He set his own land all on fire.

There was a man all full of fun
Who made a fire to see it run.
But as it did not act so good
It ran about and burnt his wood.

Because of the fires and the shipping industry's systematic
deforestation, lumber was scarce, which is why many people
were skeptical when Deacon Joel decided to add a sawmill along
the side of the gristmill his father and grandfather had operated
for years.

Every weekday and some Saturdays, Deacon Joel fed logs into
the blade. He controlled how the water was let down, the waterwheel turning six thousand revolutions per hour. He would eventually replace the mill's vertical blade with a circular saw that had
inserted teeth, metal tongue, and guard, and later, after the Deacon was long dead, his son Samuel would hire a man who drank
too much, who one time, in a sleepy gesture, or perhaps off balance in his drunkenness, would place his hand down on top of
the whirring blade and watch his palm divide in half.

In August 1827, Joel's wife, Huldah, passed away, and seven
months later, he married Rebekah Hatch, a distant relative who
could also trace her bloodline back to Walter.

Around this time, one of Deacon Joel's older sons built a
large white house of twelve rooms less than four hundred feet
away from the Red House. With his second marriage, and thus
the establishment of his second family, Deacon Joel must have
begun deeding land to the older children, who were starting
families.

Although it wasn't much, Deacon Joel was planning on leaving the mills and the Red House to Joel Jr., who, like his great-
great-great-grandfather Walter, was interested in shipbuilding.
But when depression struck shipbuilding in the 1830s, Joel Jr.

decided to try his luck homesteading in Michigan, a move that would prove to be his undoing.

In the middle of November 1837, Joel Jr. left his small house at the end of the Hatch Mill Lane and traveled for forty-eight hours to New York. There his wife, Mary, and their teenage son, Joel Henry, joined him.

The family traveled across the state in riverboats and line boats, up rivers and through lakes, past Buffalo and on to Toledo, Ohio, where they switched to railcars. When they reached Centerville, Michigan, they had traveled more than eleven hundred miles. In a letter Joel Jr. wrote upon his arrival, he estimated that the cost of the entire journey was two hundred dollars.

In March 1838, Joel Jr. and his family built a small log cabin located four miles southeast of Centerville, Michigan. The twenty-three-acre property included a large lake from which they hauled water until they could dig a well. The cabin was one and a half stories, with one door and one window. Homesteading was a meager, difficult life-style. Joel sowed two acres of wheat, planted some potatoes. Mary, who had injured her foot on the journey, had to hobble around with only one shoe for months, until her sore healed. They survived mainly on pork and milk they begged from neighbors.

Yet, in April, having received just one letter from his brother William in Two Mile and none from his father, Joel Jr. wrote of his success at farming in this new country. He mentioned affable neighbors and "many good friends," the large crops and fine soil. "Mary likes it here quite a bit," he wrote, presumably despite her lame foot. The tone of the letter was hopeful, perhaps tinged with a bit of loneliness; he tried to convince his brother to move out with him. "I have got along much better than I expected when I got here," he wrote. "They say the fever and ague prevails here very much in the later part of the summer. . . . I don't know what to say. You can get land here for 3 to 5 dollars per acre." This letter seemed to speculate that the price of land was worth the gamble of sickness, but Joel Jr. had no idea how much that risk would ultimately cost him and his family. "Fever and ague" was a common term for malaria, prevalent in wet, swampy land in the summer. But Joel Jr. had no idea that mosquitoes carried this disease, and others, like yellow fever; if he had, perhaps he would have thought twice about building near such a large lake.

Back in Two Mile, Joel Jr.'s sister Mary passed away. Another sister, Rhoda, wrote him in Michigan, bearing the sad news. Joel Jr. replied, "O may we make a wise improvement of we know not which of us will be called next."

The next person turned out to be him. On July 14, Joel Jr. fell sick with "bilious fever"—a variation of yellow fever that in the early stages was similar to malaria, including muscle cramps, violent sweats, and shakes. In its most toxic form, bilious fever progressed to running sores and bleeding from the eyes and mouth. A doctor made house calls to the cabin for the next two weeks. But by then the rest of the family had fallen ill with malaria.

That was the beginning of August; sometime in the beginning of January 1839, Deacon Joel received the following letter from Joel Henry:

To: Mr. Joel Hatch
North Marshfield, Mass

Centerville, Michigan September 18th 1838

Dear Grandfather,
*   I now take my pen in hand to write a few lines to you but they must bring mournful tidings of the death of an affectionate Father. He died Aug 3. He was sick about three weeks and had the Bilious fever—He appeared to be willing to go and I trust he was prepared. We have been sick ever since the first of August and have had the fever and ague. It*

*has been very sickly here this summer in some houses they
have been all sick and Death has taken away two of our
nearest neighbors. The crops have been pretty good. Corn is
50ct per bushel. Wheat is 50. oats 20. Beef 5 cts per pound.
Pork 18. We intend coming to Marshfield next fall.*

*December 23—I now have a chance to send this letter to
the post office tomorrow. The reason I have delayed writing
so long is because I have had the fever and ague. Mother
has the ague every other day and is so sick that she does not
sit up but very little. Mother joins me in sending her Re-
spects to all friends (PS write soon).*

Yours, Joel H Hatch

In the next letter to Two Mile, dated March 1, Joel Henry describes himself as recovered, but his mother is still so ill that she
"cannot but sit up long enough to have her bed made." How they
survived for six months in the grip of fever and disease is un-
clear. The farm was in disarray. In this letter, Joel Henry tried to
establish himself, in his grandfather's eyes, as the new head of
the household, and he went into more detail about his father's
death the previous August. "It was the general opinion of the
people here that he was killed with calomel!" he wrote. "His
tongue had several holes in it as large as a bean, also a hole in his
elbow which run most of the time." The letter goes on to mention the burial and the fact that they could not afford gravestones—this was the first of many times he would ask for money.

On July 23, Deacon Joel sent a letter to Joel Henry containing five dollars, which he had to "go abroad" to get, indicating
that the Deacon did not have much money either. The letter also
tells of his aunt Rhoda's death, apparently of a stroke—"the
disorder was on the brain." She had given birth to a baby boy,
Joel Henry's cousin, only two weeks before.

Within one year, Deacon Joel had lost three of his children—

Mary, Rhoda, and Joel Jr. It is obvious why he clung to the fate of his grandson Joel Henry. On August 8, a year after his father's death, Joel Henry admitted defeat and wrote to his grandfather that he and his mother were selling items from the farm and making their way back east to Marshfield. "Money is so scarce that we should not be able to get enough to carry us there." So Deacon Joel sent more money.

Joel Jr.'s dream of westward expansion and escape from the rut of Two Mile had turned into a sad, slow tale of sickness, poverty, and struggle. It took Joel Henry and his mother twenty days to travel from Michigan to a relative in Vermont. It took them even longer to gather the strength to make it back to Marshfield from there. The last letter Joel Henry wrote his grandfather from the journey was dated November 5, 1839.

Joel Henry and his mother eventually made it back to Marshfield, where they spent time recovering in the Red House. Six years later, Joel Henry wrote his grandfather again. After staying in Marshfield for two years, it seems he had returned to Michigan.

Mr. Joel Hatch
North Marshfield, Mass

Sherman July 12th 1845

Dear Grandfather,
I now take my pen in hand to write you a few lines and let you know that I am still in the land of the living. I have not heard from you in four years and I want you should write to me as soon as you receive this and let me know all the news at Marshfield. I have been here most of the time since I left Marshfield. I worked on a farm about one year and in a store two years. The rest of the time I have been in different kinds of businesses. I am now to work at the Carpenters trade and get $1.00 per day. They commenced harvesting here last

*Monday. The wheat crop is the best it has [been] since I have
been in the country. It will average about forty bushels per
acre. Almost every farmer has from forty to sixty acres and
some more one man here (Judge Sturgis) has three hundred
acres. The other crops look remarkable well. Sherman has got
to be considerable of a village there is two meeting houses here
one Baptist one Methodist and six stores one furnace etc. etc.
Centerville too is growing some there is four meetinghouses
there is one Baptist, one Methodist, one Episcopal and one
Dutch reform. Two publick houses, nine stores. One large
flouring mill, one saw mill etc., etc. There are other villages
near as large as that such as _____ 16 miles northwest on
the St. Joseph River. White Pigeon 12 miles west and Motte-
ville 18 miles west. Sherman is only fifty miles from Hillsdale
the termination of the southern railroad from Lake Erie. I
could go from here to Boston in four and [½] days for $18.00
and I think I shall come down this fall and spend a few weeks
about the time fruit is ripe. . . .*

Presumably, Joel Henry had held on to the log cabin and the
farm. Although he had to supplement his farming with other income, his prospects in Michigan were probably better than anything he could find in Two Mile, as his return after his father's
death probably proved to him. In the letter, he enclosed a few
kernels of winter wheat from the year's growth, so that Deacon
Joel could "have specimen of Michigan wheat." The seeds
dented the letter's paper where they had been sealed and pressed
into the envelope. Joel Henry instructed his grandfather to sow
the seeds between September 1 and 5. "Please write soon," he
continued, "and do not put it off because I have."

Thinking of his family, the Red House, and Two Mile,
everything he had left behind, Joel Henry wrote, "I want you
should send me a copy of the family record as far back as you
know about it," perhaps to keep the story straight in his mind.

Seven

The bunkhouse

In the fall of 1982, Kim returned to the Red House with a forty-foot wooden boat. Movers delivered the unfinished hull, swinging a large flatbed around the back of the house, driving it across the field, where it remained behind the barn and the stone wall, covered with a blue tarp. The boat seemed giant—a whale, an alien ship. It towered over a grove of cedar trees that stood around it like attendants.

Kim moved down from Maine with Ted, a boyfriend whom she soon married. In the previous four years, I had seen little of Kim; she would arrive on holidays, or in the summer for a few weeks, always involved with a nautical project, always with a Jimmy Buffett–like boyfriend—a returning sailor, a merchant marine, a bohemian salty dog. Her projects were bigger than life—she was crewing on a millionaire's yacht; she was shark fishing from helicopters; she was restoring the *Mayflower II*; she was building her own boat with Ted.

When she returned home this time, Kim was very thin. Nearly six feet tall, she had long arms roped with muscle, a collarbone like a shelf. Her face had lost its baby fat, leaving her wide-set eyes above cheekbones that sloped down to a square jaw. She had cut her long hair into a bowl cut, which made her face seem even more angular and striking, made her smile bigger, broader. She arrived tall and toothy with Ted, who was short and stocky with shoulder-length curls, dark eyes, and teeth like a collapsed picket fence—a look of someone perpetually about to laugh.

The day Kim returned, she wore just a scarf wrapped around her breasts. I was surprised by her near nudity, the casualness with which she stood around in low-slung jeans and waved to the boat movers, yelling and directing with her arms. Ted, in contrast, was wearing a dark turtleneck, even in the heat. They were arranged like opposites on either side of the hulking blue shroud that was slowly unloaded and released from the trailer.

The boat was "a half-finished cedar-planked hull," I had heard Kim say to a friend over the phone, "a transom, but no sheer clamp." Its ribs were steamed and bent white oak secured with copper rivets. My sister had heard about the boat from a friend, and when the original builder decided to abandon the project mid-construction, she stepped in.

Kim and Ted revamped the bunkhouse room where Kim had lived as a teenager, years before. The two other rooms in the bunkhouse had been taken over by my father's tools and lawn mower—a workshop of sorts that still housed his old truck. Kim and Ted ripped out the floor in the old bedroom, opening up the foundation as a lower level, and raised a loft bedroom with a futon mattress. When I visited Kim there, I felt as if I were aboard a pack-rat vessel, or inside an adult clubhouse—every corner was occupied with shelves or cubbies. Wind shook the blue spruce that towered above the roof, the tin pipe of the new woodstove flexing its robot elbow into the chimney.

I had never seen anyone live this way—on a boat or otherwise. Suddenly the rooms inside the Red House seemed warm and airy—what had seemed cramped compared with the neat houses of my friends no longer seemed unlivable. The Red House was outflanked by a smaller dank space—the bunkhouse, painted in matching red with white trim, a miniature patchwork version.

If she wasn't in the bunkhouse, I'd find Kim under the large tarp she'd built around the boat, listening to the radio and clamping pieces of wood to a workbench. Work on the boat went slowly. Ted turned the tarp into a weather-tight shed; they worked on the hull, filling the rivet holes with cedar, then cutting off the plugs and sanding the planks. They built a catwalk made of staging and boards placed three feet below the upper lip of the boat. On this small bridge, I could walk the perimeter, staring down at the ribs and frame molds, the guts of the unfinished boat.

That year, I was a junior in high school, and spent a lot of classroom time staring at the dingy squares of linoleum floor beneath the modular chairs. Every chair had a half-desktop, as if it were pulling its elbow up in defense. But defense against what? Kate had married her high-school sweetheart at the Red House in the summer of 1981 and then moved to Vermont, Patrick had graduated and gone to college, and the house was filled with a new batch of haughty, more contentious teenagers. In an attempt to get us out of the house on time, our father had bought us each the same version of a Timex clock radio, a decision he soon regretted. The second floor became Radio Zone where local stations WBCN, WCOZ, and Kiss108 battled for airtime.

"Endless Love" transmogrified into "Another one bites the dust" as he progressed past the thin colonial doors, yelling to us over the noise not to leave our wet towels on the wooden floors. Suzy couldn't sleep unless her radio was playing. I couldn't sleep with it on. Bored, Bekah recorded herself singing Blondie's "The Tide Is High" on the handheld tape recorder my father used for Mobile X-ray.

Each morning, we carried Kissing-Slicks and tiny cans of Aquanet in our purses past the abandoned Hatch Mill on the way to the bus stop. All the high-school parties seemed to take place outside, in locations called "the Pits," "Garbage Gut," "the High T's," or "the Spit." Inside the high school, they banned video games, and in retaliation some pranksters Superglued shut the locks on a hallway of lockers.

My history teacher, Mr. Sanchez, had a graying walrus mustache and talked a lot about an operation he was going to get to replace his knees. "One more week until my new knees!" he'd say. The class was mid-afternoon, right after lunch, and everyone always fell asleep or passed notes. That year, I often got in trouble for picking lint balls off my sweater and trying to blow them across the aisle. Tim McNally, fresh from art class, had a spherical sculpture made of card stock and cellophane on his head.

"I'm Mork from Ork," he said, "Nano-Nano," turning around to shake my hand.

"Miss Messer!" Mr. Sanchez barked. "Please do us the favor of taking your feet off the desk." I took them off slowly, one by one, like a spider stepping out of its web.

We were learning about the Revolutionary War.

But then, suddenly, Mr. Sanchez was saying, "Governor Winslow House . . . the oldest house in Marshfield . . ." And I raised my hand.

I told him that my house, the Walter Hatch house, was the oldest house in Marshfield.

"Yes, I know some people think that," Mr. Sanchez said. The air went still in the room. I felt instantly adult, as if great matters were at risk.

"But the house was built in 1647," I said. He had said, moments earlier, that the Governor Winslow House was built in 1699. Clearly, I was right.

"Yes," he said, "that's when some people claim your house was built. But I'm not sure those people are reliable historians. This topic has always been under some debate."

I didn't know what to say. So I said nothing.

Then he added, as if just now aware that I was a kid, "It *might* be older than the Governor Winslow House."

But in that moment I knew he thought I was an idiot, and in terms of a debate, I had lost. My face felt hot, and the air in the room started shifting again.

Mr. Sanchez said, "Well, now . . ." and the lecture moved on.

At home that evening, I confronted my father: "Mr. Sanchez says that our house is not the oldest house in Marshfield." I said it in an indignant tone, as if to imply, *He's wrong, right?*

But my father said, "I never told you it was the oldest house in Marshfield—I told you it was the Oldest Continuously Lived-In House in Marshfield."

"Oh," I said. Thinking that I was, perhaps, sort of right. The house was *something*. But what did "continuous" mean? By the same family? By anyone? I wanted to add more qualifiers: "Oldest Continuously Lived-In and Owned by the Same Family," versus "Oldest House That Always Had People Living in It." Or perhaps: "Oldest Continuously Privately Inhabited House in New England Haunted by Members of the Family That Built It."

Really, I had no idea what he meant.

———

Soon after her return, Kim re-established a relationship with Richard Warren Hatch, who had moved to a retirement home in the Cape Cod town of Orleans. Kim drove down every two weeks to visit him and talk about shipbuilding and the history of the house.

A local paper had recently profiled Hatch as "yearning for an earlier Marshfield," when "people grew their food, got shoes from the town shoemaker, medicine from a friend at the local pharmacy." "Towns were self-contained," Hatch was quoted as saying. "Now everything is owned by outsiders. . . . Families are scattered all over the world and we are poorer for it." The article concluded with a plea to readers with clout in the publishing world to bring Hatch's books back into print.

Kim saw Richard Warren as a grandfather figure from whom she could learn things. She would arrive in a battered VW Bug, and Hatch was always happy to see her. He would speak to her in a guiding and abbreviated way. She liked to believe that Hatch could see her imagination, her hunger for history and fact. He would tell her stories about the house, stories about being a young boy in Gloucester and seeing for the first time the fleets of fishing schooners, about keeping a boat on the river, about leaving home at sixteen or seventeen to go to sea as a crewman on a Gloucester fishing schooner. He'd written a children's book, *All Aboard the Whale*, about his experience with Boston tugboats, but mostly he talked about life on the North River when shipbuilding still thrived, before the industrial revolution. His novels about the Red House and the fictional Bradford family were filled with yearning and descriptions of a time that no longer existed. Yet, despite his nostalgia for the Red House and Two Mile, Hatch had spent little time there as a child. His father had been the first of the Red House Hatches to marry outside of Two Mile and successfully leave New England. And now, in his conversations with Kim, Hatch spoke continually of return.

"Before I die, I must go aboard a Gloucester fishing schooner again. Then I could die a happy man," he told her.

And through it all, Kim seemed happy. My parents were

gone a lot, and when I came home from school, Kim and Ted were often the only adults around. Unlike my parents, who often seemed distracted, Kim and Ted sat around the table in the kitchen and talked to us about school, boyfriends; they brought art projects into the house, unfinished pieces of the boat. Kim had always been a prankster, and Ted seemed perfect for her, her ideal victim. And we were the captive audience. She would make a banana-cream pie with the express purpose of shoving it in Ted's face, smearing the whipped cream over his head while she laughed and snorted out her nose. Sometimes she laughed so hard that no sound came out, her mouth flung open and her body in a big laugh-cramp. Then Ted would take handfuls of ice from the freezer and shove them down her shirt.

———·———

Ted had a job at the Quincy shipyard but spoke little about his work. One day he returned with a badly broken front tooth. Kim asked what had happened, and Ted shrugged it off—an accident at the shipyard.

"Well, if it happened at the shipyard, you should have your insurance to pay for it—you should collect Workman's Comp," Kim had said.

Ted said that he would handle it. When several more days passed without his calling an orthodontist, Kim called the Quincy shipyard to ask about the status of her husband's insurance.

"Oh, he doesn't work here," they told her.

"How long hasn't he worked there?" Kim asked.

"About a month or more," they replied.

———·———

Around this time, Jessica, twelve, threw a slumber party and fogged up the kitchen with strawberry incense, Tears for Fears, and Love's Baby Soft perfume. The party's theme was

Sarah Messer

"communicating with the dead," involving seven preteen girls, a case of diet soda, and, predictably, a Ouija Board.

Perhaps my sister and her friends were imitating the plots of horror movies they'd seen—teenagers in a creaking house, hormonally primed for freakout, watching as the Ouija shuttled across the game board, spelling out a dead person's name, crossing a spectral-respect boundary that paved the way for unleashed ghoulish hordes—vampires, ax murders, etc.

But according to my sister, that's what *did* happen. At least the first part. Responding to the question "With whom are we speaking?" the porthole eye of the game piece moved. It spelled out the letters H-A-T-C-H.

"That's the last name of the people who built this house," my sister gasped. Then her friends gasped too. Was it a trick? No one was smirking. "How did you die?" They asked the Ouija, and the porthole zoomed over to the letters W-E-L-L . . . The well out behind the house that was now covered by a Jack-and-Jill-ish stone wall and geranium planter, or *Well* . . . meaning the beginning of a longer story? Maybe a kid had fallen down the well and drowned? Maybe . . . The phone rang. It was our mother calling from Florida, calling to tell Jess that she had a bad feeling and knew she was up to something. "Don't mess with the house," our mother said into the receiver two thousand miles away.

"Really? Did that really happen?" people would ask when the story was told and retold later, asking about our mother, not the Ouija Board. And we would nod our heads yes—unbelievable but true. "Is your mom psychic?" one of the friends had asked on the way out the door the next morning. "How did she know what we were doing?" they asked.

The house, Jess always believed, had ratted her out.

Late one night about six months after the Ouija Board incident, Ted was drunk and reeling through the Red House. He was distraught—he had moved out, it had been storming thunder and sheets of rain all night, he and Kim were getting divorced, and it was his birthday. An hour earlier, he had pulled his car up crookedly on the back lawn by the bunkhouse but found that Kim was in the Red House, housesitting for our parents, who had gone away again for the weekend. Jess was at another slumber party, and Suzy, Bekah, and I were upstairs, isolating ourselves in our usual radio wars.

Ted wanted to talk. Kim went with him out to the bunkhouse, telling him he was too drunk to drive. *"It's my birthday,"* he kept saying. Then she took his car keys.

Perhaps he had wanted to leave, had come stumbling after her looking for his keys. His voice labored as he negotiated the dining-room table, turned right through the living room. Perhaps he had wanted to talk to her once more, to try to fix things between them. Or maybe he was just drunk and wandering, not knowing what he was doing, guided by some other force that took him out of the bunkhouse and into the Red House; he dragged his muddy boots, his shirt and pants damp with rainwater, into our parents' bedroom, where he collapsed beside Kim on top of the bed.

Out like a light. Out cold. Out of the storm and the bunkhouse. For some reason—she can never say why—Kim let him stay. She pretended to be asleep. It was nearly midnight, and the radios had all turned off. The storm outside had gotten worse, and wind whipped against the windows, pelting rain.

Kim lay still in the darkness as Ted, lying on his stomach, arms at his side, began to snore. She must have fallen asleep, because at 4 a.m. she found herself jolted upright in bed as if someone had touched her arm. Ted was still beside her, lying in the same position, breathing heavily. Her heart pounded and she felt alarm, and what she says she saw then defies rational thought. Out the small panes of the north window, the sky was just beginning to lighten. She saw the dark shape of the hillside, behind which she knew was the mouth of the North River. Then, above the hill's silhouette, a cloud opened, broken by a flash of light.

The ball of lightning moved horizontally. Kim had risen to her feet from the bed and was at the window. She heard a crash that sounded like a truck being driven into a brick wall and felt the whole house shake. Then she felt a second, smaller crash. Then the fire alarms went off.

———•———

Lightning forms when a cloud is pushed too high up, when it looks like an anvil in the sky. Inside the distant anvil, rain collides with ice crystals, producing positive and negative charges; electric sparks release from the bottom of the cloud, which becomes a conduit to earth. The earth responds with a positive charge back to the cloud, a current that can reach up to thirty million volts at a hundred thousand amps. It all takes a fraction of a second.

Lightning, the firemen would later say, is made up of two twisted strands of energy—one all heat, and the other all force. The bolt struck the chimney and ricocheted off the roof, breaking several slate shingles. It then split in two, the heat strand hitting the converter box at the side of the bunkhouse, and the force strand driving into the giant spruce tree, splitting it down the center.

Bekah, Suzy, and I left the Red House through the door on the south side. Ted stumbled in the doorframe, reeled through the door, then collapsed face-first on the lawn.

The house was hit by lightning, Bekah was saying; the chimney was hit, Kim was saying, thinking that there must be a secret fire hiding somewhere above us, on the roof. Rain came down in sheets as the four of us, in drenched nightgowns, slowly stepped backward over the man passed out on the lawn, our eyes tilted up to the roofline.

I was the first to turn my head away from the house and look toward the barn, where flames leapt in the windows.

"The barn is on fire," I yelled, and began running. Bekah and Suzy ran with me past the bunkhouse and toward the flames rising up the windows, but as we came within twenty feet of the barn, the flames disintegrated, a mirage. An orange glow still hung in the sky, and we turned around once more to see that the fire was not in the barn or the house, but in the bunkhouse.

Flames were already leaping out the windows. Not only was the bunkhouse old, the wood dry and porous, but inside it were cans of paint, and on the outside wall, a 250-gallon tank of kerosene.

Kim dragged a garden hose to the kerosene tank strapped to the side of the bunkhouse.

"Keep water running on the top of this tank," she yelled, passing off the hose. She carried a fire extinguisher under her arm as she ran to the back of the building, to the door of her house. The fire had not yet spread through the wall to the workshop where our father's truck was stored. Kim opened the double barn doors enough to slip a rope around the heavy chrome bumper, then she closed them again.

And now she was running back to where Ted was lying on the lawn.

"Get up!" she yelled. "Our house is burning. Help me move the truck out."

The keys to Kim's car were burning up in the bunkhouse apartment, and Ted's car was too small to tow anything. In that instant, as she was pulling on Ted's soggy arm, trying to sit him up, she realized that she had heard no fire trucks. They weren't coming. Inside the Red House, the phone line was dead. After the 1971 fire, my father had installed a system that automatically called the fire department whenever the alarm went off. But despite this elaborate setup no call had gone through. Kim ran over to the neighbors, and stood where our father had stood over ten years before. And she too was yelling up at the windows, at different neighbors, yelling at them to get up and call the fire department.

When Kim stepped off the neighbors' lawn and back through the hedgerow, she saw the spruce go up like a torch, and flames now burning through the bunkhouse roof.

Kim returned with Linda, our neighbor, who was wearing a rain slicker and had given Kim a windbreaker.

"We need to get away from the bunkhouse," Kim said. "You guys go with Linda."

Frank, Linda's husband, was getting a vehicle to drive across the lawn to help tow out the truck, but before he could get out of his driveway four fire trucks appeared and surrounded the bunkhouse.

"The first thing we need to do," Kim said to the fire chief, "is tow my father's antique truck out of the shop. I already have a rope tied around the bumper."

"Listen," the chief said, "if you open those doors, the whole place will go up and nothing will be saved."

She tried talking to other firemen, the men in slickers and boots who were uncoiling yards of hose and passing it off to each other, but they all ignored her. Ted was between the fire trucks, completely sober now and trying to be helpful. Some of the firemen were talking to Ted, asking him exactly what was in the workshop, what was in their room.

Ted was saying, "Refrigerator, meat freezer, a push mower, an old car."

Kim realized that Ted actually looked normal—slightly sleepy and concerned, standing in the clothes he had been wearing for hours while passed out on the bed—he was fully dressed.

Kim, on the other hand, was wearing a boy's-size windbreaker over a heavy and drenched terry-cloth robe and thin cotton nightgown trailed with mud. She was barefoot, her hair plastered to her face. She looked hysterical, she realized, and the chief approached her the way someone might approach a trapped wild animal, saying, "Listen, everything is going to be OK. I know how to fight this fire. Just let me fight this fire."

We spent the night with the neighbors, lying on couches under afghans or in spare rooms. The fire burned all night. Less than an hour after they arrived, the firemen saw the futility of saving anything and simply aimed their hoses at the blaze. The firemen stayed until 9 or 10 a.m., when the fire was out and the bunkhouse was completely gone save several blackened beams that rose out of the wreckage like swamp cedar. The air was bitter and filled with micro-blizzards of ash.

The next day, Kim dug through the cellar hole. Richard Warren Hatch's book *The Curious Lobster's Island* was intact, but twice burned, the edges charred. When she climbed out of the hole, she passed over where the car would have been and noticed that the chrome bumper had not burned, and the piece of rope was still looped where she had tied it.

Later, in her shock, she would wrap the book in a plastic bag and place it on top of shanks of beef in the coffin freezer in the basement of the Red House, trying perhaps to preserve it. A few days afterward, the *Marshfield Mariner* would run a brief article about "the summer's first attention-getting electrical storm of powerful proportion," which resulted in two burned buildings and fourteen lightning-damage reports. A man on the other side of town watched as a lightning bolt shot through his house, cracking a tree in the backyard in half. Lightning had also struck the steeples of several churches, and emptied the harbor of boatmen. The paper, misidentifying the bunkhouse, would say that the storm "caused the destruction of a barn on

385 Union Street belonging to Ronald J. Messer. Inside the barn and lost in the blaze was an antique car belonging to Messer." No mention would be made of Kim and her lost belongings.

Beyond the flattened rubble of the bunkhouse, the charred grass, the unzipped and splayed spruce, sat the boat—all that Kim had left.

Israel H.
1837–1921

Carrie

Israel H.

Lulu, Rebekah, and Thomas

Thomas

Why are the bones of man not on the outside?

If bone was all over him, as it is
over an oyster, he could have no
feeling or knowledge.

When a carpenter builds a house, he makes
and raises the frame first. Bones are the frame
of the body. The skin and flesh
put on them, as the carpenter puts on boards—

What are these bones made of?

They are made of food.

> —Mrs. Jane Taylor, *Physiology for Children*
> (New York: Saxton & Miles, 1846)

In 1843, after Deacon Joel's grandson Joel Henry had returned to Marshfield and left again, Marshfield shipbuilders tried to dig the North River a new mouth. The shipping industry was failing, and shipbuilders estimated that it cost $125 for every hundred-ton vessel to get out the last three miles of the river. Sometimes it took seventeen days to get a ship out completely, the most difficult passage coming at the mouth, where a large delta of sand accrued through storms and tide had blocked the exit. The ships had to be turned on their sides and dragged like giant snails across the sandbar by oxen. The shipwrights placed the inflated stomachs of animals beneath the sides of ships—to make them easier to roll over, to protect the planking. They argued for a channel between Third and Fourth Cliffs that would divide the joined mouths of the North and South Rivers. Finally, the shipbuilders made an appeal to the government for support.

Ex-President and then–U.S. Representative John Quincy Adams arrived at the beach in Marshfield from his summer home at the Glades, to see the site of the proposed cut. A large party of shipbuilders and farmers met him there. Those who supported the cut had brought with them teams of oxen and horses. They carried shovels, hoes, and axes. John Quincy Adams and other authorities heard arguments for both sides of the issue. Eventually, the proposed cut was declined because of the vocal presence of farmers who feared that the fragile salt meadows upriver in Two Mile would be destroyed by the increase in tides. The president left, and the mob of shipbuilders and farmers went home.

That night, a mob reconvened. In the darkness, they marched through Two Mile and back to the beach, carrying lanterns on poles, shovels, and hoes. They stopped at a few houses along the way and asked to borrow teams of oxen.

The men worked at digging and hacking until morning but were unable to complete the cut: the thin piece of meadow dividing the river from the beach and the ocean was too thick and hard. In the morning, the town witnessed their half-finished attempt: the river flowed partially through the cut, until it was filled up with silt and sand again, becoming only a shallow scar.

———·———

On winter nights, Israel H. Hatch followed his brother Walter to the river to spear eels through the ice. Fishermen had erected small sails around the fishing holes to act as windbreaks. The sails, lit from behind by lanterns, could be seen for a mile, glowing in the darkness along the hairpin curves of the river and low salt marsh. With the help of some other boys, Walter and Israel cut holes in the ice and used long poles to net the eels. Israel liked to glide along the ice or stand with his back to the sail stretched between the poles over the fishing hole, his feet on either side of the lantern. Walter worked the net and, drawing up eels, placed them in a bucket or a tin pail. Israel stared into the blackness of the water running under the ice. Once he had watched a young man fall through a hole and be carried by the current to another hole, farther downstream, only to lift himself up and out of it, frozen yet generally unharmed. Everyone at the time agreed it was a miracle.

In July 1849, when Deacon Joel keeled over in his pigpen and died, Israel was only eleven years old. The youngest of Deacon Joel's ten children, he had been raised in the Red House with Walter and their sister Rebekah. The Red House estate could not be legally divided until Israel was twenty-one. Deacon Joel's older children, satelliting around Two Mile, had become surrogate aunts and uncles to their younger half-siblings. But, given the choice, most Hatch descendants wanted their own new start, not the ramshackle house and the surrounding acres of over-farmed land. Only Deacon Joel's oldest daughter, Huldah (who never married and was called "Aunt Huldy" by everyone), planned to spend her entire life in the Red House, along with the newly widowed Rebekah (who was only one year her senior) and her three teenage children. So, by a process of elimination, the Red House, once intended for the oldest son, Joel Jr., had ended up in the hands of the youngest, Israel.

Israel got the dregs—not enough land or money to allow him to be landed gentry, an intellectual, or even a decent farmer. As Richard Warren Hatch would eventually write about his grandfather: "What Israel inherited, aside from a house that was considered no good, was the smallest and most worthless piece of land; hardly ten acres of upland, whereas three other pieces of the original property averaged over seventy acres."

Fatherless preteen Israel grew up to be a frustrated intellectual, innately aimless, spending his time triangulating between the Two Mile School House, the post office, and Hall and Weatherby's Confectionery, the first chain store on the South Shore. Unlike his contemporaries, he did little manual labor. He always seemed to be visiting people and buying pieces of candy.

At fourteen, Israel left school in Two Mile and moved to New Bedford, where he worked for the office of the *New Bedford*

Standard for two years. During that time, he received letters from Rebekah and Walter, who had both married and moved out of the Red House. When he wrote, he made jokes with himself, and entertained a witty repartee with his brother and sister as well as the whaler Thomas Oakman, who had married Rebekah in 1850 and was often away at sea.

On November 23, 1855, Thomas wrote, "I feel very bad," saying that he was just getting over a bad case of the "Boo-hoo fever," an actual illness, it seemed, that had him lying on his back "for seven days in the greatest of agony." In his letter to Israel he described Hawaii as filled with "great times— theaters, circuses, fairs, drunken carousals and fights every night." He referred to news that Israel had written him in his last letter, commenting that men like his brother Walter (who was "driving cows") would be making more money than he, Thomas, would. He concluded the letter with mention of Honolulu and the large quantity of pretty white girls, saying, "Kiss sissy [meaning Rebekah] for me if you do that sort of thing, and if you don't, never start."

"Israel," Thomas wrote at the end of the letter, "my eyes are aching."

Israel, however, was lazy, was always resting his eyes. He was not a whaler or a shipbuilder; he had no desire to travel or homestead, and was uninterested in Two Mile trade. When he returned to the Red House at sixteen, he fell into the popular temperance movement. He attended private school for a year and then taught "singing school," instructing local pubescent girls and boys in a collection of temperance hymns and ballads. When Israel began planing boards in his uncle David Hatch's mill (a job for which he was paid), he wrote:

Oh! what dreadful sport! Everything to bother and no one to help. How much pleasanter to sit in Roger's Hall with the best girls in Marshfield opposite where you cannot

look up without seeing lovely faces. How I do want to see
some of them.

After a month of planing, he wrote: "Planed a while this morning and then came home and went to bed. Feel as though that is the best place for me."

He entertained himself by conducting pseudo-scientific experiments. He kept a "diary and cash book" with a column on the left-hand margin for wind direction followed by the barometric pressure, which he measured outside the Red House four times a day, at 9 a.m., noon, 3 p.m., and 9 p.m.

On July 4, 1856, the *Pembroke Union* recorded: "**Returned Whaleman**—Mr. Thomas R. Oakman of Marshfield, returned to his friends on Sunday June 22nd, after an absence of three and a half years. He came home as second mate of the ship Saratoga, Capt. Harding, of New Bedford." Israel, stuck in the overfarmed fields of Two Mile, must have deeply romanticized Thomas's life-style, even though it meant leaving his family for long stretches of time. When he returned, Thomas may have brought Israel the pair of whale's teeth covered in scrimshaw figures that were eventually passed down through the Hatch family—three women engaged in domestic activity, and one whaleman.

In a sense, the teeth illustrated Israel's life: he was destined to live thirty of his adult years with his mother and aged aunt Huldy while the men in his life, like Thomas, traveled. To make matters worse, the house Israel had inherited was dilapidated. Water was pumped from a well twenty feet from the back door. The giant fireplace in the 1790s kitchen ell had long since been covered up, replaced by a smoky cast-iron cookstove. The closets and parlor walls were papered with Sears Catalogs and Marshfield Fair posters. All the decorative fireplaces in the house had been covered with tin to keep out the cold. At night, light came from oil lamps glowing from the dimly lit passageways that connected house to shed, shed to barn. The barn sat aslant under umbrella elms, while the house rambled with uneven floors through the parlor and the living room, past the narrow couch with a blue-and-white coverlet and the abandoned foot-pump organ. Perhaps this was why four times a day he took the pulse of the house, the speed of the wind whipping by. Perhaps he realized that it was now an old creature.

The winter he turned twenty, Israel began his journal: "The year opens with a slight snowstorm. Thermometer last night at 9pm 30—Cloudy. About an inch of snow fell in the night which has considerably improved the dubious sleighing." It was 1857, the year that would beget trouble in Kansas, the Fugitive Slave Act, but that January 1, the papers began only with Tennyson's poem "The Golden Year"—" 'We sleep and wake and sleep, but all things move; The Sun flies forward to his brother Sun; The dark Earth follows wheel'd in her ellipse . . . ' " Israel continued his entry, mentioning some "work on the highway" where he "froze an ear," an experience he described as "pretty tedious," the temperatures averaging eight degrees. In the next three days, two more storms would dump a total of sixteen inches of snow on the Red House, isolating the Hatches from mail and travel. Inside the Red House, ice formed over the mouths of sleepers; even the spiderwebs froze.

Around this time, the siblings sat for daguerreotypes—Rebekah, like Israel, was interested in history, and had begun to collect the bride's towels of her mother and grandmother, going back through the matrilineage to 1690. When she married Thomas, she had embroidered her new initials on a machine-woven towel run with red thread.

To entertain himself, Israel stayed up until midnight reading three or four different newspapers—*The Shipping List, Museum,* and the *Farmer.* He would later write about his newspaper addiction as a "piece of foolishness deserves special condemnation." The headlines reported: "Mexican Priesthood," "The Secret of Warm Feet," or "The Value of Liquid Manure." The papers included national news about a strain of hog cholera; the discovery of giant man, animal, and bird footprints in limestone rocks, in Cincinnati, Ohio; a two-and-a-half-inch codfish found inside a sealed oyster shell; a snake caught in Mississippi with a head at each end; a man found intoxicated and whitewashed by a pair of rogues; a man found frozen in a swamp, his hands clasped in prayer. The papers ran ads for pianos and nerve tinctures, a popular children's magazine called *The Little Pilgrim*, and a dissertation on "How to Cure Frozen Feet," which included cutting an onion in two, dipping it in salt, and rubbing it all over the foot.

In his journal, Israel wrote between the lines, a subtle love song. Although Thomas warned him against it, most of Israel's attention focused on catching titillating glimpses of Carrie B. Oakman, Thomas's cousin. Describing another temperance meeting, he related a quote of Reverend Leonard: "One bad woman is equal to ten bad men." In his journal Israel ruminated, "Whether he was willing to reverse the statement—one good woman is equal to ten good men—was unanswered."

Then he wrote in a smaller script, "My kingdom for a wife [crossed out] woman [crossed out]."

On July 18, 1857, Israel described a visit from one male friend with whom he went to the mill; here they joined another party, and all wound up at Thomas's father's house, where Israel "got to meet _____."

For a while, it seemed that he couldn't speak or write "Carrie B. Oakman"; her name in his journal remained a blank line. Would she be at this event or that? There were outings, tea parties, temperance rallies. An Independence Day parade during which the town was mobbed. Was _____ there? One more trip past Hall and Weatherby's to—what?—buy a few stamps, of course, a piece of confectionery. Who might be sitting on the steps? Who might be? Later, after crossing some threshold, receiving some acknowledgment from her, he wrote "Carrie B. Oakman" over and over again in the front of his journal. What was he invoking? Israel was hiding his desire from himself, the way he would write and not write about her, using a large loopy script for daily details, and a minute blocky print for his confessions, the subtext even he could not keep inside. "But I guess you stopped somewhere else on the way home didn't you?" his scripty conscious inquired, tiny, in the margins, a few centimeters high.

Israel, in his journaling, began to see himself as part of a historical continuum. His oldest brother had struck out from Two Mile and had failed. Nine children down the line, Israel was left with a house that was worth nothing. And so he began to turn to the house itself—a lineage of sorts, the fabric trail-marks, the stories of his ancestors. Israel became a historian, a chronicler of the past. The house, he realized, gained significance merely because it had lasted. He kept meticulous notebooks, and traveled around the South Shore of Massachusetts collecting vital records of Hatch descendants.

While the Western frontier expanded, cities teemed with immigrants and industrial capitalists, and the South threatened succession, New England focused on being old—the site of America's beginning. In Plymouth, planning and construction began for an eighty-one-foot-tall monument to the Pilgrim Forefathers on a hill overlooking the harbor, an endeavor that would take thirty years to complete.

Yet, in spite of itself, Two Mile was modernizing: Schools now contained atlases, steel pens, lead pencils. There were wood saws, lamps, coal stoves, ruled notebooks, church organs. There was a superintendent of a school committee, female teachers. Manners had run their course. No longer was it in fashion for boys to take off their hats and bow, or for girls to curtsy when they met an acquaintance or a stranger in the street. Children no longer rose when a visitor entered the classroom.

Now there was a cast-iron plow, a screw auger, threshing machines, winnowing machines, corn-shellers, hay-cutters, mowing machines, and hay rakes. There were washing machines and clothes-wringers, sewing machines, churning machines, apple-parers, meat-cutters, sausage grinders.

In houses all over town there were sofas, vases in the parlors. Daguerreotypes, ambrotypes, photographs, tintypes, and pictures hung on the walls. There were cookstoves and friction matches; coal, whale oil, and kerosene for heating; butcher carts and baker carts in the streets. Guns had percussion locks.

Wagons, buggies, and carriages drove past houses painted white with green shutters flanking large-paned window glass. There were buffalo robes, daily newspapers, printed posters, a list of town voters, envelopes. There were dentists, false teeth, patent and quack medicines.

The town had a meetinghouse, an almshouse for the poor. Two new bridges spanned the river.

When Israel finally romanced his love, Caroline B. Oakman, he was working as a grammar-school teacher, making thirty-five dollars a month. They were married on August 9, 1859. Months later, when Caroline was three months pregnant with their first child, the notice came that he was drafted to fight in the Civil War. The draft record listed him as five feet seven and three-quarters inches tall, approximately 130 pounds with dark skin, high brow, long nose, and hazel eyes. In a daguerreotype, he is pictured in civilian clothing, with a ruffled bow at his collar, short-cropped hair, high cheekbones, looking slightly off to the left, his cheeks painted a flush pink. Israel would try anything not to go to war—he claimed flat feet, paid a substitute three hundred dollars to go in his place. Eventually, his options expired, he enlisted in Company K, 38th Regiment of the Massachusetts Volunteer Infantry, and left Two Mile along with Thomas Oakman and many other neighbors—not knowing if he and those most beloved to him would ever see each other again.

Eight

The tall ship *Spirit of Massachusetts*

Isn't it the father's job to dive down into the conch grass at the bottom of the ocean, to dive while his daughters watch, floating at the surface of the Caribbean like pieces of paper, like notes to themselves written on their white T-shirts and tossed there with their bikinis, snorkels, and masks? One of his jobs, anyway—to retrieve the conchs that move slowly in a herd through the undulating grass some twenty feet below the water, which looks as clear as wiper fluid. This is what he told us anyway—our father of the extreme gesture, our father the romantic, who had decided "you can't take it with you," who told us that we would have no inheritance, that he was spending it all now—*carpe diem*—by taking the teenage half of the family, finally, on vacation to St. Thomas.

The four of us floated by, kicking our feet and moving our hands at our sides like small fins. We could see him plunge below us as if suddenly beneath blue glass, the bubble-trail from his snorkel. He swam down and away until his body was smaller than ours, down among the parrot fish, and the sunfish and the fish whose names we never learned, his hair swirling above his head like seaweed, his arms pushing out in front of him as if he were sweeping a table with one broad gesture, clearing things away.

Earlier, on the beach, sorting snorkel gear, I'd watched the sailing yachts drop anchor. They were tourist day-sailers with names like *Night Wind*, *Slip Stream*, or *Margaritaville*, promising jaunts to St. John or St. Croix with a gourmet lunch, visits to exclusive snorkel reefs. The sun gleamed off the chrome rigging, the fiberglass decks. Tanned bodies moved back and forth, scrubbing, washing, coiling rope. A young man stepped to the end of one bow and cupped his hands to his mouth. Then we all heard the long moan of a conch shell being blown—not the sound of a horn exactly, but of air and breath being pushed through a tiny spiral of shell. With this, the tourists were called back, to gather on the sand at the edge of the water. They waited with their shopping bags, like a line of construction horses at a curb, for the dinghy to row in from the yacht and pick them up.

"I'll dive for them," our father had said. "I have the best lungs." This is what he told us after we had swum out together beyond the reef to the patches of conch grass. We couldn't remember where the idea had come from, about the conchs. Occasionally we raised our heads and rolled our eyes at each other behind our masks. The snorkel mouthpieces made our lips pout out, grimacing and blue.

Unwittingly in the Hatch tradition, Kim had gone to sea after the bunkhouse burned. We hadn't seen her in years. She sent home paychecks to help pay down the loan on the boat that sat unfinished in its shed behind the Red House. The smell of the burned bunkhouse hung in the air long after the bulldozers had plowed the foundation into the ground, as if the fire remained but had changed elements, drifting like a fog from the absent

bunkhouse to the Red House. Because the house fire had happened when we were children, it seemed that we entered our
teenage years wearing halos of smoke. We read the smoked
pages of books, looked at smoke-tinted photographs and paintings, and stared at our faces in mirrors where the smoke had
been rubbed off the glass in smudged ovals. Now, since the
bunkhouse fire, events just happened to us within a familiar
haze, until life itself assumed a different shape, just as, for years,
favoring an injury, the body shifts and muscles atrophy.

Below us, the conchs moved very slowly across the ocean
floor, but even so, in the clear water, we could not tell exactly
how deep they were. They moved like dark-green thoughts
through a thinning head of hair. They plodded like tanks, ancient armored creatures. Our father swam down, and the distance became distorted. The conch shells appeared larger than
they were, and he ran out of breath. They were always just out
of his reach, his lungs pinched as his hand reached and finally
snagged one from the grass, feeling the living animal withdraw-
ing into the shell as he shot up to the surface like a cork, bubbles
streaming from his mouth. He swam toward us with the shell
held aloft above the water, a waiter carrying a piece of cake.
When he reached us, he placed the shell in a nylon mesh bag,
slipped the handle over Suzy's wrist, and dived again. A shell for
each girl, bigger than our two hands clasped together, bigger
than a man's hands: King Conch. We realized now what he was
doing—he had seen them at the hotel gift shop, empty and polished, the smooth inner surface pink as a sunset. Jess had said
they were pretty, hoping he'd buy her one. And now we were out
harvesting our own. Perhaps he thought that, like the yacht's
call, these shells could bring us all back from wherever we had
drifted. Or maybe he imagined them in a row along the dressers
in our bedrooms, or beside our heads on nightstands—
conchae—giant ocean ear next to a smaller human ear, listening.

He dived to the bottom and came back up. He dived so

many times, he told us later, his head ached. Most times he surfaced with nothing, smiled at us, and quickly dived again. He placed each spiky shell into the nylon mesh bag. It wasn't until later, when he tried to pay the bill for sandwiches at the pool bar, that he would tell us the truth: while diving, he had lost his money clip, leaving fifty one-dollar bills floating at the bottom of the ocean. Then we all swam back out to the conch grass and dived again and again for the bills, which rolled along the bottom of the ocean, snagged in the long spikes of sea urchins. The money drifted; we each came back up with a few dollars, our lungs expanded like sails. I kept diving until I snatched two dollars that waves were sucking in and out of a small reef under prongs of fire coral. When we got back to the hotel, we spread the wet dollars to dry on the glass patio-table. "Hey," our father said, his face lighting up, "I only lost two dollars!"

We all loved this side of him—the childish optimism, the pursuit of the beautiful story or the impulsive fantasy. It was this quality, after all, that got us the Red House. At least this is what we believed. And for the most part, we indulged him, played along. But sometimes his plans sputtered and failed.

Like the conch shells. In the days following the diving, our father became fixated on getting the animals out of their shells. He pointed out which shell was for each of us, commented on how tenacious each particular conch was. "Jess's got a tough one," he'd say.

Fact was: none of them budged. He tried jabbing a knife into one, but the animal retreated, put up some kind of hard snail shield. He tried to freeze them in the tiny hotel freezer, then bake them in the sun on the balcony, then freeze them again, thinking that the conchs would loosen their grip on the shells and be pulled out easily. He tried pouring rum into one, salt into another.

"You're torturing them!" Suzy said.

174

"Well, you have to get the conchs out, honey," he'd say, "otherwise they'll stink."

"They already stink," Bekah said.

Desperate, he began asking advice of anyone who seemed to be a native islander. "How do you unconch a conch?" he'd ask the hotel desk clerk, the cute guy renting out Windsurfers on the beach. We'd cover our faces with our hands. One day, on the way back from the grocery store, he stopped a Rastafarian goatherd who was shooing his goats along the road.

"You take him by the foot and hang him in a tree. Then the shell falls off," the goatherd said as if it was completely obvious.

"Isn't that great!?" my father exclaimed, riddle solved. But when we got back to the hotel, all the shells but one were gone.

"What happened to the conchs?" he asked. Our mother and Jess had been the only ones left behind. Our mother the gun-slinging biologist, I mused, but then thought better of it. She never interfered with my father's schemes. There she was, cooking something at the stove, not looking at us but holding her palm out flat in a Diana Ross and the Supremes gesture, as if to say, Stop . . . Keep me out of it.

"I let them go," Jess said. And, true, her hair was still wet, the snorkel gear and nylon bag in a puddle on the balcony. Jess, the youngest, the one whom nobody ever blamed. She did it because she was the only one who could.

"Except for that one," she said. "It was already dead."

———

Not much transpired in Two Mile after we returned, save one more tedious year of high school for me and a plague of gypsy moths for the town—an epidemic that ruined many outdoor weddings and caused homeowners to ring every tree trunk in Vaseline, like so many giant raccoon tails. Our father maintained a postvacation pout for at least six months. I met my first boyfriend dancing to "It's Raining Men" at a high-school prom, and suffered the inevitable breakup a year later, walked to the North River, and threw his letter jacket off the dock, then thought better of it and fished it out. Boys from the neighborhood—Mike, Sully, Kevin, Beaner—came over sometimes to flirt with Bekah and play pool in the basement. Then, at the end of my senior year, while waitressing at an Italian restaurant off Route 3, I met someone.

He was the new bartender. The feel of his name in my mouth when I spoke it was like one of the harsher elements of nature, like a crag or a knoll, claiming the one-syllable authority of a rock or a bend in the trail. Speaking his name was as stiff and sharp as swallowing salt water.

So I never used his name when talking to him. We created our own language and traded it back and forth like a secret slipped beneath tongues—outside the restaurant bathroom, the chrome kitchen, standing next to a line of coffeepots and folded napkins. We wrote blank lines instead of names. "Have you seen this movie, _____?" And I would respond, addressing him the same way, a mirror, a blank.

It was his words I had met first anyway, his slanted script on a square napkin slid across the lacquered bar as I paused at the waitress station. He wrote:

> Our understanding rises from such vast spaces
> where things waver and vanish
> > > waterily

I imagined the note had appeared in a gust of wind from the overhead fan, or perhaps my own thoughts suddenly materialized. "Waterily"—it was a word that I studied with both anticipation and fear. At first, I could hardly look at him.

Of our first encounter, I remember little, partly because I was drunk, or driven, or both. Delirious before slide photos of his bicycle trip to France. He was staying in an apartment off the side of his parents' house—a house like mine, constructed by shipbuilders—in Scituate Harbor. But in the slides he stood tan and smiling before churches that rose up against the French backdrop, wind catching a tuft of his hair. At one point in the evening, I awoke with his arms around me. My T-shirt had been turned inside out and backward. For a long time, I squatted in the hallway in the bathroom's wedge of light, pinching the leaves of a succulent plant. Later, I stumbled, swearing, to the bathroom and knocked the same plant over, black potting soil fanning out over the wooden floorboards. In the bathroom, he stood behind me, our faces reflected in the dim fluorescent mirror. My back fit snugly against his slightly concave chest. And I kept thinking of the word "waterily"—our underwater movements, our damp, fishy skin.

He was the kind of man whom women touched and left their palm prints on, who seemed alien—unbearably tall and thin, with long, pale fingers and a body like a stalk pushed by the wind; a man who ate with his hands and licked his fingers, who looked entirely out of place under neon, behind a bar.

When I first met him, he would say: "Would you like a steak, some grapes? Would you like to lie down under the sky?"

He was my first real lover. It was the spring when my father and mother were having problems, problems they never talked about. I would see them walking back from the river together, their faces stony. That last semester of high school, when it seemed my family would break apart, I concentrated on my art class. One assignment: "Make a collage from family-related objects." In the midst of my halfhearted search, I asked my father for something from his life or history, or the Hatches', anything. He gave me the following X-ray and exam:

Sarah Messer

INDICATION: Annual Examination. Four films were obtained

Slight prominent ductal tissue is noted bilaterally. There is stable asymmetric fibro-glandular tissue in the 6 o'clock position of the right breast and laterally. This appearance is unchanged from prior studies. Coarse calcification associated with a subaureolar nodule on the left is unchanged as well. This most likely represents a fibro-adenoma. Rare bilateral benign-appearing calcifications are seen. No suspicious clusters are identified.

IMPRESSION: No evidence of malignancy
Written recommendation for one-year follow-up given to patient.

Only after the assignment was handed in did I realized that the X-ray was the bilateral mammogram of the patient Patricia Messer of Box 3646, North Marshfield Mass., DOB: 3/5/38, PHONE: 747-2233. My father, ever subtle, had sent me the results of my mother's most recent breast exam. I'd asked for a "family-related object," and this was the only mammogram, if you believe in antiquated views of marriage, that he rightly "owned." At least for that tenuous moment.

My father had sent an X-ray, a glimpse into my mother's body, as if his body extended into hers, just as I knew the house included us and all the Hatches. The house was bodily ours, if not waterily; it was the space we all inherited and inhabited, swam in. Yet now I wanted to get away from the house, from its history, its family importance, and my father's nostalgia.

But in the end it was my parents who left. My father moved out in fits and apologies, returned, and left again, and finally my mother left too—to England, to see some castles. Jess was packed off to summer camp and friends, and Suzy, Bekah, and I were left to care for ourselves in the huge, empty house.

In the beginning, it was a relief to be separated from the agony of my parents. My boyfriend whittled small wooden boats and gave them to me as presents. We drove down abandoned mill lanes and made out in the back seat of his car, an old monster Impala. He smelled like geraniums, screen doors, metal screws. Once, while walking, he grabbed a handful of apple petals and stuffed them into a hole in a tree. "There, this is you," he said. And when I frowned, he picked up a stick and said, "And this is you too." And he poked me with it. We kissed again. Sometimes my mouth tasted faintly of chlorine; sometimes his mouth was like a dog's mouth, watery. I would suck my braid absently; he would suck the corner of his finger. Later that fall, when he asked me to drop out of college and move to Utah with him, of course I said yes.

———

Kim was at sea when I made these decisions, living months at a time on water, staring at the horizon where the sky met the ocean. She was the second mate of the *Spirit of Massachusetts*, a 125-foot reproduction of the two-masted schooner *Fredonia*. She traveled down the coast to Virginia, North Carolina, Louisiana, Texas—the ship a sort of "goodwill ambassador" for the state of Massachusetts.

In September 1985, the *Spirit* returned to Cape Cod for Wellfleet's tercentennial celebration. Papers advertised Wellfleet's "Spirit Weekend"; T-shirts were sold out of the backs of station wagons in the harbor, and the Congregational Church planned a "Bach to Bluegrass" concert. Kim put a call in to the head of the committee in Wellfleet, saying that she had an elderly friend who was in a nursing home in Orleans and she really wanted to bring him aboard the ship; was there any chance she could get a rental car? In the years she was away, Kim had not thought of Richard Warren Hatch. When she first went on board, she sent him a brief postcard, but never told him that she was "driving" a Gloucester fishing-schooner replica. Now, perhaps guided by nostalgia and memory, Kim called Hatch and invited him to have lunch aboard a boat. He agreed.

That summer on Cape Cod, papers had been consumed with the story of Myles Standish, the last survivor of a pod of stranded pilot whales that had beached themselves the previous Thanksgiving. After a year in captivity in the care of his keeper, George King, Myles Standish died suddenly. The irony of the whale's name versus his keeper's did not escape Kim. "Get it? George King . . . King George?" she wrote in red pen in the margins when she sent me a copy of the newspaper in the mail. Below the article ran an ad for menswear—"Puritan Clothing of Cape Cod"—a line drawing of a man in a windbreaker and very short striped athletic shorts. "Aye-matey!" wrote Kim.

That Saturday in September, the *Spirit* entered the harbor and was met by more than one hundred local vessels, which, like some nautical fan club, had motored out to greet the ship. Cruisers, Boston Whalers, fishing boats, Coast Guard Patrol, charter boats, and Windsurfers escorted the ship to the dock. The town offered prizes—"Most Decorative," "Most Original," "Most Patriotic"—as if it were a boat prom.

When they pulled into port, the committee head met them at the dock, telling Kim that she could borrow *her* car to drive to Orleans and pick up her friend. By then Kim had told several people on board about Richard Warren Hatch—that he was a writer who had spent a few of his teenage years aboard the same sort of vessel out of Gloucester. She told them about the lobster books, and his novels about the house.

When Kim picked up Hatch the next morning, he was wearing loose, baggy clothes, looking, Kim thought, like an old salt.

On the drive over, he told her that he was going blind, could no longer read; because of his failed hearing, he was no longer able to listen to books on tape.

Kim turned off Route 6 and drove past the salt marsh toward Wellfleet Harbor. As they approached the pier, Richard Warren Hatch inhaled sharply. "Stop, Kim; stop one minute." Kim slowed the car.

"Look over there," Hatch said. "It's the mast of a schooner. It has the same rig as a Gloucester fishing schooner."

He could see the outline of the masts in light and dark shadows on the horizon, and he knew exactly what it was.

"That's the boat I told you about," Kim said, "where we're going to have lunch."

Hatch turned to Kim and said, "My dear, you are the son I've always wanted."

That weekend, twenty-three hundred people paid two dollars each to board the schooner and walk around the deck, visit the library with its collection of books of Massachusetts history, and talk to the crew about how great Massachusetts was. "It's like a traveling gift shop," one tourist remarked, milling about the crowded deck.

Hatch boarded the *Spirit*, sightlessly negotiating his way around the deck from memory, feeling his way with his hands, his long arms outstretched. He asked many questions of the skipper and crew. Lunch was served, and he sat at the base of the mast, on top of the ditty box. Tourists and young couples and groups of schoolchildren were coming aboard then and touring the vessel. Hatch stayed in his seat and began to tell stories of his boyhood aboard a similar vessel, stories about fishing, about earlier times, and stories about the house, and the Curious Lobster, the North River, the shipbuilders.

A small crowd had formed around him when a reporter from the Barnstable paper noticed him and began to take notes. Hatch glanced up at the reporter.

"Excuse me," the reporter asked, "who are you?"

"Son, I'm nobody," Hatch replied.

Soon after the reporter left, Hatch said that he'd had a wonderful time but he was tired now and would like to go home. While Kim was driving him back to the retirement home, Hatch spoke animatedly of what a great time he had had, how wonderful it all had been. He emphasized how much he had wanted to go aboard a Gloucester fishing schooner again, and now his dream had been realized. Then he fell into a very long silence. When Kim asked him what was wrong, he replied, "Nothing, dear, I'm just tired."

After its stay in Wellfleet, the *Spirit* sailed to Lunenburg, Nova Scotia, for repair work before setting off again for the Caribbean.

One evening a week after the event on Cape Cod, the skipper told Kim that she had an important phone call up in the shipyard office. It was our father.

"I have some bad news for you," he said. "Richard Warren Hatch is dead."

"What are you talking about?" Kim asked. "I just saw him."

"He killed himself," our father said.

It was exactly a week since he had gone aboard the *Spirit*; a week since he had recognized, through blurred light and shadow, the rigging of the Gloucester fishing schooner of his youth; a week since he had stepped on board.

———

My father phoned me too. He and my mother had reunited, worked things out, he said. I had stuck with my plan—dropping out of college, living in Salt Lake City with my boyfriend. Because my father did not approve of my choice, we hardly spoke anymore. When he relayed the news of Richard Warren Hatch's death, his voice sounded heavy and sad, and it seemed that he was calling more for himself, in his own grief, than to inform me of the death of a man I hardly knew. Having told me the story, he was now silent.

"It's OK, Dad," I said.

"He was a great man," my father replied. "It's just so sad. Such a waste."

I hung up the phone and looked around my grim apartment—the beige walls, the doors painted chocolate brown. The floor was carpeted in worn shag, the room otherwise empty except for a couch, a few dying spider plants and coffee cups, a waterbed in the next room. Something seemed subtracted from the air.

My father told me Hatch had grown almost completely deaf and blind. He could see shadows and white patches of light at certain angles, the fringe of shapes, isolated movement. The sound of his own voice and that of others must have reached him as distorted and haunting—a static roar pressing against the back of his head where far off he knew people were talking. My father told me that Hatch took a taxicab and had the driver drop him off at one of the beaches in Orleans. Then he walked into the ocean. I tried to imagine Richard Warren Hatch blind and in a taxicab. I imagined the taxi slowing to let him out in the empty beach parking lot, leaving him to walk over the edge of dunes. Just a month before, the same parking lot would have been full of dogs, coolers, umbrellas, children running without shoes on the hot tar. But Hatch wouldn't have been able to see or hear any of it.

Even as an old man, he must have towered in the parking lot as the taxi drove away. Perhaps the driver said, "I can wait with you for your friend," aware of the man's infirmity; but maybe he was distracted, had another fare waiting, or sensed beneath the frailty some sort of anger or sadness or desire to be alone that told him *go now* from this man, thin and tall as a tree with his broad shoulders and large hands.

It was sometime on September 21, my father had said. There

weren't any witnesses. The taxi driver might have asked nothing, or spoken only of the fare, handing back change that Hatch held in his hand, placed in his pocket. To Hatch, the taxi driver's face would have been a blur; his voice, a dime tossed down a well. Maybe Hatch thought of his wife, Ruth, who had by then lost her mental faculties; she had already floated away from him, away from the absence that had become her face. My father told me that Hatch had tried to care for her himself, but they had taken her away. And now he could no longer type, listen to recorded books, or read. For years, his life had been about words, letters, stories he had written and sold.

I tried to imagine how he could have waded into the surf, feeling the cold water soak through his shoes, his pant legs, his torso. He must have fallen forward into the waves, or bent his knees sinking backward, or struggled to swim a ways. My father had said that it was a waste, a shame. But, staring out my window in Salt Lake City that fall, I wondered, simply, how he had done it.

The body tries to live no matter what the cost, and perhaps there was pain, the lungs collapsing, pressure at the throat's automatic closure. Then breathing in.

It is impossible to know what his thoughts were, if there was hesitation or joy or fear. Or if there were no thoughts. The body might sink or float. Action completes itself. Water becomes air, a desire to live under the ocean, a desire not to live on earth, a desire to step off, step into the place where a person walks and breathes. When all seems lost—past, love, sight, sound—the body continues.

I remembered how it had felt to save Suzy, to reach down and grab her hair. I thought about grabbing Hatch by the hair and pulling him back. But his body was heavy in my mind, drifting deeper, legs scissoring or dropping limp, arms rising from the torso and floating as if in greeting, fingers clenched or opening, the pant legs billowing, the clothing clinging to his body like a flag wrapped around a pole. Perhaps Hatch wanted to stop all this—to stop the body. Because that is what he did, that is what happened.

———

It seemed to me that Hatch's death was a reversal of his lobster: when it was time for him "to be gone," he walked out of the house and into the sea; when Mr. Lobster wanted to be gone, he walked into a house that was pulled up out of the sea into the air. What I hadn't realized was how far I'd gone, how long I'd drifted away from who I'd always been, like a dory slowly carried away by the current. One day, you look up and it's just gone.

At some point in the months following my father's phone call, I realized that my boyfriend and I had stopped talking. I developed insomnia and began getting up in the middle of the night and walking around the city until light filtered into the sky. I'd walk out of the apartment with nothing—no money, no identification—with at most a T-shirt. No jacket. I guess part of me knew how dangerous it was: we didn't live in a very good neighborhood. But my body felt empty, hollowed out. Nothing seemed to matter, and my boyfriend never said anything. If someone had offered me a ride, I would have gotten in his car and gone with him, wherever he was driving.

Eventually, I ended up in the hospital, and used, by way of payment, the only thing I'd ever stolen from my father—his Blue Cross Blue Shield number. I was nineteen years old, not technically a dependent; but the doctors said that if I didn't contact my parents they would. This led me to phone my father and recount the details of the hospitalization, what the doctors had said, that I'd suffered some kind of extreme dehydration and toxic shock from taking too much speed and not eating for days, then swallowing fistfuls of Valium, resulting in massive hemorrhaging (a "spontaneous abortion," they had called it), because I had been pregnant and not even known it. In one phone call, I'd fulfilled every parent's worst nightmare of teenage trauma—anorexia, overdose, pregnancy. I was terrified that my father would be angry with me, but instead he kept asking, "Are you all right? Are you all right?"

"Yeah, I'm OK," I said. "I mean, physically OK."

He said he would call me right back. An hour later, he called and said, "Go to the airport; there'll be a ticket waiting for you."

"I don't want to go home," I said, thinking that I just couldn't face the Red House, my sisters, that all those old things would smother me. Mostly, I felt deeply embarrassed.

"You're not going home," he said. "We'll meet you in Charlotte Amalie."

My father was taking me to St. Thomas. I immediately thought of the botched former trip, how much of a failure it had been. But already I knew this was different, and somehow I made it to the airport.

"Suzy will be there," he had said before he hung up, "and your mom."

Before I left, my boyfriend sat on the edge of the waterbed and methodically rolled ten joints, put them in an empty Marlboro Red box and handed them to me.

"You'll need these, baby," he said. He brushed his long blond hair out of his eyes and smiled.

"Thanks," I said, knowing that, in his own strange way, he was just trying to help.

The trip involved several planes: from Salt Lake to Miami, from Miami to Puerto Rico, from Puerto Rico to St. Thomas. From the plane, the pinprick lights of Charlotte Amalie Harbor formed a U in the petri-dish ocean.

In the cab from the airport to the hotel, my father sat in the front with the driver, and the rest of us sat in the back seat. There was no meter, no divider between front and back, no identification tag. The driver quickly repeated our destination and adjusted his White Sox cap. When I tried to roll up the window, I realized it had no glass. The driver wore dark-brown pants and a short-sleeved cotton shirt. He played loud calypso music and drank pink liquid out of a grubby coffee cup. Air blew in the open windows, the same temperature as the human body, ninety-eight degrees. My father kept turning around as if to talk, his arm stretching along the seat, but nobody said anything.

When they met me at the gate, my mother, taking one look at me, had burst into tears. "What?" I asked. "Nothing," my mother had said, "it's good to see you."

"She thinks you're too skinny," Suzy whispered to me now, in the back seat. "But I think you look good." I knew she was lying.

We passed a Pueblo Supermarket spray-painted with the words "Some people are racist," and "This is our home." "I could take you tomorrow," my father said, "to a ruined fort—someone built a shrine to the Virgin Mary. The statue has been stolen, but the fort is still there." The driver stared straight ahead and said nothing. He tapped his long fingernails on the fuzzy steering-wheel cover. Traffic was blocked for miles by what seemed to be road construction—large shadows of backhoes and cranes rose above the string of cars and the bright lights of machinery. I watched a kid in a parochial uniform buzz by on a scooter and ascend beyond the crawl of cars into the hills. "Sound good?" my father asked, looking at me. I thought: Bless that kid on the scooter, the one who has escaped. I didn't answer.

"Is this all road construction?" Suzy asked, changing the subject.

"No," said the cab driver, "Carnival." As we drove closer, the shadows in the distance become people with giant masks walking on stilts lit from behind by flares.

It was late by the time we returned to the hotel. I shared a room with Suzy, and in our bathroom I sat on the closed toilet seat and lit a joint. I hadn't even thought to shut the door.

"Hey, Mom and Dad are next door," Suzy said. She grabbed the joint out of my hand and stubbed it out on the sink. "Where did you get this?" I offered up the cigarette pack, half thinking that she was jealous, that she wanted one. She took the pack from my hand, made a gesture meaning "get up," and then flushed the joints down the toilet.

"What's wrong with you?" was all she said.

Right before dawn, I left. I simply walked around the back of the hotel, past clipped hedges of hibiscus, down a path hazy with gray light. I walked out of the parking lot and onto a small road pocked with holes. A streetlamp illuminated a corner at the base of a hill, and I turned right, past a building advertising bait and Budweiser. I walked under canopies of tamarind trees, past houses made of layers of plywood and metal sheeting. The road ended at a local beach unused by tourists, its edge ringed with crushed soda cans and overturned boats. In the water, some people were swimming. I could see them clearly: four men, their heads and arms moving in dark shapes. But there was something else swimming with them, a large animal caught in the circle of their bodies. The men clapped their hands and yelled to each other. I realized that the swimming animal was a horse, only its long head visible above the water. The horse circled and tried to reach shore, laboring through its nostrils, its ears pinned back, but the men kept cutting it off.

One of the men waved and yelled something. I sat down in the sand. It was now almost daybreak. From where I sat, it seemed that the horse was very old—as old as my horse had been when we had walked him in circles in the paddock, when he had been sick, before we had put him down. For a moment I thought it was my dead horse out there swimming. But the horse in the water was very young; the men were exercising it, swimming it on long lines of rope. As the men led the animal out, it jumped and stumbled in the surf, held by two of the men. The horse was sleek, a young Thoroughbred awkward on its long spindly legs. The four men trotted the horse down the beach, laughing and gesturing to each other. As they moved past me, I thought I recognized one of them as the cab driver.

When I returned, my family looked at me with careful faces, as if approaching a cornered animal. "Well, we're off to Red Hook," my mother said, in a scripted tone that told me all decisions about the day had been made. I went to bed.

I woke up a few hours later to the sound of a blender. My father was trying to perfect his piña colada recipe.

"Which do you think is better—coconut ice cream or pineapple ice cream? Here, I've made two batches." He handed me two small glasses. "They're virgin, of course. Come on, try one," he said. He kept handing me different drinks, all sweet, cold, and frothy. "Now try this," he would say, handing me another.

He was different from any way I'd ever seen him, more tentative, as if he'd made a mistake and felt sorry about it. He didn't say it, but I knew it was true.

"I was wondering if you could help me with something," he said, "out here, on the balcony." I didn't say anything but followed him anyway. On the patio table, he'd arranged a vase of red hibiscus flowers. Next to it sat a watercolor pad and some paints, two brushes.

"I've been trying to paint this flower all morning," he said, and flipped the cover of the pad over to reveal a runny red blob. It was terrible. "Maybe, if I watch you paint it, I'll learn something," he said.

So I sat down, and he sat next to me, and I painted the flower. "Oh, that's great," he said when I was done. "Now watch me while I try." He tore off the page and started painting.

"Be careful not to overmix the paint," I said, "or it'll become mud." I realized that this was the first sentence I'd uttered to him since arriving.

"Am I holding the brush right?" he asked.

"Try that," I said, moving his hand. We talked about the pigment, how it was carried in the water and how the paper absorbed it; how you only needed one brief gesture to capture the essence of the flower. At some point, my mother and Suzy returned, only to say that they were going out again, were leaving us alone.

And the afternoon continued this way: I painted a flower, then he painted a flower. "Now paint the vase," he had said. And then: "How would you paint that railing?" I don't remember when I realized that this was all part of the plan—that he had never needed any help. Eventually, I was painting the flower, the vase, the railing, and what stretched beyond it, the deep-blue bay, the white yachts, and the green hillsides of the distant chain of islands. And this was how we made it through the day and into evening, painting landscapes, until the color we needed for the sky grew flush pink, then deeper and deeper blue, and the houses made of plywood and tin, which earlier were just brown dots on the hillsides, began to light up from the inside, and we left them white with perhaps a tinge of yellow, so they would shine from the painting exactly the way we saw them. Then, while we sat next to each other in the dark, everything else except for the glowing houses disappeared.

PART TWO

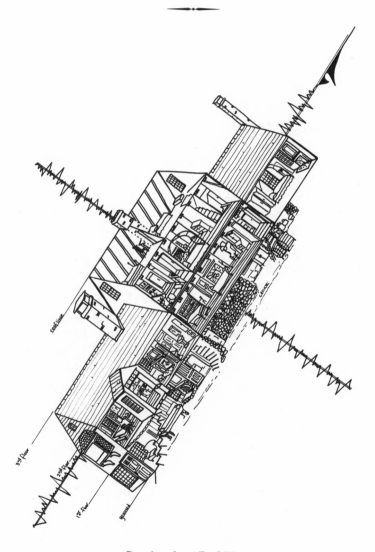

South side of Red House

HOUSE *beautiful.* HOUSE *by the churchyard.* HOUSE *by the river.* HOUSE *by the works.* HOUSE *in town, a sequel to Opportunities.* HOUSE *of Commons for the people.* HOUSE *of Commons on stimulants.* HOUSE *of correction.* HOUSE *of danger.* HOUSE *of fulfillment.* HOUSE *of grass.* HOUSE *of hidden treasure.* HOUSE *of Israel, a scripture story.* HOUSE *of quiet, an autobiography.* HOUSE *of Raby, Our Lady of Darkness.* HOUSE *of reform.* HOUSE *of the misty star.* HOUSE *of the strange woman.* HOUSE *of wisdom, the house of sons of the prophets; house of exquisite enquiry and of deep research.* HOUSE *on the marsh.* HOUSE *on the moor.* HOUSE *on the rock.* HOUSE *on the sunless side.* HOUSE *on wheels, far from home.* HOUSE *opposite.* HOUSE *party.* HOUSE *that baby built.* HOUSE *that Jack built.* HOUSE, *the garden, and the steeple.* HOUSE *with a history.* HOUSE *with the golden windows.* HOUSE *with the green shutters.* HOUSE-BOAT *boys.* HOUSEFUL *of girls.* HOUSEHOLD *angel in disguise.*

—Titles beginning with the word HOUSE, from the
*Dictionary of Anonymous and Pseudonymous English
Literature,* 1929

Nine

1996 restoration of Red House

At low tide, the river beneath the Route 3 bridge smelled like a burned match. The smell drifted up to the bridge, and because of wind or tide, because of the glide of traffic, the air also smelled like clams. The air wrapped around itself—insular, thick, drifting in from the river's mouth past red-winged blackbirds, marsh reeds, a Boston Whaler's gas rainbow.

After many years away from the Red House, I was returning—June 1996. According to Kim, the house was falling apart. Kim was there now, having cleared out my parents, and a month earlier had started to reconstruct the house's south side, a project that would eventually span three years. I told myself that this was the reason for my return, that I was going to help Kim and her new husband, Philippe, try to save it. The house would basically be empty except for me, Kim, and Philippe.

Driving over the bridge, I could see the river side-winding through a plain of marshes. Looking down at the marsh cliffs,

I thought, *Clam flats, muck,* imagining knee-deep mud that would be gone six hours later, when the tide returned and the air was filled with salt. Beyond the farthest bend in the river, the Red House waited in the woods and could not be seen from the highway.

I had left Salt Lake City soon after the trip to St. Thomas and moved every six months for the next ten years—back to college and then graduate school, journalism assignments, teaching gigs, and grant-writing—almost as long as I had stayed still in Marshfield growing up. I became very good at moving. When I left Salt Lake City, I also ended my relationship with the man who had once helped me escape. It had been years since I had seen him, and I had no idea if he had left Salt Lake, and if so where he had gone. Finally, I found myself facing the decision to return home as if I were a passive observer, not someone making a conscious choice. In this state, I often told people that I felt "underwater," which I thought was an apt metaphor for my murky existence, my slow, undulating movements toward nothing in particular.

I was traveling with my new boyfriend, James, who was as different from the first as anyone could be: loud, funny, and wildly moody, he grew up in Los Angeles and knew nothing of New England, three-hundred-year-old houses, or the two-mile plot of land where I was born. Even now, he stared out the window appearing not to notice anything, perhaps because it was getting dark, or—fingers tapping on the dash—because I had just flipped on the local radio station that was playing Abba's "Knowing Me, Knowing You" segueing into Lou Rawls. We took Exit 12 to Route 139, a potholed ribbon of tar. Turning onto Union Street, the main thoroughfare of Two Mile, we drove beyond the lit placards of Mobil and Gulf stations and into stands of white pine, houses set off the road, a "Slow Children" sign, a giant cement frog with a mailbox growing out of its head. One house, painted chocolate brown and constructed from curved pieces of corrugated tin, had been there for years. It looked like the product of a bad holiday-cake book. The road passed colonials, developments marked by carved wooden signs. James's fingers tapped the dash, his crossed leg. "You'll never find another love like mine." We passed the Pembroke-Marshfield town line and the beginning of Two Mile, the road progressing through a dark corridor of trees.

"Didn't that house look like a cake?" I said.

"Where?" James asked, looking out at the darkness.

"A Yule log. Didn't it look like a Yule log?"

I was trying to imagine the landscape from the eyes of a stranger. When my parents bought the Red House, the town was still relatively small; its center then was the beach, with lines of cottages and summer people. Brant Rock Beach had a bowling alley and a movie theater, and Rexham Beach had the Rexicana Ballroom, which featured big bands and dancing on weekends. A few businesses sprang up: First National Market, Toabe's Hardware, Buttner's, a state-run pheasant farm, and a pharmacy and gift shop called The Ordinary. I told James that celebrity lawyer F. Lee Bailey had lived here in the seventies and had a helicopter-landing pad next to his pool; that my mom often saw Steve Tyler of Aerosmith in her aerobics class. I rattled off facts, that the town's main employers were still: (1) the town of Marshfield; (2) Purity Supreme Supermarket; (3) Marshall's Department Store; and (4) WATD, the radio station to which we were listening. Marshfield, I insisted, was not the Currier and Ives version of New England that James imagined it would be—no picket-fence-sleigh-apple-crate-rosy-cheeked-toboggan nostalgia. And yet sometimes it was—inescapably New England, like a cartoon of itself. We passed a street named Chowdermarch.

I turned left into a driveway marked by a painted boulder,

onto the Red House property. To our right, James had a clear view of the neighbors' front field, which continued back toward the White House, the Red House just beyond it.

I told James that the Red House was being restored, that the entire south wall needed to be shored up. Because of this, I reminded him, some stuff would be out of place. From the driveway, I could already see that the south windows had been removed and covered with plastic sheeting. My parents had left the house dismantled; Kim and Philippe were already working steadily. I had not, until this point, described the house to James at all, except to say that it was built in 1647, and that, as long as anyone could remember, it had been painted red.

A brick pathway progressed toward the house and widened into a patio at the west ell. The house stretched its two and a half stories away from the path, wings spreading east and west. It loomed above me now—shelter for centuries of New England gentry on decline, scratching out the same patch of earth—my adopted historical family.

"It's red," James said as we got out of the car. The sun had gone down, the sky grown gray. He had no idea how red it really was.

Moths batted the lamp where swags of wisteria hung over the doorway. In its halo, the side of the house appeared shiny and dark. I had forgotten the wasps, the mosquitoes, the brilliant green flies, the vines covering the north side. The house was humming, alive. In an earlier phone call, Kim had told me of a six-foot water snake summering in the basement. The snake left white powder trails down the stone cellar walls each night when it ventured out to do its snake business, sliding down to the wet floor of the wine cellar. And recently the trees had let loose a yellow dust that covered everything. Before the pollen, a plague of ladybugs blown north by El Niño crawled up people's arms and helicoptered through rooms before they dried up in the windowsills. Without my parents around, the house became its own creature.

Stepping into the kitchen, I saw tracks winding through a thin veil of pollen to a note on the chopping block: "Welcome home! Went out, be back late. K and P."

In the past ten years, the house had grown thick with objects. Above our heads hung pewter mugs, shellfish steamers, the six-foot sideboard of the 1871 schooner *Helena*, a cranberry scoop, two Revolutionary War muskets, a goatskin flask, a cloth wine-carrier suggesting "A Grape Idea," a hanging wire fruit-basket, three dusty woks, and eighteen tin lanterns. Corners housed a tin flour-sifter from a general store, a pastel drawing of the Matterhorn, a handful of Betty lamps and tobacco-cutters, a collection of wooden rolling pins on top of a microwave. My dad had recently begun wood-carving, and clamps and hand tools lay stacked on side tables. On top of a cupboard, carved figures stuck out of about twenty liquor bottles—animals, arms that moved, twisting human heads.

Each hour, approximately nine clocks in the house bonged loudly, their tones overlapping. Now, according to the clocks, it was 8 p.m. James stood in the rings of a braided rug, dangling the strap of his backpack, as the clocks chimed. He had experimental facial hair and the eyes of a cartoon lion.

"Do I get to meet any ghosts?" James smirked.

"Don't be dumb," I said.

I gave him the tour, starting with the basement. Past the hammered-tin door before the tunnel opened up into the small room with a floor that was part brick, part cement, part scraped earth. James noted the wine barrels, their cracked spouts, the staircase with the heavy hatched beams.

"Like the Flintstones," he said.

I told him the house had probably begun here—in the cellar hole. I told him about the fire in the central chimney in 1790, the addition of the east ell, the subsequent building of the breeze-way to the barn. I told him that electricity and plumbing weren't added until 1940. Then the barn was torn down. The east ell was turned into a bedroom, the breezeway into a kitchen, and a bathroom was installed on the second floor. I told him all of this from underground, looking up and pointing left and right, feeling the weight of the house.

"It's kinda musty down here," he said.

I led him upstairs again and found that the dining room was consumed by the construction project—an orange extension cord coiled on the sideboard next to quartered pieces of sandpaper, a cordless drill. Furniture had been pushed to the corners, covered in plastic sheeting, and the room smelled of sawdust, machines. On top of the dining-room table, someone had streaked three fingers through the dust.

In the living room, the couch and tables had been pulled away from the wall, the window plastic whirring like insects. Hurricane lamps lined the mantel below a hand-tinted photograph of the last launching of the *Helena Foster* on the North River. In the photo, behind a split-rail fence, about sixty people stand shoulder to shoulder along the mastless deck of a boat. An American flag, raised on a pole from the deck, whips in a nearly invisible blur.

We moved through a parlor to the north side of the house, the entryway, the bolted door we had all learned to pull as children, where now a rein of sleigh bells hung from a nail. Now, with James beside me, I was acutely aware of how fragile and precarious everything seemed—the dust on the decorative fire-grates, the thinness of doors, the way the uneven floorboards caused everything to rattle as we walked through. On the second floor, we entered the Borning Room, from which my things had long since been boxed and removed to the barn with the X-rays. Now it was a guest bedroom. I wound the handle on the music box, and it began its repertoire like an off-kilter cyclone.

Rooms led to other rooms. On the bathroom door someone had taped the sign: "Please do not use bathtub for bath. Take only three-minute showers."

We stooped into and then out of a converted crawl space we had called the "corn chamber" as kids. It was the only room that we were allowed to decorate, to paint. The room remained unchanged, filled with our seventies artwork—orange walls with a giant snail, a gnome napping under a mushroom, a rainbow stretching across an eave. A yellowish-green carpet covered the floor. Along a baseboard I had painted a diorama—hunters on horseback chasing deer who ran with sock-monkey-looking legs across rolling hills.

"OK," he said, "this is weird."

After that, the maze of rooms disoriented James, reducing him to monosyllables—"wow" or "huh." We had gone up and down staircases, into the eaves of the attic, continually passing through doorways. Like most visitors, he commented on the small rooms, how dark they were.

"It's night," I said, trying to joke. But he kept reaching out toward the wood-paneled walls stained by smoke or use. Perhaps he had expected something grander, like a high-ceilinged Victorian—something more classically haunted. Not this labyrinth that spiraled around itself, that had spiraled around me when, as a child, I put my head down to sleep each night. The house in my head. And now I moved through it, remembering the choreography, the feel of every latch in my hand.

That night, we slept on the second floor, in the northeast corner of the house. There were sheets on the bed and a bathroom with running water, but in places only plastic stretched between nature and us. Outside, the frog volume was amped to ten. James said it felt like camping.

I realized that I had been using the house in various ways my whole life—to scare girlfriends, to impress teachers, seduce boyfriends. But now the house was half exploded and as jumbled as a junk store—the basement was just a basement; the attic, an attic. Throughout the tour, James had seemed bored and cold. And now he was apparently asleep, breathing softly.

Whenever I returned to the house, I couldn't sleep. A mosquito whined in my ear, and I got up and moved to other beds. I wandered the house, my hands finding the places I used to touch as a child. As an adult, when I was away from it, I thought about touching these places—fingers across plaster, the two-inch wooden latch at the corner of each doorway. I walked through a doorway and my hand would glide up the doorframe to the latch, which I pushed with my fingers as I passed through. I knew that it took ten steps from the back stairwell, around the corner banister, through the doorway of the room with the twin beds—right hand grasping a bedpost—and across the uneven floorboards to the far doorway into the next room.

I went into my old room. The twin bed's mattress was horsy and sunk in the middle. I ran my hand along the length of the bed-runner, and found the indentation of teethmarks I'd made there as a child.

I slept and woke again. I dreamed of the century before the elms were cut down. A man stood in the doorway, dripping from the ocean. He was wearing a ship captain's uniform. He smelled of brine and fog, the storm that had taken his ship down. The floor was an unsteady deck floating beneath him; he weaved, holding the door latch, water pouring from his sleeves. His eyes were spectral; his hair was matted around his face. He had a fever, his body was boiling, he was drowning. *Thomas,* I thought, saying his name. He was the first boyfriend, the one who helped me escape, whose name I never used—he was Thomas. Tom now, in my head, in history. As far-gone from me now as this sailor, a man I could not reach. I knew then that if I searched the entire globe I could never find him, except here, in this dream, standing in the doorway. I tried to reach out to him, but my body would not move, and I could not speak. I knew him, but he was not from this century, he was wearing such strange wet clothes.

———•———

In the morning, I found myself back in the room with James, not sure that I had ever left.

James stretched, rolled over, said, "Who was that man you were talking to last night?"

"That was me," I said. "I left in the night and came back."

"No, you were here," he said. "There was a man standing at the edge of the bed."

I told him he must have been dreaming. A man in his head, maybe? I remembered the dream about my ex-boyfriend and felt guilty. I was worried that I might have said something in my sleep, and now I'd have to tell him the dream. Even though it was a dream, I felt I had cheated on James.

"I wasn't dreaming," he said. The man, he insisted, had been talking to me.

"What was I saying?" I asked.

"You kept saying that everything would be OK. That everything would be put back."

I looked out the window, beyond the glassy surface of the pond, to where a hill rose to a shed, an orchard. James wondered if the man had been Philippe.

"What did he look like?" I asked, realizing that he had no idea about my dream.

"He was wearing a dark wool coat. And he had a long white beard. It was halfway down his chest. Thin face, high forehead, long nose."

"You're kidding," I said, but could tell by the look on his face that he wasn't.

"What does Philippe look like?"

"Philippe is *French*," I said, but that didn't seem to mean anything. I had had a long conversation with a man who had stood by my bed. It was a conversation that I couldn't remember. I remembered the dream and realized that James was talking about someone else, a different man.

"You were sitting up and talking to him," James repeated.

"What did he say?" I asked.

"I couldn't hear him," James said. "But he seemed upset about something."

That morning, we went downstairs to the kitchen, where Kim and Philippe were seated at the table eating mangoes.

"Did you come in the room and talk to Sarah last night?" James asked Philippe, immediately after being introduced.

"No," Philippe said, "we got in late."

"There was a man in our room last night," James said.

"Maybe it was the smothering ghost," Kim said. She told how, the week before, a friend of hers had seen a man in the room who continually tried to climb in bed on top of her.

"She felt like she was being smothered," Philippe added, "like the ghost was trying to get in his old bed and she was there. Or he was trying to *get with her*, you know."

"No, not like that, Philippe. A smothering ghost," said Kim again, turning the skin of a mango inside out, "not a, what do you call it . . ."

"Succubus," I said.

"Yeah, right. What did he look like?"

"A *mothering* ghost." Philippe snorted.

"Come on," Kim said.

James then described the dark coat, the beard, the face.

"Oh yeah," Kim said, "that's him." And then she and Philippe were nodding and claiming that the man the friend had seen also had a beard. And this seemed to confirm it, the situation as banal as spotting someone across a crowded room.

"Oh yeah, that's him," they repeated. "The ghost."

James looked as if he were trying to swallow a walnut. He glanced at me. I decided not to mention my dream about my ex-boyfriend as a drowned nineteenth-century sailor—the conversation seemed strange enough.

"I don't think anyone came into the house last night," I said. Yet part of me wanted to believe Kim, to believe in ghosts, to believe that I had been talking to the ghost of a Hatch. She had already launched into a recipe for ridding oneself of a smothering ghost. Something to do with a bathtub filled with milk and rubbing yourself all over with white carnations.

"But that bathtub upstairs is broken," said Philippe.

"Oh yeah, right. Well, James, I guess you're going to have to use your own bathtub for the ritual, then. It's OK, do it when you get home," Kim said.

———·———

For the next few days of his visit, James remained convinced he had seen a man, not a ghost. I went looking for evidence that the man who stood by the bed was someone who had lived here before, a deceased Hatch.

I began with the closet in my father's study. The narrow door reached halfway up the wall, stopping at eye level. Beneath an old stethoscope I found two printed sermons, from 1753 and 1766; a proposal to build a bridge; a thumbprint in wax, 1778; my father's arithmetic tests from 1940; a photograph from 1976 of my sister Kerry sitting on a high-school bleacher; a nineteenth-century letter from a sailor in prison in Peru; a silver bracelet inscribed "Shirley"; a diary from 1857; a picture of a

turkey that I had drawn in third grade; an inventory of Marshfield's Civil War dead; my mother's childhood copy of *Winnie-
the-Pooh*; and six Bibles dating back to 1701.

Then, on top of a box of party gags, I found a sky-blue letter
about a woman and child on fire. The letter was written in tight
script on paper creased with squares where it had been folded
into an envelope. A burning mother and child had been carried
out of their house this way—folded, like their story. The return
address was Marshfield. "Dear Brother," the letter began.

On October 23, 1853, Sarah Stoddard had tried to put her
ten-month-old baby to sleep. Because the girl was fussing, and
perhaps because her husband was away fishing, Mrs. Stoddard
lay down with her child. She later awoke to find the fluid low in
her only lamp, and stood to fill it so she would have light. While
she was pouring the quart can into the lamp, the fluid caught fire
and exploded, engulfing Mrs. Stoddard in flames. In her confu-
sion, she grabbed her sleeping child (who would have been fine
if she had left her alone) and held the baby to her breast as she
ran flaming out of the house. A neighbor doused them with well
water and rolled them in a rug.

The letter had been written by Rebekah R. Oakman to her
brother Israel H. Hatch (Richard Warren Hatch's grandfather)
about their neighbor. "From the time of the accident 'till Thursday morning," the letter continued, "the child never cried or
spoke but laid as if stupefied, excepting when in fits, of which it
had several. And of course no one thought it could live. But
Thursday it came to, enough to cry, and can now talk, and seems
more likely to live than her mother. . . ."

The mother's body was burned everywhere except the place
where she had held the child close. She carried the map of her
child's body upon her own, a silhouette—breast, part of a rib
cage, a hip left unburned. So engulfed, Mrs. Stoddard forgot
whom she was saving; she forgot that she was the one on fire.
The letter concludes with a description of the mother and

daughter still alive and lying naked over bedsheets, their burns dressed hourly with cotton and turpentine by the local doctor. "Please excuse all mistakes, of which there are many," Rebekah wrote to her brother, "if I do not tell you everything you need to know, please write me and I will answer."

Israel H. Hatch, the recipient of the letter, was the last Hatch to be born, live his life, and die in the house. My sister Rebekah had been named after the letter's author, Israel H.'s sister.

I had always known about the old letters and documents, but for some reason, until that afternoon, I had never looked at them, or made this kind of connection. I had always taken the house for granted; the people who had inhabited it had seemed dreamily distant. Besides, I preferred to imagine the Marshfield where I grew up as just a suburban landscape: diesel and grass-clippings, the Rod n' Gun Club, boats on blocks, Dunkin' Donuts.

Except now there was this letter.

I began to feel the pull of two opposite attractions: one toward a house that seemed fixed and immovable, the other toward something more transitory—the woman on fire, the idea that anything or anyone at any time could ignite. I also couldn't ignore the result of the woman's actions: trying to save the child, she burned the child, but in failing to rescue the child, she had saved the house.

Beneath the blue letter, I found Rebekah Oakman's Bible and, in the back, read the names:

Lizzie Agnes Oakman
Born April 7th, 1857
Died Aug 27, 1863

Ellen Richmond Oakman
Born December 6th 1859
Died Aug 21st 1863

On the next page of the Bible, Rebekah had written: "Thomas R. Oakman, died Dec 26th, 1867."

Thomas. Rebekah's husband was named Thomas.

Within a four-year period, Rebekah had lost two children and her husband. In the Bible, she had underlined a passage from Psalm 139:

> *If I take the wings of the morning, and dwell in the uttermost parts of the sea; even there shall thy hand lead me, and thy right hand shall hold me.*

I drew out what I expected to be another collection of children's primers and catechism books. Instead, I saw faces. The same neat script as in the fire letter identified them as Rebekah, Thomas, Israel, and Deacon Joel Hatch, layered in glass, staring out at me from the dusted shells of their covers. In one daguerreotype, Rebekah is posed next to Thomas, holding an infant, Lulu, who escaped her sister's illnesses. On the stuffed silk opposite the glass was a braided wreath of infant hair. Rebekah had clipped her baby's hair and sewn it there so she and others could touch it. In another daguerreotype, Israel sits alone looking off to the right of the frame. Another of Thomas alone, staring straight ahead before the painted backdrop of a schooner.

Rebekah held innocence in her face, her mouth partially open as if about to speak, her black hair parted in the middle and drawn back in tight-looped braids. The infant on her lap was blurry from fussing, unable to sit with the stillness required of the exposure. Israel resembled his sister and her plain openness; he had a round face with prominent cheekbones, dark shining eyes. Even when he was a young man, his nose had a ball on the end, his lips were thin and pursed.

I remembered Roland Barthes: "That terrible thing which is

there in every photograph: the return of the dead." And it felt like that, looking at the Hatches and them looking back at me. The daguerreotype repeated a moment to infinity—Thomas, Rebekah, and Lulu sitting together—that only happened once. The daguerreotype was an opening into history, the way that a wound or an X-ray was an entrance to the body. The daguerreotypes, in this sense, were miniature rooms opening into the past, were ghosts.

It was Thomas, however, whose face leapt from the inked and mirrored surfaces. He had wide-set almond-shaped blue eyes that glowed in contrast to his dark skin and even darker hair, which was cut in pageboy bangs across his forehead. Both Israel and Thomas wore muttonchop sideburns, goatees, limp bows tied at their necks. But Thomas was at least twice as beautiful as both his brother-in-law and wife combined. His face glowed.

Thomas's brother, an Oakman, had built the house a mile up the road where Mike, one of the pool players, had lived when we were in high school. Years after this daguerreotype had been taken, I had been the ghost wandering through Thomas's family house.

Finally, tipped behind a stack of crumbling Bibles, I found a final framed black-and-white photograph. It showed an old man and six children posed in a square rowboat on the banks of the North River. The three girls wore skirts, blouses with bunched sleeves and double rows of buttons, hair ribbons the size of Ping-Pong paddles, typical of the 1900s. One boy sat at the back of the boat wearing knickers, suspenders, a shirt with the sleeves rolled up, and a cap. This boy had one hand on an oar and the other at his mouth, as if he was chewing a piece of grass. Beside him, the oldest girl reclined. At the front of the boat, the two other girls dangled their bare legs over the edge, and the boys, the youngest in the group, stood in the middle of the boat, next to the man, who held the second oar out against the shallow marsh. It was a sunny day; the children squinted at the camera, and the man wore a wide-brimmed straw hat. The boat cast a reflection in the water, broken up by reeds and marsh grass. The river stretched back beyond the boat to the other bank, the water line bisecting the man's shoulders with its perspective. No planes dragging across the distance. The photo captured the marsh beyond the other bank, a row of white-pine and hard-wood trees, the sky hazy with a few clouds.

But it was the man in the photo who captivated me. He wore a white long-sleeved shirt beneath a black button-up vest, grasped the oar, and looked off the side of the boat in the direction of the tide, his face shadowed by the brim of the hat. Caught by the wind, a blizzard of white beard blew halfway down his chest.

I brought the photo to James, who was packing in a room upstairs.

"Was this the man who was standing by the bed?" I asked. James grabbed the photo and stared. Then he handed it back to me.

"That's him," James said, "that's the guy."

I flipped the photo over. While James had held it, I had noticed writing on the back. It was handwriting that, in the next few years, I would learn to know well, to recognize by sight. A carefully scripted "Israel H. Hatch." The brother of "Dear Brother," brother-in-law to Thomas. Here he was suddenly an old man. Israel had written, perhaps for posterity, his own name.

Then it occurred to me that the two small boys in the picture—the taller, dark one staring confidently at the camera, his hand in his overalls, and the smaller, shiny-haired blond—were Israel's grandsons, Richard Warren Hatch and his younger brother, Tracy. Here was Richard Warren Hatch as a *child*. Richard Warren had passed away more than ten years ago, Tracy in 1960, and Israel in 1921.

"These people," I said to James, "they're all dead."

Israel H.
1837–1921

Israel H. Hatch with grandchildren on North River

But it is the maid with the stoutest heart who fears not her fate—and whose desires are great—who dares to put it to the touch of the cellar stairs' visit at midnight. The proper form is for her to let down her back hair, then "dressed all in white" with uplifted candle, a la Lady Macbeth, in the left hand a mirror, she proceeds to wend her way slowly—and alone—down the stairs backwards to the cellar; it is then when the final step is reached and the critical and dramatic moment arrives, that she will see the face of her future husband in the mirror she carries in her left hand. It is only for those possessing great faith that the face in the mirror will materialize. If the maiden reading this doesn't believe in the efficacy of this special rite, let her try it for herself—seeing is believing.

—From discussion of love divinations and folk rituals,
in *The Ladies World*, November 1892

In early December 1867, roses appeared on Thomas Oakman's chest. Pink lesions bloomed in a rash on his torso, then moved down his abdomen—they looked like roses in the long-handled mirror Rebekah brought him. He had felt it first as a slight tug in his joints, an ache that turned into a fever hot around his temples. This was how he first realized that he had typhoid, an illness he could have picked up a year earlier through contaminated food or water, or by touching infected earth and rubbing his mouth with the back of his hand. He could have walked around for more than a year shedding the bacteria without showing any symptoms.

His fever would have turned hot, turned into pharyngitis, constipation. For a few days, he would have lost his appetite, complained of a tender and sore stomach. When Rebekah offered him a plate of food, he would have swallowed only one bite.

By the time the roses appeared, he would have lost all control of his faculties. Prostration. Delirium. Stupor. Constant diarrhea, containing blood. Coughing up blood. The sheets would have been continually changed and replaced, visitors trying not to wipe their mouths or touch their faces; the sheets would be stained badly with shit and blood. In the advanced stages of the disease, it was not uncommon for the patient to bleed from the eyes, nose, and mouth.

Israel, standing at Thomas's bedside, would have known exactly what the disease raging through his brother-in-law's body felt like. Having entered active military duty in August 1862, Israel only made it as far south as Washington before he fell ill. Carrie, five months pregnant, had taken a train down to the Baltimore Hospital to nurse him. He had typhoid fever and chronic dysentery. Carrie took care of him by day, slept in the hospital with him at night. After three months, he was honorably discharged as unfit for duty. In October, the first sergeant in Company K filed a disability form for Israel, stating, "He became very sick and weak from long continued diarrhea, being at times very feverish and at other times suffering from the chills. His condition became so alarming that he was ordered to be sent to the Regiment Hospital, where he was left when the regiment left for the front."

When Israel returned to Two Mile, he had to confront more illness. Rebekah's children, Lizzie, six years old, and Ellen, four, had died within six days of each other—of the same thing: typhoid and dysentery. In November 1863, Carrie and Israel's nine-month-old son Israel Ellis also died of a fever. Thomas's brother Otis Oakman, who also enlisted in 1862, never returned to Two Mile, dying from wounds and illness he acquired in battle. Israel had survived, but it seemed no one else had.

With great trepidation, and still weak from months of chronic illness, Israel re-enlisted, in Company C, 61st Regiment of the Massachusetts Volunteer Infantry, and was immediately promoted to corporal. In 1864–65, he saw Petersburg and Appomatox, built fortifications at Fort Mahone, known as "Fort Damnation," and dug cannon-proof holes in the earth, dirt hills surrounded by logs called "breast plates." He wore the suspenders and the high-waisted pants given to him by the Union Army, the boots shipped in wooden boxes from the Two Mile Mills, ate the hardtack. In 1865, when the Confederacy surrendered, he marched all the way back home through Virginia, past the looted houses and farms, through burning Richmond, and on past the capital. And then just two years later Thomas lay dying, looking up at him with those eyes that had always seemed to glow but now were lost somehow. It was so strange that Thomas had sailed all around the globe, been so near death and disease on the ships but survived it all, and now the war was over and Thomas was finally home, but here, in Two Mile, he was dying. At Christmas, they knew he'd be lucky if he made it to the next day.

"Israel," Thomas said, "my eyes are aching." Somehow, he made it through Christmas to December 26. Then his pupils turned from white to red. And then he was dead.

———•———

Israel remained in Two Mile, but he made little money. He had three children and earned an income constructing wooden boxes at the box mill, though he was also a self-described "one-horse farmer and dairyman," running a milk wagon to Marshfield Hills. "With no mill and a mere patch of upland," his grandson Richard Warren Hatch would later write, "Israel had to augment his income with town jobs, and mortgaged the place."

In 1872, George Leonard, the pastor of the church Israel attended, gave a lecture entitled "Marshfield Sixty Years Ago Today." Leonard concluded with his main concern: that all the young men were leaving Two Mile; no young men had gratitude, no one wanted to stay. "A large number of our enterprising young men leave the place and go where they can find more business and make more money than they can in Marshfield," he stated. "They do not like to work in our bush pastures, sandy plains or wet, low lands. They do not see much money in our salt marshes. . . . They find but little mechanical business here which they consider lucrative; so they conclude to go to Boston or some other city, or go to the West, where there is better prospect of realizing a fortune; and no doubt many who leave Marshfield do better than they would by remaining here."

And, true, while the rest of the country modernized, Two Mile stayed the same. Raccoon and skunk pelts hung in the dooryard of Hall and Weatherby's store the way they had at the old meetinghouse, two hundred years before. By 1890, the telephone and the light bulb had been invented, and the railroad connected both sides of the country, but the Red House remained unchanged from the house Israel had inhabited as a child—vegetation embroidered the south side, the barn slanted dangerously, the water pump rusted. Israel kept a trout swimming in the well to warn of toxins, his own canary in a coal mine. He inhabited the Red House with Carrie and their daughter Alice, who had never married and was called Aunt Alice by everyone, growing wide in girth like her mother, canning, baking, attending church. Israel had long since given up teaching singing school or planing in the sawmill, which was now run by Decker Hatch, his cousin once removed. On the ten acres of land, Israel dug ditches and farmed a "dyke meadow," grew some corn.

Inside the house, he worked on small inventions, kept the John Bailey clock wound, stored his papers in the highboy in the old kitchen that had been turned into a parlor, with the old flax wheel and piles of books. Israel, sitting by the light of a lamp, wrote poems about clams, thinking about the river, humoring himself like an internal castaway:

> From grass the meadows are bereft,
> Our commerce proves a sham—
> What is there for old Marshfield left
> Except the patient clam?

We want a lighthouse on the beach,
A fortress on the land;
A wharf and drydock within reach,
A drum corps and a band.

Don't be afraid to make a move
And call on Uncle Sam!
Don't always run in the same groove—

In short, don't be a clam!

When Israel couldn't get the paper, he probably read old ones, read them over and over again, even the ads—"The great cure for rheumatism and loss of manhood—Kidney Wort." "Daisy and Philadelphia Lawn Mowers." "Grindstones." "Salt-glazed drain pipes." "Mother Swan's Worm Syrup." "Four-Point Barbed Wire." "Corset Hospital." He read the news too, the dates fixed; this allowed him to return to the way it was before. Each day was the same. Each day, Irish immigrants built moss shanties on Jericho Beach, thirty-five thousand lobsters were sent away by rail, the sloop *Annie Lee* got a continuous coat of new paint. Each day, the same woman was thrown from the same horse, the same girl bitten by the same dog.

In 1916, *New England Historical Genealogical Register* published the following confirmed genealogy, submitted by Israel himself:

Walter Hatch settled in the part of Scituate called "Two Miles," which was joined to Marshfield in 1788; and the house which he built there is still standing and is the residence of Israel H Hatch, his descendant. A will of Walter Hatch, dated 3 Mar. 1681/2 and signed 4 Mar. was never proved; for after this will was made his son

*Antipas became of unsound mind, and his father made a
new will, providing for the maintenance of Antipas but
leaving his brothers the land formerly intended for him.
This second will was proved. The unproved will is now in
the possession of Israel H Hatch of Marshfield, Mass.*

Israel was researching his personal history at the same time
as he was applying for disability pensions from the government
for the injuries he accrued in the Civil War. He had always been
involved with civic affairs—an overseer for the town Poor
House, a justice of the peace, secretary of the Marshfield Agri-
cultural and Horticultural Society, clerk of the Second Congregational Church. He was fifty-four when he applied for his first
pension, which included the testimony of his neighbors on the
subject of his compromised health:

*17 October 1891—Deponent John Grover has lived
about two miles from the home of said soldier. For six years
from 1883 to 1889 said soldier was Supt. of Town Farm
and lived next door to me. During that time he was several
times unable to leave the house for weeks at a time and was
reduced from 184 lbs. to 125 lbs. in weight. I have heard
that the physician Dr. Eckert, who moved from the state
soon after, attributed it primarily to rheumatism of the
muscles. At a later period he was laid up with conjunctivitis
or inflammation of the eyes, which Dr. Stevens thought to
be the result of rheumatism. I have heard that he was the
subject of occasional attacks of diarrhea.*

*Deponent Sylvanus Shedd lives within about [½] of a
mile of said soldier's home. I can certify to the above
statement and know that at one period the friends of said
soldier thought he would never recover. From general
intercourse with him as a neighbor I know him to have
suffered with rheumatism in one shoulder and one leg. For*

six years past he has been unable to do an able-bodied man's
work and is prevented by weakness of eyes from doing office
work for which he is qualified.

Israel joined the New England Geneaological Society in 1911
and was a member until his death, ten years later. He had traced
his family roots back through Walter's voyage on the *Hercules*,
to County Kent. He pored over map after map of his family
tree—expanding circles of names cycling out from his own like
a giant spiderweb.

At the end of his ninth personal notebook, Israel wrote perhaps his own best epitaph: "Happy. Bright. Alert. Not at all
pert. Vigorous and Vivacious. Worthwhile brains dressed in
grand rags. Needs no reform."

In his old age, he grew his beard long and white, slept by an
airtight stove with his mouth open. Otherwise, he remained a
hack poet, an organ player, a rescuer of doomed horses from the
slaughterhouse, putting sweet fern in their forelocks, taking
them out in the chaise, moving at a slow crawl. Or perhaps a
standstill—in the middle of the road, or at the end of the sandy
lane, talking to a neighbor, the horse shifting from one back leg
to the other, hips cocked below the cloud of flies, sweet fern, and
blinders, grayed forehead and lip drooping below the long
yellowed teeth.

On August 9, 1909, Israel and Carrie had been married fifty
years. Friends and family threw them a "Golden Wedding Celebration." Rebekah Hatch Oakman Woodman, remarried eight
years after Thomas's death, read her brother a poem she had
written celebrating the heritage of the Red House:

They built the house that is here today; the centuries are
ripening its walls
That keep the secrets of years gone by, for the past knows
no recall.

*Here three generations were born and wed in the old
Colonial days;*
*Oh, for a record, that we might read of each one's works
and ways.*

*Vain is the wish—but the old-time home, where the family
tree begun,*
Is the home today in line direct from Puritan father to son.

*Though many the changes time has wrought in the house-
hold ways we know,*
*May the old-time hearth-stone never grow cold, or the
altar-fire burn low. . . .*

Israel, who had now progressed to the role of grandfather
and great-grandfather, kept hard candy in his pockets for children, and cranked the Victrola while Carrie stood before the
cast-iron cookstove melting lard on the griddle and frying
doughnuts with melted cheese.

When he was seventy-eight, he was still clerk of the Congregational Church and a commander of Post 189 of the Massachusetts Grand Army of the Republic. He placed the Red
House on tours of historic sites of Marshfield. The local paper
described the tour as a "peregrination":

> *The Two Mile home of Israel Hatch of the sixth
> generation here down the little lane by the saw mill and the
> pond. Linen, spun, woven and marked by the women of six
> generations, a spinning wheel, flaw wheel, carder, winder,
> reel, fireplace baker, wood and pewter dishes are shown.
> Mr. Hatch is an authority on local genealogy and history.*

Pensions had been furthered for Civil War veterans on
May 11, 1912, but government red tape slowed the process con-

siderably; Israel was still filling out forms in 1915. When he died at the age of eighty-four of chronic congestive heart failure, he was receiving fifty dollars a month.

June 25, 1921, the day Israel died, grandchildren were visiting next door, but they were not allowed to run through the thin divide of bushes to the Red House, even though all the women were crying and men were coming and going down the lane in chaises and carts and on foot and sometimes in automobiles. Someone came to "lay out" the body, to shave Israel for burial. Blocks of ice arrived in a wagon, along with a coffin and straw to pack around the ice, and a long pan to drain the water out when the ice around the body melted. Everyone, they said, stood outside the south side of the house, singing "Nearer My God to Thee" over and over again until late in the evening.

Ten

Kim and Philippe Villard

The house was keeping its mouth shut. The sill, the base support beam that ran along the house's south side, had gone to powder. Kim and Philippe looked at the twenty-foot boards that extended from the base of the sill to the rafter beams and were confused. No vertical studs existed between the framing beams, so the wall of boards that was once attached to the sill was now attached to nothing. On the other side of the boards, they found plaster and lathing, no insulation, no wind block, no space stuffed with hay or batting. The entire wall, from the living room to the outer layer of shingles, was only as thick as a man's wrist.

Over the years, the south side had begun to bow, the living room to slump. When leaned upon, the wall rocked, and the floorboards cracked. If a ball fell onto the floor, it always rolled to the same spot. In December 1995, my father had been putting up a Christmas tree, lost his balance, and fell against the wall. The wall moved out slightly with his weight, then back again, the windowpanes jangling. He pushed on the wall again and felt it give. Then he trudged out the back door in his slippers, through a drift of snow, finding he could push the house with both hands and move the outside wall too. When he stood outside the back door and looking west, eye pressed to the doorjamb, the side of the house was a series of red-shingled waves rippling toward the lilac tree and the west ell, a funhouse mirror.

Inside, the five windows along the wall in question had begun to push out of their frames.

"Look at those ceiling beams," Kim said. We were now standing inside the living room, assessing. Somewhere in the distance, a weed-whacker buzzed.

I took a few steps back. The ceiling hung like a belly.

"What's above here?" I asked, moving directly under a section of paneling that stretched across the living-room ceiling. It was also the floor of the hallway upstairs. The edges of the beams bloomed yellow stains into the ceiling plaster. Water damage. The bathtub.

The bathtub was dangling precariously between two ceiling beams, and at some point in the past someone had removed a twenty-foot framing member that held up the house. In short, nothing but a floor joist and some plaster prevented the bathtub from falling onto the piano that sat beneath it.

———

Over the next few days, Kim kept the cordless phone in her back pocket or pressed to her ear. She talked French and English, sometimes both. When she was wearing a tank top and a long piece of printed cloth wrapped around her waist, she held the phone under her arm like a clutch purse or a thermometer, or she shoved it into her skirt hem. She wrapped her long brown hair in a bun secured with a pencil. When she needed to write something, she would pull the pencil from the bun and her hair would unloop in a scroll down her back.

We needed to get supplies.

Our daily trips were recorded in receipts, what was bought to fix the house, an ever-expanding list. From Woodworker's Warehouse, Kim bought drywall screws, pigskin gloves, a rosewood bevel, a toxic respirator, a tooth blade, a steel blade, a fourteen-tooth wood-carving disk. From Somerville Lumber she bought supply line ($.89), elbow insert ($1.32), piano-hinge nickel ($12.49), white blank ($.43), sixteen-inch energy barrier ($17.84), pump jack ($52.24), beetle trap attack ($3.76), plastic tarp ($33.24), half-inch wire staples ($5.18), 20D galvanized common nails ($6.20), 3 × 100 Tyvek House Wrap ($37.29), 1 × 3 × 8 strapping ($8.80), and deck screws ($2.37). Also: primer and sealer, wood filler, foam brushes, paintbrushes, five-in-one tools, scraper blades, scrapers, a 15-ounce can of wasp-and-hornet spray.

Then she made lists of projects: sill project; window project; bathroom project; other projects. House of Carpet and Flooring ("Since 1940, Your Total Floor Store") delivered and installed a new carpet in our parents' bedroom in the east ell, a shag style called "Mirage Supreme," the color Vintage Plum. She rented a drywall gun and a stapler from J&B Power Equipment. She serviced the vacuum at Vacuum House of Marshfield, ordered five boxes of nails from Tremont Nail Company, brought the rotten sills and the old aluminum storm windows to the dump in three carloads in the back of an old Volvo station wagon.

The project was accomplished incrementally. Kim and Philippe and their crew had dragged two giant round bushes away from the side of the house. A truck with "Triple G Scaffolding Services Corp" stenciled on its side pulled up the driveway, and a man with a clipboard asked me to sign. Then he gave me the receipt with a yellow flier attached—"Do not get caught with the wrong planks under your feet; Demand OSHA stamped"—and I told him to drive his truck across the lawn to the side of the house, where Philippe was shirtless in boots and shorts, up to his waist in a ditch, his face covered with dirt. He was holding a square-tipped shovel. From the open door of the Volvo, the radio played Jimmy Cliff.

"This entire sill—it's rotten, totally gone," he said.

"The staging guy's here," I said.

"It is unbelievable. I mean, if a very large person were to lean against this wall, I think the house would fall over." The earth had been pulled down from the side of the house the way one would, with finger in lip, expose a gum, molars. On top of the granite foundation, a horizontal layer of pulverized wood lay where the sill beam should have been.

"Where do you want the guy to put the staging?"

"Tell him to drive across the lawn but not to run over the rhubarb, OK? I am coming."

I worked on the other side of the gravel driveway, opposite the house. Philippe had stretched a canvas tarp between two trees. He had cut down several long pine limbs, then placed four posts along the length of the tarp, stretching the canvas into a roof. Drop cloths covered the grass, and plastic sheeting rolled down the sides. This became the "window reconstruction area," or the "window tent," and I was the "window queen," sitting in front of a workbench made of two doors and four sawhorses.

Kim and Philippe removed all the windows on the south side of the house and stacked them in piles. Each window had two sashes, and each of these sashes had twelve panes, which were held in by pins and hardened glazing.

I began my window-work day by placing a window on top of two long, thin blocks on the worktable with the glazing side up; then I gouged out the glazing with a stumpy knife. I moved the knife between the glazing and the mullion, trying not to crack the glass beneath, trying not to cut into the wood, prying with the palm of my hand. Sometimes the glazing would slide out like a layer of frosting; other times it would be so dried and hardened that it had already separated from the mullion and could be picked out by hand. Sometimes the glazing was moldy and hard, an encrusted cement that had to be shaved away or pried from several angles, chipped, and hacked.

Once the glazing was removed, I'd carefully lift the glass pane out. *How many centuries of eyes have looked through this?* I'd think sometimes as I placed pane after pane in a stack at the corner of the workbench. Later, after sanding and painting each window, I'd have to put them all back in.

———

Days fell into a pattern: breakfast, lunch, dinner, interrupted by windows and more windows. Hours spent edging around panes of glass. From the tarp on the other side of the yard, the house yawned in advanced stages of surgery—the flapping plastic, the bowed side propped with ladders, shovels, and pickaxes. I inhabited the house with Kim and Philippe, who kept large cases of mangoes and pineapples on the steps of the root cellar and ate mostly fruit. We ate the mangoes and pineapples with avocados, and cucumber salad with vinegar. Watercress. Spaghetti squash.

Monday through Wednesday during the restoration, my father would return to check on the progress, often staying a few days. As my father aged, he had begun to look more and more like the actor Charles Bronson, so much so that people stopped him in restaurants and said it to his face. *Charles Bronson*—mashed nose, mustache, broad-shouldered; a little grayer and a lot taller; without the attitude but with, in fact, a certain broken-nosed boyishness, swinging his arms as he walked. He'd come and go in his short-sleeved cotton shirts, carrying his briefcase, and being very specific about his breakfast, asking about the misplacement of his glasses, his keys, his favorite juice cup, then about what kind of materials we had bought for the house that day, where we had put the receipts, cooing to his big white dog, scratching its ears, and feeding it pieces of cheese.

Behind his back, Kim and I talked about how the dog smelled, was a nuisance, mopey and depressed perhaps, yes definitely depressed, especially at night when he crashed through rooms and snuffled to bedsides with watery, needful eyes. Out of respect for our father, we split the duty of training the dog to the invisible fence. Every day, one of us had to walk him around the edge of the Red House property that was marked by tiny white flags that indicated where the electric wire was buried. The purpose of this was to "introduce" the property boundaries. During the day, the dog walked the perimeter of the land, and at night, he circled the inside of the house. Kim said he was chasing ghosts. At his neck, he wore a nondescript gray rectangle box equipped with two half-inch metal prongs. But because of the thick fur at his neck, the shock didn't seem to affect him much. The dog labored heavily in the heat as we walked slowly around the flags—which looked to me like a ring of flapping surrenders.

But Kim had her agenda and my father had his. On nights that he was home, we abandoned the fruit diet in favor of takeout pasta or Chinese, and sat at the long kitchen table talking about the house. My report was always the same. "Windows. Yeah, it's going well." Then Kim gave her report, punctuated by Philippe. Besides repairing the sill, my father wanted beaded clapboard covering the entire house; Kim never wanted to paint those high peaks again. She thought clapboarding the whole house would look ridiculous, especially the ells and peaks. "How can you clapboard a peak?" she asked. Then she found herself saying, "The ells would never have been clapboarded, they were shingled," even though she was the first to admit that she really didn't know how the Hatches had originally sided the house, or how they had changed it over the years.

When she discussed these things with my father, it seemed

that Kim was arguing with him for some sort of aesthetic or historical authenticity, but really there was no dispute—in the end she'd do whatever he wanted. Both of us would. He had sent for Kim when she was down and out in Berkeley, just as he had sent for me in Salt Lake City. But he didn't expect either of us to come home for good; he let Kim camp out in the bunkhouse, and he took me to an island. And although we never admitted it to each other, we both recognized that we owed him.

———

At night, the window plastic fluttered and whirred. Mosquitoes held tight in the corners of the humid ceilings, and the white dog roamed each room, a silent night-watchman. Sometimes I'd wake to find his pot-roast-sized head inches away from my own, as if he had been watching me sleep. "Shoo," I'd say. Then he'd whine and shuffle away.

I had returned home committed to restoring the house into the place I had remembered as a child, the place my father wanted it to be. But now that I had been back for a few weeks, it seemed that perhaps I'd been the one fueling a fantasy. My parents had left the house when they separated from each other, and since getting back together, they seemed to heal their wounds by traveling as much as possible. Now my mother was running a B&B in Vermont, and my father was trying to spend as much time with her as possible and still keep the Scituate office going. I had returned believing that Kim and I were rescuing the house the way our father had once rescued both of us. But really he was just relinquishing the house to our care. When I returned, the house had seemed like a living, vibrant creature, but, dismantled, the house acquired a slightly desperate countenance.

Each day, the house seemed more and more abandoned, entered and exited by a series of young neighborhood men who had been hired to mow and chop things. They used chainsaws in the woods, drove large lawn tractors, dug up and hauled away stumps in makeshift trailers, always stopping and having a beer with Philippe, who played fast and loose with his French accent and would talk to anyone.

"OK, dude," he would say. "See you later, dude."

But he would say it in a French way that seemed sweet, almost feminine, as if "dude" were someone's name and not an erasure of name and identity.

The workmen had weeds in their hair. They were sunburned, with thin torsos, ponytails, and dreadlocks, hemp necklaces at their throats. Philippe had found them at the beach, the gas station, the local health-food store. Their faces were always changing. They were hired for discrete jobs, for a week or two at a time, paid cash. Philippe created time sheets for them, titled "Red House Project/Summer '96," with the date and their project description, the hours they worked.

Mostly they rode lawn mowers, moved brush, carried castoff shingles from the house to the dump. They wrote in blocky letters on the time sheets—"mow and trim river road"; "weeded driveway"; "shingle removal"; "cut fallen branch from yard—large logs for f.w. hauled away small."

One of them was a dark-skinned Frenchman named Pascal who spoke no English and went about on the staging on the outside of the house in a quiet way, smiling and nodding.

Theo, equally silent, was our next-door neighbor, a sculptor on break from art school. Some days he was there, and some days he wasn't. When he wasn't ripping off shingles or digging with Pascal and Philippe, he was building tiny sculptures of cast-off material. A tower of fanned shingles on the edge of the stone wall. Stacks of cement bags. He wove an arc of reeds, fastened it to a board and several empty twenty-ounce. Coke bottles, and let it float out into the mill pond. When the water was very still, the arc and its reflection created a complete circle.

All day the sun stayed on the south side of the house; the staging heated up like the racks of a broiler. After three days of digging a trench in front of the sill, Pascal's back was a deep red-brown. I was often next to him on the aluminum ladder that bounced when I leaned it up against the side of the house. Sometimes we were five inches apart—Pascal moving up the layers of the house, ripping off strips of shingles, while I was prone on the ladder, scraping the window moldings, pulling out nails. Sometimes the ladder was tilted far away from the house, so that the top could reach the highest rain-gutter along the roof, and it stretched over the staging, where Philippe and Pascal walked back and forth, facing the side of the house all day, their backs to the sun.

"Don't drop any shit on our heads, please," Philippe said.

The shadow of the ladder fell on the staging, the men working, the side of the house, and the pit where the sill had been exposed. The shadow moved across them like a sundial. And I watched flakes of paint flutter down like confetti to the levels below. My arms were covered in a fine layer of gray sanding dust.

Philippe kept his hair in a ponytail, carried a cordless drill, and practiced what I would call "Xtreme Carpentry," hanging off scaffolding by the edge of a boot. He was always running past the tarp, backing the Volvo across the lawn, or climbing up the slate roof without a rope to look at the cracked chimney plate.

"Phi-leep!" Kim would yell in a high-pitched scream whenever she saw him doing something too dangerous. I had never heard that tone from Kim—a strange combination of fear, devotion, and annoyance. Once, while a few of us were under the window tent, Philippe skipped across the roof's ridgeline like a gymnast on a balance beam.

"Phi-leep!" Kim yelled again. Then "Jesus," under her breath.

"What—is he auditioning for *Fiddler on the Roof* or something?" Theo said.

"In France, he was a paraponter," Kim said as she opened a can of primer with a screwdriver. "You know, hang-gliding with a parachute. Done on skis. Off the side of a mountain," she said, as if this explained everything.

1646. The date that was suddenly in the air and on my father's tongue. And soon: "The house was built in 1646," Kim was saying to someone on the telephone who was advising her about plumbing, drainage.

I knew that the house's earliest date was 1647. For years it had been on the sign at the curve of the driveway; I had sung it in jump-rope songs.

But now my father was making new signs for the front and back driveways. Large carved wooden signs, painted dark red and gold. The signs were going to read: "Red House, 1646." There would be no Hatch names on the back.

This wouldn't have been a problem, except that the town of Marshfield had become involved. My father began his subtraction when he was approached by Betty Magoun Bates and Cynthia Hagar Krusell of the Marshfield Historical Commission. Bates and Krusell worked as a tag team—the Holmes and Watson of Marshfield history. Not only had they published numerous books and articles on the area, but they were both the genetic progeny of old Marshfield families.

"I'm a Hatch, you know," Betty said the first time I met her, only a few weeks into the restoration project, standing on the south side of the house in a pile of dirt next to Cynthia, who was holding a clipboard. Wearing jeans, tennis shoes, and bright cotton shirts, they struck me as curious—not typical Marshfield turtleneck-and-pearls types. Cynthia wore a Patagonia windbreaker, and Betty sported a giant ring of New Mexican silver.

For years I had heard about the Bates-Krusell team and wanted to impress, even with my meager knowledge. The Marshfield Historical Commission was in the process of hanging small hand-painted signs on the sides of houses, and they needed to know the exact date the house was built. My father had told them 1646 on the phone, a date they said didn't match any of their records.

I knew they were right, of course. And I was embarrassed by his made-up date.

Fortunately, Kim had already engulfed the historians in a conversation about a stone by the back door. While digging the trench along the sill, Kim and Philippe had discovered a stone that had been acting as a doorstep.

"I think this is where Walter Hatch is buried," Kim had said to me earlier in the day. "Richard Warren Hatch always said that Walter was buried somewhere on this property. And I think he said he was buried under a large stone. Wouldn't it make sense that he'd be buried here?"

I noticed that Kim, like my father, often claimed authority by mentioning Richard Warren Hatch's name.

"So people left the house and walked over Walter?" I asked.

"I don't know," Kim said, "but where is a better place to be buried?" And she pointed to the carvings on the stone—a circle with a tiny line etched through it.

"I think it might be Native American," Cynthia said, successfully distracted. "You should talk to someone over at the Mass. Historical Commission. It certainly could be a native carving."

We stood, through awkward moments of silence, on our mounds of dirt. Cynthia and Betty seemed very clean in their windbreakers, their graying hair whipping in the wind.

Betty told a story about the Marshfield Historical Commission at the turn of the century, and its efforts to dig up Myles Standish. Perhaps the Commission, in its infancy, had dug up the past just to see if they could. "He had said in his papers that he had wanted to be buried between his daughter and his daughter in-law," Betty said. Apparently they had found his remains, complete with good teeth and wisps of reddish-blond hair. "He was a short man," Betty said, "but, then again, everyone was shorter then." True to his request, Myles Standish had been buried between two skeletons of younger females. The ground had shifted them slightly over the centuries, but the configuration remained.

While Betty talked, Kim drew a picture on a piece of scrap paper of where she thought Walter was buried. The drawing detailed an upside-down triangle "rock" and a tiny pile of bones beneath it, and a skull and cross bones; and then she sketched the house beside it to represent where we were standing.

"Well, I *think* Walter Hatch is buried over at the old Second Society Meeting House," Betty said. She was trying very hard to be nice.

Suddenly I realized what amateurs we were with all our conjectures.

"You just let us know about that date," Cynthia said, as they walked away.

I glanced at Kim, dismayed.

"They were nice." She shrugged, handing me the drawing. In the little pile of bones beneath the cartoon rock she had drawn a grinning skull with "X"s for eyes.

———•———

Sometimes, on the ladder, facing the red side of the house, I would become angry. There was never a specific reason. Sometimes I would be angry at my father about the dates; I'd be angry with Kim and her fruit diet, her phone monopoly, her Walter-grave theory. Stuck as I was on the ladder, my mind roiled. Sometimes I was mad at the house itself—*big red thing, giant rotten myth*. What if the dates were phony? What if Hatch had duped my father, sold him only a great story? The thought made me feel terrified and thrilled at the same time. Once, without thinking, I threw my hammer at a bee. The bee had been hovering to my right, divebombing my head. Then, for a moment, it balanced next to me in the air. I threw my hammer, one swift movement. The bee moved aside, and the hammer tumbled end over end to the dirt below. "Hey, watch it up there!" yelled Philippe.

Sometimes I thought about James. "So—you think an old

guy with a beard just broke into our house? Just to stand by my bed?" I would ask him on the phone at night.

"Well, he *could have*—the house is half torn up." And then I would ask him again what the ghost looked like. "How tall was he? Are you sure he had a long white beard?"

James was teaching at a junior college in Salem, the town where, in 1692, twenty people and two dogs were hanged for witchcraft. James wasn't interested in colonial history; he was interested in kitsch.

"They have silhouettes of witches on brooms on all the cop cars," he'd say. "The paper comes out *at night*."

He had no use for my gravity, my concern over dates.

"It's just one year," James said. "Give your dad a break."

"But it's the wrong year," I always replied.

———

"Why are you so serious?" Philippe would ask when I was up on the ladder with my hammer.

"No reason," I'd say.

"There must be a reason," he would say.

"Nope," I'd say.

These questions went on for a few days, until the shingle removal was halted in exchange for more ditch-digging. Kim had discovered that the wiring attached to the back of the house was not up to code and all of the cables had to be buried. This set Philippe, Pascal, and most of the crew digging up the backyard. They were digging a line right past the old well toward a telephone pole in the neighbors' yard, a distance of more than thirty-five yards. I was left up on the ladder, watching the furrow inch farther across the grass, the men bent in their mad gopherage. The furrow was a dry river, a tiny gorge, a new esophagus. I played games in my head, recited famous palindromes, sentences that could read both backward and forward, a hangover from my mirror-writing days.

Sarah Messer

Rats live on no evil star
A man a plan a canal Panama

Abandoned to my own devices, my thinking became more abstracted and obsessed. A man. A plan. The house contains both the living and the dead, and there are always traces, because the house is not separate, has not one owner but many, has many beams, many different panes of glass, the way a body might have many lovers, the way each owner might look at the house as if at the body of a lover. If the window is removed, is it still a part of the house? If the fireplace swing-arm is taken and put in a museum, is it no longer a part of the house? Can the house be removed from itself? The owner, the past, the parts of the house. I thought: Who can steal a house? Who owns the lover but the loved?

In the early 1990s, I had arrived late at a dance performance only to be locked out of the first act. The performance was in a museum, and I found myself stopped before a life-sized plaster sculpture of a horse. The horse—hanging from the ceiling in a sling of canvas fastened around its girth—seemed as if it were from another century, lifted from a cargo hold, the way my old horse had been lifted when the backhoe carried him to his grave. I traced my hands over the entire sculpture—sinews of pasterns and hocks, the muscles of the shoulder, the flat cheek and nostril, the dipped spot above the eye that can catch rain. How many times had I run my hands over my horse's body? I realized that I could still trace each part blind. It was like seeing the body of someone who had been lost for years—the body of a lover returned from the dead.

If I touched every shingle of the house, every pane of glass, wouldn't I know the house with the same kind of intimacy? Wouldn't it reveal all its secrets to me?

Sometimes when I got down from the ladder, everyone was gone. Perhaps they had all slipped away quickly, driven off in

234

cars without leaving a note. Or they left a note that said simply, "Please water the garden." Or "Close the windows if it rains." And then it was just me and the house. I felt shy, exposed, as if the house could read my thoughts.

During these absences, my family was often replaced by sur- rogates, the workers and crew.

One evening, I came off the ladder, dirty and tired, with the word MEAT scrawled across my hand in black Sharpie. A crew member named John was leaning against the chopping block in the kitchen in landscaping shorts and boots, reading a note that Kim and Philippe had left.

"Hey, what's that?" he asked, pointing at my hand. I said that I had to remember to get my father's deer meat out of the freezer in the basement. I told him about the bat in the basement, the one that divebombed people—"like a bomber plane." He said that he wasn't afraid of bats, he'd done a lot of camping. He walked over to the sink and fingered the dog dish on the counter. My father's big white dog rushed into the room from elsewhere, and John bent down, said, "Here you go, boy, here you go!," and gave him a handful of kibble.

"I'm not here long," I heard myself say. "Just helping with the house over the summer."

"Oh yeah?" he said, looking up from the dog. "Where are you going?"

I didn't answer. He was wearing an orange wind-shell, the kind Coast Guard rescue crews wore. He said he was only doing the Red House job to supplement his work building stone walls. He was waiting for a big job to come through building a wall for a lady down the street. He said that he and his buddies might drive across the country. "Have you ever driven cross-country?" he asked. I said I hadn't.

He sat at the kitchen table, his fingers webbing and unweb- bing like nets underwater. His nails were clean and square. He said when he worked on the stone walls he wore Carhartt gloves or no gloves at all. He said his work involved building a series of piles that led to other piles that then became a wall. The stones he used came from other walls—old farm boundaries that now led into highway rest stops, housing developments, cul-de-sacs, the back of the new high school. He said no one cared that he took the stones.

Usually, he said, he worked at night, wearing a flashlight strapped to his head. He'd park his truck at the side of the nearest road from which he could walk straight out through the woods. If there was a trail, he would push a small wheelbarrow in. The best way, he said, was to put as many rocks as he could into a canvas sling and walk them out, the sling thrown over his back. To get enough stones for twenty feet of wall might take him all night. When he stole a wall, he told me, he liked to imagine what that wall had once contained, what was there before the trees—not parking lots, but farms and square white churches.

The night of my junior prom, I had changed out of my prom dress and into jeans in the back seat of my date's car—tossed the pink taffeta dress with the thirty-two covered buttons in exchange for a night of drinking cheap beer in the woods. The prom's theme, "We've Got Tonight (Who Needs Tomorrow?)," was inspired by the Bob Seger song. I had taken it literally, wandered off, and fallen asleep in the trees, to wake up the next morning with my head rolled against a stone wall behind a housing development.

I wondered now if John had stolen that wall. Or if the wall had been built by a Hatch, built perhaps by Israel. I wondered if John had slowly been erasing the Hatch boundaries, moving them somewhere else—to rock gardens and treed islands at the mall.

"So—you don't remember me from two summers ago?" he asked. "I was the same grade as Jess."

He said his major in school was acting, the stone thing was just temporary. He said that when he drove through town he liked to think about his rebuilt walls. He drove past all the lawns, the driveways, pointing to his friends and saying, "My stones are there, there, and there."

I said it was cool that he rebuilt stone walls, because, you know, nobody did that anymore.

"Yeah," he said, "nobody does."

———

"How do you say when you have a tear in your eye?" Philippe asked, standing in the dining room the next day. The table was arranged with the framed wills from the living room, along with crowbars and shims, a handful of screws.

"Choked up? Teary-eyed? *Moved?*"

Philippe held to his chest some undisclosed items. After they had put up scaffolding and begun stripping the shingles off the outer wall, they had found a few things.

"Cows," he said.

Beneath the shingles was tarpaper, and beneath that were layers of lithographed cows. Old Marshfield Fair posters. The posters were late nineteenth or early twentieth century, some colored with reds and greens, disintegrated and torn. When he opened his arms, bits of paper stuck to his T-shirt. He put the layers down and moved the pieces around with his hands on the top of the dining-room table. The posters had been placed in the wall as a windbreak, the paper shredded, stained, and bug-holed: the half-head of a cow, a sheaf of wheat, a team of oxen, a man pushing a plow, half of the side of a woman's laughing face as she watched a horserace in the distance, block letters, words cut off.

Behind the posters, they had found vertical boards tapered the way a tree is tapered, growing smaller at one end; the boards were installed top to bottom in an alternating fashion, to make them snug. Between the wallboards and beneath the floorboards, Philippe found an Indian-head nickel, a marble, a clay pipe, some pieces of glass and pottery, shreds of newspapers from the early twentieth century. He held these small items in his hands.

"But this is nothing," he said, putting the pile down. "Wait. Now come in here."

I pushed aside a curtain of plastic sheeting to get into the living room. A large circle of plaster on the south wall had been ripped off, and beneath it was an exposed board of leopard-spotted painting. The decorated side was the back side of the board that faced out, covered in the cow poster and then shingled. This meant that the entire living room, the walls and ceilings, as Richard Warren Hatch had said, had once been decorated with these painted spots.

The vague story of the discoveries after the fire, the image of Richard Warren Hatch crying in the living room, suddenly felt like a myth coming true. It was true, the story of the painted room, and I could suddenly see it: a room of leopard spots, swirling. And we had found more of what Richard Warren Hatch thought he had lost. I ran my hand along the wall, then picked up a wooden mallet, wrapped the head inside a T-shirt the way Philippe showed me, and lightly knocked on the wall. Cracks spidered from the blows, and pieces split off in chunks. Lathing packed with horsehair lay beneath the plaster like a tiny corral. Philippe removed the lathing boards by hand, slowly, dropping the chunks of plaster and broken boards into a bucket. He blew the dust away from what was beneath, the hidden painted surface.

If it meant anything, it meant that the house was very old. Nothing but shingles on the other side of these boards, and people had lived in a room like this—every surface leopard.

I reached out to touch the wall, the expanse of newly exposed boards, but Philippe stopped me, pushing my hand down. "They have been untouched for so long," he said, "I don't want to ruin it."

Harris
1866–1934

White House and Red House, circa 1900

The Cause of Sighing:
Professor Lumsden says that sighing is but another name for oxygen starvation. The cause of sighing is most frequently worry. An interval of several seconds often follows moments of mental disquietude during which time the chest walls remain rigid until the imperious demand is made for oxygen, worrying. One may be anxious, but there is no rational reason for worrying. A little philosophy will banish worry at once. Worry will do no good. It will rod one of the pleasures when blessings do come, as one will not be in a position to enjoy them.

—*Popular Science Monthly*, November 30, 1900

On November 8, 1895, physics professor Wilhelm Roentgen saw a faint outline of bones when he placed his hand between a black cardboard box and a barium-coated screen. When he moved his hand, the bones moved, and he realized he was seeing through his own skin.

At the time, Roentgen had been experimenting with vacuum tubes in his laboratory at the Royal University of Würzburg. The tube, when connected to a source of high-voltage electric current, caused a pear-shaped bulb enclosed in a cardboard box to glow in the dark. When Roentgen looked up from his work, he noticed that a screen lying on top of a table on the other side of the room was also faintly flickering a fluorescent-green color. The screen emitted light only when the tube inside the box was supplied with an electric current. After placing several objects, including his hand, between the table and the box, he realized that invisible rays were traveling from the tube to the screen. He wrote: "Behind a bound book of about one thousand pages I saw the fluorescent screen light up brightly, the printer's ink offering scarcely any physical hindrance."

Sarah Messer

The first X-ray developed and published was of his wife's left hand—her wedding band and the bones of her fingers and palm, the only mass that the rays could not penetrate.

Meanwhile, up and down the East Coast of America, a new wave of immigrants arrived from Europe, and cities grew crowded—America's interest moving beyond the ostrich plumes, badger shaving-brushes, and bust cream of the Gilded Age to steam engines and sky bicycles. Two Mile unfolded with telephone poles. Houses started sporting green shutters, local bandstands played "Cupid's Garden"—"I want you honey yes I do." The X-ray had come to America, transpierced documents and letters, paintings, a mummy, diamonds and other gems, plants, wood, and, of course, human and animal bodies.

Some English manufacturing firms had advertised X-ray–proof underwear, suggesting that the X-ray would be used to see through ladies' clothing: "I'm full of daze / Shock and Amaze; / For now-a-days / I hear they'll gaze / Thru' cloak and gown— and even stays / Those naughty, naughty Roentgen Rays."

Harris, the first and only Hatch industrialist, had believed in progress enough to leave Two Mile at the age of sixteen. He worked as a printer's devil, or a chore-boy, in a Boston printing shop, a job that included straightening type that had become mixed up after use. While in Boston, he attended the Congregational Church, where he met and courted his future wife, Susanna. He proposed to her when they were both nineteen years old; as an engagement gift, he gave her a wooden box he had made from nineteen pieces of wood.

Harris, unlike his forefathers, led a peripatetic existence. He worked for a calendar company, as a salesman for a company that made paper-folding machines, in the publishing business. The jobs took him to Framingham, to Buffalo, to Chicago, to

Hyde Park. In 1910, he landed a job as general manager for the Royal Electrotype Company in Philadelphia.

Harris and Susanna had six children in twelve years, but only four of them survived to adulthood. One died as an infant of meningitis, and Lawrence, their second child, died at the age of four of scarlet fever. That left Helen, the oldest, followed by Esther, Richard Warren, and Tracy.

Sometime around the turn of the century, Harris inherited the Red House. He never lived there, immediately turning the deed over to his mother, Carrie. Harris's children, particularly his sons, Richard Warren and Tracy, spent a lot of time at the Red House with their grandfather Israel. Richard Warren loved haying and weeding the garden, feeding the chickens and cows and the horse that his grandfather would harness to the chaise and drive down the lane. In keeping with Hatch tradition, the Red House was filled with widows and virgin aunts—Aunt Alice stepping into the role that Huldy had filled for so many years.

———•———

After rising to the rank of president of the Royal Electrotype Type Company, Harris bought the White House, next door to the Red House. He retired to Two Mile in 1928 and built, on the rise of a hill, a small hunting cabin. Harris picked for the cabin the highest spot of land from which he could see the Red House, the White House, and lanes leading past the mills to Union Street on one side and the river on the other. The cabin sat squat on the hill, a square of large round logs, chinked and stacked. Four logs made up the roofline, which rose to a peak above a porch overlooking a small cleared lawn and a ring of pines.

While Harris was digging postholes for the cabin, he found remnants of other inhabitants—arrowheads, shards of bowls, and the bones of small animals that had been butchered and eaten. He also found part of a skeleton, a human jawbone that had been wired and drilled—an early form of dentistry or a postmortem ritual. He kept these things in the cabin along with bird feathers, several mounted deer heads, and bird guns above the granite fireplace, and thought, perhaps, of his findings as "archeology," imbued with the history of the place, people who had vanished. And perhaps the cabin itself was a testimony to this, a reaction against the factory where he had worked, the pressure of progress.

Harris's youngest son, Tracy, and his wife moved into the White House below Harris and Susanna, who occupied the second floor. Together they started a cut-flower farm.

In the 1930s and '40s in Two Mile, Tracy Hatch and his wife, Betty, were a seductive pair—the dark and the light, titillating. Tracy, the product of the farm-boy-father-makes-good-in-the-city, the son returning home to "the land"; and Betty, a brick-house, fiery Christian who drank vodka and took her top off any time she was around water. They raised gladiolus, or "glads." They called the planted back field "the glad rainbow." Entering the greenhouses, any visitor would be knocked over by the intensity of the perfume, the color, the bright light. All summer, Tracy cultivated the flowers, picked and cut them, tied them in bunches, and shipped them to the Boston Flower Market. Glads were easy—tender perennials with erect sword-shaped leaves. He planted them in long rows, three feet apart, which took up the length of the fields behind the Red and White Houses, filled the southern view from the cabin. The plants grew waist-high, the blossoms opening from the bottom up, each stalk its own bouquet of brilliant trumpets, a stacked row of fringed skirt. The field was layered rainbow, with the colors spotted like a paint palette—Beauty Cream, Daydream, Goldstruck, Highstyle, Joyful, Lemon Twist, Mr. Lincoln, Summer Rose, True Love—colors Tracy and Betty had ordered the winter before from catalogues. The bulbs had arrived packed in peat or sawdust, like boxed eggs.

In the spring, they hung a sign on the side of the barn visible from the road—"North River Farms." The southwest side of the Red House faced the outdoor growing fields and the newly constructed rows of greenhouses. The glass roofs of the greenhouses were cantilevered, motors opening and closing the panels automatically in the heat. The greenhouses contained the tulips, iris, and daffodils with white, orange, or yellow centers. In the barn, Tracy built a cool room and a cold room for buckets of flowers cut from the greenhouse. Four large spools of string hung from the rafters and let down tendrils where the workers would sit and cut the stems off flowers into a bucket, then wrap the ends with string and tie it off, clip it, and pull the tendrils down again. The workers squatted on a line of stools, their buckets of flowers between their legs, arms reaching up to pull more string as if they were puppets tied into some larger, hidden mechanism. Behind them, in the vast empty space of the barn, was a rope where nieces and neighborhood children would swing. Betty filled the White House with flowers.

It was well known in Marshfield society at the time that Tracy and Betty Hatch were "naturalists." Precursors of the nudist movement of the 1960s, the Hatches and a small group of friends believed in swimming and sunbathing in the nude. They often relaxed this way along the banks of the river on weekends, to the shock and consternation of most of the town.

In the fall, after the glads came and went, Tracy and Betty dug up the bulbs and planted mums. The first year, Tracy and Betty probably worked alone, carefully digging the bulbs. They piled the clods of dirt on long, flat trays that they pulled behind them down the rows and then beneath the barn to a series of underground rooms. The space was called the "underground barn," where more long boxes on metal rollers sat filled with dirt. At night, long rows of lights placed inches above the planted bulbs were switched on, connected to a generator and a timer.

Sarah Messer

In the underground barn, Tracy began the slow process of cleaning and pruning the bulbs. Each glad grown a year or more in the field left a tuberous stem, topped with rotting brown leaves where the plant had been. Tracy would slice the old bulb or corm off, and pack the new corm in sawdust for the winter.

———·———

Of course, there were problems—the generator failed, employees quit, a gear jammed in the pump house, and bushels of flowers were not ready when the eighteen-wheeler lumbered across the field from Boston. But for at least a decade, the fields behind the Red House were filled with various flowers—such as pompom mums grown in long rows and covered at night with cloth to protect against frost. At night, Betty and Tracy would walk out to the fields and stand facing each other on either side of the row of flowers, gripping the end of a broad black cloth that was rolled and tied. They'd walk the length of the row, holding the cloth tight and aloft, a long black ribbon. Then they'd lay it down, fasten each corner to the ground with stakes, and walk back up the row, occasionally tying the cloth down at a stake. Beneath the cloth, the mums made bulbous silhouettes like small grounded clouds. When hurricanes rolled in, the cloth was ripped from the stakes and would fly thirty feet into the air, uncoiling from its spool, leaving the plants battered and flattened. From the Red House, one could see the storm roiling the flower fields, as the horizon behind the stone wall unspooled— giant black ribbons whipping over thirty feet into the air.

Eleven

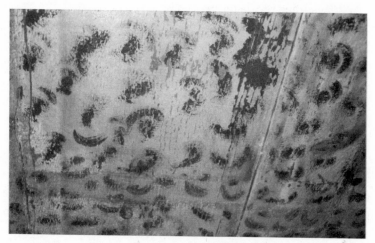

Leopard design on Red House wall

When I wasn't working on the house, I'd walk down the half-mile dirt path past the Hatch Mill and one mile up Union Street to the Hatch family burial plot.

There I'd find them: Deacon Joel Hatch, Israel H. Hatch, Thomas Oakman, and, near the back of the cemetery, Rebekah R. Oakman. Before a line of hedgerows I found the graves of her children, the two who died within six days of each other at the ages of four and six, their headstones like buried hat rims, granite laced with lichen.

I didn't find the graves of Mrs. Stoddard, the burned woman, and her child, but searching for them led me back to the letters and wills, and the letters and wills to the house where they had been found. The Red House finally held my attention, because it seemed to defy the number-one law of reality: impermanence. *Nothing lasts forever.* The Red House had outlived every fretful human who inhabited it, outlasted all our dramas and imaginings.

If the letters, the daguerreotypes, were ghosts, then the closet where I found the documents was a little grave. Both Israel and Rebekah wrote letters about the tragedy of Mrs. Stoddard and her burned child. Ten years later, they would lose their own children, and perhaps in these earlier exchanges they had some glimpse of their future grief. I couldn't help thinking about my own parents—my father's paranoia about fire and drowning, Suzy's near drowning, my mother swirling to catch Jessica as she was thrown over the banister during the 1971 fire. Perhaps the gesture of grasping a child in a moment of trauma is what connects humans throughout history. The child represents a figure in relation to a future—a person saved becomes a person written about in a letter, becomes a discovered letter, and becomes a story saved, a part of history.

Searching, I followed two trails in particular: Israel H. and Richard Warren Hatch, who had arranged all of the documents before me. I found scraps of wills and receipts glued or Scotch-taped to legal-sized pieces of construction paper, as if from a giant unbound scrapbook. Each document was described and labeled, either in Richard Warren Hatch's handwriting or in the thin font of an old typewriter.

Some letters were grouped in series, fastened with a large paper clip, beneath which was a small typed square: "This is a series of letters 1837–1839 to Deacon Joel Hatch." Other letters were from Richard Warren Hatch to my father, including several that alluded to a dispute about the ownership of the wills:

Richard W. Hatch
Orleans Retirement Center
Daley Terrace
Orleans, MA 02653

RED HOUSE

December 13, 1982

Dr. Donald [sic] J. Messer
385 Union Street
No. Marshfield, MA 02051

Dear Dr. Messer:
 SUBJECT: TITLE TO THREE HATCH FAMILY DOCUMENTS
VIZ; DIVISION OF THEIR FATHER'S PROPERTY BY WALTER
AND WILLIAM HATCH DATED 1651, A LATER WILL OF AN
OWNER OF THE HOUSE YOU PURCHASED FROM ME, AND A
LETTER OF A SEAFARING MEMBER OF THE FAMILY.

1. When you purchased my house I loaned you the said documents on the condition that you have custody of them while you retained ownership of the house.
2. Recently, for personal reasons, and having in mind the several articles from the house that I gave you at the time of the sale and subsequently while I was in Barnstable, I request you forego that balance of the term of the loan and return the documents to the family if my son John C. Hatch of Dover, Massachusetts desired them.
3. I understand you have refused my request.
4. This is to notify you that I have transferred title to the said documents to the above John C. Hatch.

Yours Very Truly,
Richard Warren Hatch

(As I no longer read, please address any reply to James A. Brink, Hale & Dorr, 60 State Street, Boston, Mass. 02109)

Sarah Messer

[no date]

Dear Ron:

I am writing to you because you said that you and Pat might try to get down here sometime and there are things that I could not tell you over the phone. Ruth is a victim of senile dementia, the effects of which are progressive, varied and unpredictable. At present I am carrying on as sole care-taker and attendant, but I do not know from week to week how long it will be before I shall have to make a drastic change in our situation.

However, I do know that with preparation and a favor-able day Ruth would get great pleasure from seeing you both. As for me, you have aroused my curiosity and interest, and I not only would like to see you but have a lot of ques-tions to ask about the schooner project. I am always here, but as I wear head phones for listening to the records and cassettes that are my reading I do not hear the phone. So the times to call me are at the noon hour or between 6 and 7 pm.

It occurred to me the other day that the professional photo copyists do remarkable things these days with making facsimiles of old documents. I have no way of making in-quiries or even locating a good photocopier, but maybe you could locate one and ask if it is possible to make a photo-copy through glass. If it is we could make two copies of the 3 framed documents without disturbing them, and I could send them along too with other family materials that I have given the boys as obviously I have no use for them. Just an idea, but I would appreciate you inquiring.

You seemed skeptical about the value of Joseph Hagar's History of Marshfield, which is surely available in your lo-cal library, but I think you would both be amused and inter-ested in the chapter based entirely on written material from the attic of your house.

As I cannot see what I am writing, please make due allowance for errors in typing. For what it is it comes with my best to you and Pat.

yours,
RWH

A letter typed a few months later, on thin onionskin, detailed the lineage of the owners of the Red House, occasioned, apparently, by my father's desire to repaint the sign at the end of the driveway. Hatch wrote:

I have forgotten the exact arrangement of the lettering on the sign. If HATCH appears at the top it need not be repeated below of course. In any case, I believe the date when Walter Hatch took up his share of the TWO MILE grant and, presumably, started his house was at the top of the sign:

1647

Walter	1623
Israel	1667
Israel	1701
Israel	1730
Joel	1771
Israel	1837
Harris	1866
Richard W.	1898

You will have to work out your own design. Now for the first time in about 50 years I do not own more than an acre of land or a shingle on the roof over my head, and have come down from a house to two rooms, I guess the next compression will be the grave. You should call here before we make that move.

The severity of the first letter and the desperate resignation of the second and third struck me as incredibly sad. I also wondered why my father, knowing that Hatch had wanted his family letters back, would refuse to return them. I wondered if the wills and letters were the cause of a "falling out" I knew my father had with R. W. Hatch right before his death.

———·———

"You got into a legal battle with Mr. Hatch?" I asked my father one day.

"No."

"These letters say you did—a fight about the wills."

"Oh, that, yeah; that's right."

"What happened?"

"Mr. Hatch wanted the wills back. Or, actually, I think his son did. Anyway, I said he was going against his word, that he had given me those documents when we bought the house."

"But he wanted them back, and they were his family documents."

"But he didn't own them anymore. He gave them to me; he said that they should always stay with the house, that they belonged to the house."

"So, if you sold the house, the documents would stay here too?"

He didn't answer.

"Was this what caused your falling out with Mr. Hatch?"

"No. Our falling out was about something else."

"What?"

"I don't want to talk about it," he said. Something in his tone told me that he would go no further. The subject needed to be dropped.

———·———

Jean Hall, effusive, dark-eyed, with a voice half laughter and half drawer of cutlery, arrived on the tail of Cynthia and Betty on a fact-finding mission for the Massachusetts Historical Commission, and inhabited the rooms as if she had lived in them for years. She was invited to come in, and to stay, of course, by my father, because he was always the host, always eager to talk about the house, or have others talk about it.

"Please stay for dinner," he said, and Jean, not missing a beat, replied, "Sure, why not."

I had been out in the window tent watching the sky grow dark, my hands caked with glazing. My father made dinner, which consisted of grilled fish and lots of white wine. At ten o'clock, Jean was still there, bending over documents in the living room that she had spread like a tailor's dress pattern over the back of the couch, saying "Amazing" and "This is so great," and my father looked on from the doorway, grinning, a glass of wine still in his hand.

"What's this project you're doing?" I asked, leaning in an opposite doorway. Jean turned her head, fixed my gaze, and then launched into a talk on the Historical Commission and their first-period house-catalogue project on the South Shore, and how she had attended the North Bennet Street School, had a degree in historic preservation, and was now at Boston University studying preservation architecture. Then something about the Historical Commission's desire to prove or disprove dates in the area and to get the record straight. First period, Jean explained, was prior to 1720.

"This house was built in 1646," my dad said.

"Yeah, that's what you said," Jean replied.

Jean wanted permission to do an in-depth study of the house. This is what she said when she called the next week, her voice fast-paced and excited. I had spent the morning painting the belly of a claw-footed iron bathtub a color called Blueberry.

Jean thought that there was enough evidence in the paper trail my father had pulled out of the closet to warrant inclusion in the commission's study.

"Sure," I said. "Great."

———•———

"What else is lying around here that I don't know about?" I asked my father that night.

"What do you mean?"

"Well, are there any more documents or things that Richard Warren Hatch left with the house?"

"There's the original window. And the brides' towels."

"Brides' towels?" I asked.

Every Hatch woman, prior to leaving the house to marry, made a set of linen towels. Each was embroidered with the woman's name and one was left with the house. We had all of them, my father said. They were upstairs in the attic closet.

"You know about this, though," he sighed, implying that he must have told me as a child and that perhaps I had forgotten.

"No, I don't," I said. And wondered if we had the Shroud of Turin in the attic as well.

I found the brides' towels in a large garment box. The words FILENE'S FILENE'S FILENE'S fled in white slanted letters over the black box top; inside, layers of thin and folded linen towels were stacked. The off-white towels varied in size and design. Most were blackened around the edges, smoke damage from a fire. Most had scraps of paper pinned to them where dates and names had been written. In some cases, the acid from the paper had stained a yellowish square onto the towel, or the rust in a corner where the pin held the paper spread out over the paper and the fabric. The weaves varied from coarse and plain to bleached with silk scrolls and crosshatched squares. Some towels had three small initials embroidered with a series of "X"s; others had more elaborate scrolling letters—one large "H" surrounded by the first and middle initials. Some towels were stiff, some were soft. There were fourteen towels in total. One was stained with two dark-brown dots that could have been coffee, molasses, rust, or blood from the pricked finger of the woman who sewed it.

The box contained a list written in Rebekah Hatch's scrolled penmanship. When I recognized the handwriting, I thought— "Oh yes, Rebekah," as if she were an old friend or a sister. I felt I was following a trail of her clues. At some point, Rebekah had collected the towels and written:

> *Rebekah Howland, Born 1704*
> *married—Samuel Thomas—their daughter*
> *Bethia Thomas, Born 1728*
> *married—Israel Rogers—their daughter*
> *Rebekah Rogers, Born 1766*
> *married—Ichabod Hatch—their daughter*
> *Rebekah Hatch, Born 1798*
> *married—Joel Hatch—their daughter*
> *Rebekah Rogers Hatch, Born 1830*
> *married—Thomas Rogers Oakman*

After the towels, I began to find more traces of Rebekah. Perhaps more than anyone, I realized, she was here physically. The thin scraps of paper pasted on the backs of daguerreotypes were written in her small, perfect pen. She was a historian as well. The towels, no doubt, were given to her by her mother. Here, in the attic of the Red House, was the hidden Hatch matrilineage.

A week later, in a drawer in the dining room, I found a spoon with a note attached to it. The list followed the same matrilineal history as the brides' towels—"Bethia Thomas, Rebekah Rogers, Rebekah Hatch, Rebekah Rogers Hatch"—and the list ended with "Lulu," and it was Rebekah's handwriting. The spoon was heavy, a large soup- or serving spoon, made of pewter.

The earliest date placed it at 1728; the corner of the spoon's bowl was half worn with use.

A spoon and some towels. Men passed down wills, houses, land. Women, it seemed, chronicled what they could rub across their faces, hold in their mouths. I turned the spoon over; the paper with it was a business card for a horse livery in Chicago run by Walter Hatch, Rebekah and Israel's brother. He had left Two Mile for the city and had sent this card back home, perhaps as an emblem of his success. Rebekah had cut it up and used it for a list of grandmothers, a marker for a spoon.

———

Jean Hall came often. She stared at corner beams, doorjambs; she knelt and scraped bits of plaster from the wall behind the chimney with her fingernail or a small brush and collected it in a plastic baggie. She carried a clipboard with her and wrote furiously with a pencil that she stuck back in the spiral of the notebook. She snapped photos with an Instamatic camera.

It was now August, humid ninety-degree weather, and we had been working on the house for two months. Jean dressed with an impeccable yet relaxed neatness; she had the ability to be in constant motion while remaining one-pointed and still. She left traces: the white ballpoint that read "Swisshotel: Atlanta, Boston, New York"; her clipboard on the kitchen or dining-room table. Sometimes she left her notes overnight in the living room on top of the plastic-covered piano, several sheets scrawled with loopy and delicate handwriting:

> The ground floor southeast room, or parlor, has the highest level of interior finish. The frame has been boxed and a beaded detail and the fireplace wall has fielded panelling.

> The Red House does not currently have a large hearth style fireplace and summer beam that typify first-period houses in

the New England area. However, the three fireplaces in the
parlor, living room and dining room define a space that could
possibly have originally been one large fireplace.

The framing member which may be the summer beam was
not able to be viewed behind its boxed exterior. However,
seen from the other side, now buried within the back of the
closet, it appears to be of impressive height and thickness,
not inconsistent with that type of structural timber.

Renovations as indicated through documentation suggest a
pre-1763 addition (new half/old half mentioned in will),
1790s post-fire remodel, 1950s added modern conveniences
(plumbing, electricity), 1972 remodel after fire; current
remodeling using contemporary materials. (living room 25
ft × 12. kitchen 18 ft × 40)

———

"You have a hole in your shield," Philippe said. "I can see it.
This is why you have so many negative thoughts. Negative
thoughts are coming in through this hole that I can clearly see in
your shield."

We were under the oval of light, sitting at the kitchen table.
My shield, apparently, was some sort of aura. It was late, and
Kim, Philippe, and I had been cataloguing the ghost sightings.
The dinner dishes were stacked and pushed to the side. Between
us on the table sat a plate filled with ribbons of mango skin,
pineapple rinds, and the large white stone of the mango, which
Philippe had scraped clean with his teeth.

Recently a visitor had stayed upstairs and had been continually awakened by a cold draft and the sound of a window slamming shut. But when he woke up, he realized there was no
window in the window casing—that it was summer, and the
window was covered with plastic. My sister Bekah, passing

through Israel Hatch's old room and into the bathroom hallway late at night, felt that someone was staring at her. She looked into the Borning Room, where she saw a woman in a long transparent shift sitting in a chair. The woman looked away from her, stood up, and walked out of the room as if embarrassed.

"How am I supposed to fix this hole in my shield?" I asked.

"Well, I think you should have better protection around you," Philippe said. But I didn't really understand what he meant, and the conversation veered back to the house, to the south side which was still slanted and bowed. Kim was talking about the new support post that had been delivered from Vermont earlier in the day, and how the house would have to "settle into its girth" after we put it up.

"Protection? Like an amulet?" I asked.

"That might work," Kim said, although I could tell she didn't want to talk about it.

She was defensive about Tyvek, the thin paper insulation, explaining to me that it was necessary, sometimes, to use modern materials, like pressure-treated two-by-eights; that this was a choice she had made; and that the house had to breathe, needed a vapor barrier, which Tyvek would supply; and that they couldn't afford to make the wall any thicker. They had to attach it to something, and she was thinking about steel plates and bolts and maybe even the epoxy laminate used in boatbuilding.

"The Hatches," she said, "would have used galvanized screws if they had them."

"Maybe," I said, sensing that she knew I'd been hanging out with Jean and reading her notes.

"Do you believe in time travel?" Philippe asked me.

"What do you mean?" I said.

He and Kim never used to believe in it either, said Philippe—until they had this experience.

"I think you are open to hearing this story. It's a very wild story," he said. "Maybe I will tell it to you."

"Tell me the story," I said.

The story took place a few years previously. Kim and Philippe had thrown a bottle carrying a note to a time traveler off a pier in Galveston, Texas. The note read something like, "Dear person of the future, meet us at this pier at 9 p.m." Their theory was that, if a person in the future got the bottle and could travel back in time, why couldn't such a person meet Kim and Philippe at any time—even an hour hence—and in any place, like right there on that pier? They gave the date and the longitude and latitude coordinates.

From their spot on the pier in Galveston Harbor, they could see the large side of an office building where some claimed the visage of Jesus had appeared a month before. The side of the building had been sandblasted, only to have the image return a few days later in a different spot.

A person had shown up an hour later to meet Kim and Philippe; as they talked to him, they realized he looked just like the face that had appeared on the side of the building—he looked just like Jesus.

"But a lot of people look like Jesus," I said.

"Yes, he might have just been a crazy hippie," Philippe snapped, as if I didn't get it at all. He couldn't pronounce "h," so "hippie" sounded like "eep-py."

The main thing we had to do tomorrow, Kim interrupted, was to stain that beam to match the others, and then figure out a way to attach the wall back to the beam and the whole thing back to the new sill. The time-travel discussion was over. Beyond the triangle of our arms leaning on the table, the rest of the kitchen stretched away into darkness, the braided rug beyond the table circling around itself like a bull's-eye. We were all circling around the house with our allegiances: my father with his devotion to Richard Warren Hatch and his family history; Kim with her allegiance to my father and to the house itself and its repair; Jean with her allegiance to academia and historical accuracy;

Betty and Cynthia with their sign project and allegiance to local history, the town; and me with my allegiance to the whole story and, in some naïve way, to "the truth." Whatever that was.

———•———

I had been talking to Jean, and Jean had been talking to her adviser at the Massachusetts Historical Commission. The adviser was not convinced by Jean's evidence that the house was built in the 1600s. There was, for example, no "summer beam"—a support beam that typically ran from the chimney above the hearth across the ceiling of what would now be the living room. Perhaps the original summer beam had been removed, or was never there at all. The summer beam, or evidence of one, was one of the most obvious ways of dating a first-period house.

If we discovered the house wasn't built in the first period, it would surely lose its status as "The Oldest Continuously Lived-In House in New England." And if that happened, I wasn't sure how my father would react. Part of me wanted to protect my father from Jean's doubts; another part of me wanted his years of storytelling to stop.

It was mid-morning, and Jean and I were sitting behind the house on rugged patio chairs. Kim sat near us on the old gristmill stone that Richard Warren had dragged out of the Two Mile Brook and made into a flower planter.

"The Oldest Continuously Lived-In House," Jean said.

"Where did that term even come from?" I asked.

"You know—Dad, Mr. Hatch," Kim said. "And *New England*. You have to add that. The Oldest Continuously Lived-In House *in New England*."

"It's an interesting title," Jean said. She was sitting on the edge of her seat, elbows on knees, leaning toward us. "Let's break it down."

"What houses are the *oldest* in New England?" I asked.

"There's the Fairbanks House in Dedham," Kim said.

"Right," Jean said, rapid-fire, "also the Scotch-Boardman House in Danvers, the Wright House in Plymouth, the Williams House in Scituate, the Goodspeed House in Barnstable. There's also the Tilden House in Scituate. And that's just in southeastern Massachusetts."

Kim gave me a sideways look, which Jean caught. She went on to tell us that the Fairbanks House had been (like the Red House) inhabited by eight generations of the same family, until it was turned into a museum. Every year, the third week in August, the Fairbanks family held a reunion and pageant on the lawn. "When you ask preservation historians about New England's oldest house, most of them say the Fairbanks House," Jean said.

Our conversation progressed. "Continuously Lived-In" was ripe for a variety of interpretations: Continuously lived in by the same family (i.e., the family that built it)? Or continuously lived in by anyone (i.e., not necessarily the same family that built it)? And if this was the case, did renters count or just owners? Could it be a summer home, or did it have to be a year-round permanent residence?

Was a house worth more the longer it was lived in? Did this make it more of a "House"? Was the "House" that now existed the same "House" that was originally built on that spot more than three hundred years previously? The house, being continuously lived in, was bound to need repairs, and so the inhabitants could have slowly replaced parts until little of the original "House" was left.

"It's like Abe Lincoln's Ax," Jean said. "You have Abe Lincoln's Ax, but then the handle rots, disintegrates with age. So you replace the handle. Then, after a few more years, the head of the ax rusts beyond repair, so you replace it with an exact replica. Is it still Abe Lincoln's Ax?"

Jean told us that, after she presented a leaded-glass window from the Red House to her adviser, he had asked, "Did you find it in the wall?" Jean had said no—it had been a gift from Richard Warren Hatch with the documents and random pieces of furniture. "Then how do you know that it came from this house?" he replied.

But even if a definitive beam or window was found in a wall, it still might not prove anything. Houses were torn down and re-built all the time with recycled parts.

"Only one rib of *Old Ironsides* [the USS *Constitution*, in Boston Harbor] is original," Kim pointed out. "*One rib*. Do you think they should still call it *Old Ironsides*?"

I imagined another scenario. Maybe Jean, completing her survey, would find some unknown house out there, a house over three hundred years old, still lived in by ancestors of the same family that built it, unchanged, low-ceilinged, and dark, without electricity, telephone, or running water, illuminated only by an enormous supply of whale oil, which would, along with typical New England regionalism and inbreeding, explain the family's reluctance to sell the property or even "venture out"—until now, when Jean's survey landed on their doorstep, deposited by a trustworthy distant relative or local antiquarian fed up with keeping secrets. It would be only a matter of time before the fifteenth generation came squinting out of their doorway, crusty and molelike.

"Hey," they would say, "what about me? What about our house?"

While we were talking, Philippe and the rest of the crew were engaged in securing a come-along. They had threaded a long steel wire through a window on the south side of the house, stretched it through the living room and dining room and out a window on the north side. The wire was attached to bolts on the outside of the house, stretched at eye level through the rooms. In the center of the wire, in a doorway dividing the living room from the dining room, hung a hand-crank winch.

Kim, uncertain of Philippe's competence, left our conversation to join them, stood in the middle of the house, and cranked. The twenty-ton come-along acted as a toggle; she was literally pulling the walls of the house together.

I couldn't believe Kim was doing this. The torque on the house when the winch was cranked would be severe, and if it didn't work, the house might spring back, causing beams, and consequently the south wall, to fly. Kim was attempting the equivalent of stretching a rubber band tight between her fingers—a sling that could fly forward, or spring back and hit her in the eye—only the dimensions of this slingshot were huge.

The argument with my father about the particular year suddenly seemed ridiculous; now, perhaps, we would be arguing about centuries. And now—right now—the house might pop like an overwound top, all because of my sister and her schemes.

"What do you think?" I asked Jean. "Do you think the house was built in 1647?"

"I don't know yet," Jean said. "We have to look at the *fabric* of the house. And see what it tells us." As if the house knew all the answers and was just keeping them hidden.

"We have family history and good documentation," she added. "We have personal accounts of Israel H. Hatch, who was alive during the lifetime of Richard Warren Hatch, who confirmed any weak links we had with the chain of title. Richard Warren Hatch was able to confirm that Israel H. Hatch was the son of Deacon Joel Hatch, who inherited the house, and that the house in which he lived was the same house as his grandfather lived in. That takes us back to Deacon Joel's father, the third Israel."

Jean and I stood up while we were talking, wandered inside.

"So—what does this mean?" I asked Jean.

"It means that we can't put the house on the survey. It isn't going to pass."

I looked at her and said nothing.

She told me that the footprint of the original cellar was

murky, that there was no summer beam, and that some of the gunstock beams were still boxed and she couldn't see them.

She continued: "There's not enough physical evidence to prove this is a first-period home. But there's also not enough evidence to prove that it isn't."

Jean looked at me in a moment of Yoda-like composure. I was expecting to hear the house groan behind me, but it didn't. I knew that Kim and Philippe were still winching. Philippe left through the doorway quickly and jumped into the ditch running alongside the newly constructed sill. He was going to begin to drill the wall of the house back into the sill with screws and a metal plate.

"Is there more you can do?" I asked. "You know, to prove it. To get more proof?"

"No, not without completely tearing the house down, and it's half torn down already." Then she paused. "Well, there is one thing."

"What?"

"We could X-ray the house," she said.

Richard Warren Hatch
1934–1965

RICHARD WARREN HATCH of Deerfield, Mass., whose first
novel, "Into the Wind," a story of the Massachusets South Shore,
was recently published. Mr. Hatch is head of the English department at Deerfield Academy.

Richard Warren Hatch on stoop of Red House, circa 1929

Yet Two Mile lived. Delicate wisps of smoke straggled from sturdy chimneys here and there. . . . Nothing had broken the snow between houses, there was each house, a little somber outline in the morning dusk, an island of security in a cold sea.

—Richard Warren Hatch, *Into the Wind*
(New York: Macmillan, 1929), p. 18

In 1898, the year Richard Warren Hatch was born, a violent storm ripped the mouths of the North and South Rivers apart. Newspapers reported that a tidal wave crashed through the beach at Third and Fourth Cliffs, in the same spot where shipwrights, more than fifty years before, had failed to finish digging across.

The storm hit on the evening of November 27, capsizing many ships, including the steamer *Portland*. One unfortunate passenger—one of the hundred who drowned—was found with his pocket watch stopped at exactly 10 p.m. Scituate Harbor was soon flooded—heaping rubbish against storefronts, carrying livestock down flooded lanes, pulling birds out of the sky and depositing hogs in tree branches. The storm broke three hundred panes of glass in a greenhouse; windmills were knocked over, trees uprooted, chimneys blown down, electric and telephone wires dragged and tangled in roofs and bushes. All the bathhouses were toothpicked and roads swept away, bridges and docks thrown up on land.

During the night, the patrolman at Fourth Cliff Station mistakenly left his post and clung all night to the top limbs of an oak as the water rumbled past. Below Fourth Cliff, the pilot ship

Columbia was tossed ashore, crushing cottages, while other ships were wrecking all the way down to Provincetown, the beach a confetti of whiskey barrels, cheese rinds, lard and pork, lamp oil, and empty life preservers. One corpse was found inside the cracked hull of the *Columbia*, another flung onto the sand. Survivors managed to land their boats on shore, or run around near the moss shanties and cling to the roofs of houses still left standing, but even the houses eventually began to float away.

The ocean flooded quickly up the new mouth of the North River, drowning shipyards, the meadows, and cedar groves of Two Mile under six feet of water, killing trees and grasses. The Two Mile land grant is a mile wide, most houses sitting a half-mile between the river and the main road; the storm's flood covered the entire width of Two Mile, lapping at the door of the schoolhouse. The four ponds in Two Mile bled into each other, leaving the Red House an island. Many found themselves marooned. Farmers paddled boats over sunken stone walls, submerged fields, floating over the place where fields used to be, floating over rakes, a cultivator, an oxcart. They'd search for the drowned bodies of cows and horses, dragged from washed-up hillside thickets, to be thrown in piles and burned, and the air smelled like charred flesh. The Red House was surrounded by brackish water that took weeks to drain, the well gone bad with salt. The water left rings around the meetinghouse, and the trunks of trees, as it slowly receded into the river.

Even when the flood withdrew, the new mouth could not be dammed. The river was changed forever—brackish, half salt, half fresh, dropping and rising every six hours with the tide.

———

Except for summers as a child, Richard Warren Hatch had never really lived in the Red House. The family was raised in Pennsylvania, and he grew into a self-described ruffian:

A problem to my teachers in school, ringer of the fire alarm in one school when all were in the assembly room, a truant so frequently that I had to bring a report home every day to prove that I had been in school, stoning a boy I didn't like, thus bringing the police to the house, breaking the windows in a neighbor's barn, taking my lunch and going to caddy at the golf links instead of going to school, causing my father to be called from his office to bail me out of jail when he thought I was attending my college classes, arrested repeatedly for speeding and insulting police officers—and I remember no too harsh words, no violent temper from my parents, no arbitrary, unthinking penalties. How my family stood me, I do not yet understand.

Richard Warren Hatch was the first in his family to go to college, entering the University of Pennsylvania in 1916. In 1918, he left college and enlisted in the United States Naval Reserve Flying Corps. After the war, he returned to school, married Harriet Hildreth in 1922, had two sons, and lived as a teacher in western Massachusetts.

His niece Priscilla Waldron Gladwin described her uncle in this time of his life as physically and intellectually intimidating. "He was so tall," she once wrote in an essay. "His voice was deep and often carried a hint of scorn for other people, those who weren't as brilliant and able as he." His eyes were dark and bemused, his eyebrows whiskery and arching. He gave her Jane Austen, Dickens, Hawthorne, Thoreau, Balzac, the modern poets. "I was never sure whether he was laughing at me or enjoying life with me," she wrote.

There were, however, moments of vulnerability in Hatch. "The only thing in life I really want, besides peace, is home," he wrote to her in one letter. Perhaps being away from the Red House fed Hatch's nostalgia for it. His first novel, *Into the Wind,* was a thinly veiled fictionalization of the Hatch legacy. Published in 1929, the novel followed the trials of a family of farmers, millworkers, and shipwrights called the Bradfords, who lived in an old red house in a place called Two Mile in Marshfield, Massachusetts, in the 1800s.

In his second novel about the Bradfords, *Leave the Salt Earth*, he wrote:

> *One more year was burning away in the woods of Two Mile, one more year to be added to the two hundred and thirty that the house had already withstood since the first Bradford built it, and the old place seemed as secure and tranquil as ever.*

As much as these books were about the nostalgia of place, they were also about the guilt that comes with abandoning family heritage:

> *The Bradford house and the Bradfords were part of Two Mile tradition in those days when the river was a shipbuilding center . . . But not all the Bradfords had taken root in that corner of Marshfield. . . . They were a resolute, a whole-souled lot; they were workers and conscientious— these wanderers.*

Perhaps one impulse could not exist without the other. The notion of historic family home, for Hatch's characters, carried with it the ugly cousin of "burden," "entrapment"—something to be escaped. Hatch wrote about this very American impulse— the desire to "go west" or out to sea, to form an identity through separation. The novels became increasingly less about the actual Red House and Two Mile and more about the conflict between old and new, family farm versus the industrial modern world.

Yet Hatch repeated lines like: "There was always the red house. Going on two hundred years and always a Bradford in the red house." The Red House must have epitomized the declining family farm for Richard Warren—the Red House, he knew, went without indoor plumbing, electricity, or telephones for years because his grandfather and then his grandmother and aunt wanted it that way.

He had such pride in his Puritan lineage that he once paid a "genealogist of high repute" to trace his ancestry back through the *Mayflower* to England, through several earls, to William the Conqueror and Alfred the Great—a link that later relatives deemed "dubious."

When his father died, Richard Warren was allowed to choose which house he would inherit, the White or the Red. The White House was newer, clearly worth more money. But Richard Warren picked the Red House—perhaps out of nostalgia, or for posterity, because it was the oldest.

But by the time he inherited it, Richard Warren was married with two sons, and was trying to make ends meet—a goal he believed couldn't be accomplished in Two Mile. So he rented the house out and visited only for short periods in the summer. One summer, Hatch let his oldest son, Dick Jr. (as he was called), spend the entire summer alone in the old house, helping his uncle Tracy with the farm and teaching archery at the camp.

During World War II, on the *Yorkshire*, the idea of a very old lobster kept tail-fanning across Richard Warren's mind. He and the other sailors were stacked in bunks like sardines, as his great-uncle Thomas had been, hammocked in Honolulu while whale-chasing, writing about "Boo-hoo fever." In Two Mile, the ponds were quarantined for polio, off limits. Inside the Red House, a girl with polio, the daughter of renters, glided over floorboards with a skateboard-and-cane device that young sculptor Dick Jr. had designed for her. At the White House, Tracy and Betty looked out over the stone walls and the fields of flowers, watching the horizon and imagining planes over Japan, Hitler's army, a shadow extending over the body of Europe, Poland falling.

On July 19, 1940, the *Marshfield Mail* published a photo of Two Mile taken from the air. The accompanying article read: "In the distance, the winding North River, as the air men see it. . . . More of the spirals of the stream than are ever seen from the ground, or any hill, appear naturally and regnantly, to charm our souls."

Two Mile was always a charming place for Richard Warren Hatch, especially when he was away from it. In the 1930s and '40s, he published numerous articles for books and magazines on topics ranging from foreign policy to trout-fishing, as well as eight books. The lobster books, by far his most successful publishing venture, flirted with ideas of home versus adventure. The lobster, after all, succeeded in the new frontier of terra firma, yet he always returned to his underwater home beneath a clump of rocks. "Home is the best place to be after dark. Home is where you come to think over things you've found out. That's what a home is—a place not to be bothered in," said Mr. Lobster.

It seemed that Marshfield thought of itself with similar nostalgia. An ad for a grocery store in the *Marshfield Mail* asked: "Do you remember when castile soap was sold in long hunks and salt cod in strips? When the molasses keg and the kerosene can stood side by side in the back room? The glass jar of jaw breakers, the collection of hat pins and Old Honest Pug chewing tobacco? When whale oil was offered for sale in big vats?" The ad ended with "Yes, Times have changed—but our policy hasn't!"

Across the river, Scituate had its own folklorist. "Captain" Bill Vinal, a contemporary of Richard Warren Hatch, wrote wistfully about his childhood near Two Mile during a similar time period:

When a lad, my legs were long and hollow. Neighbors said better put a brick on that boys head. In school we had slates. Cash was scarce and eggs were used as money.

Shelves were covered with newspaper with scissored edges.

In January a newspaper was shoved under my shirt. We soaked our feet in mustard water. Creaky floor, howling wind, mice gnawing, and bats behind the boarded windows. Hot soapstone, flat iron, powdery snow drifting through the cracks. Hot lemonade or a drink made out of coco shells. Winnowing. Swingling flax.

Would the Indian miss the wolves, bear, wild cat and deep forest shadows? Would revolutionary soldiers be disappointed that their landscape, which was so familiar, has passed? Who would miss ox carts? Droves of swine, martins in the barn, great flocks of passenger pigeons?

It was a good time to break a leg. There was a race between filling coffins and cradles.

In the late 1950s, Tracy Hatch fell ill. It started subtly—a weakness in his arms, his hands unable to close a pair of scissors. His mind was alert as his body failed, closing in around him—like a person locked in a shuttered, unfamiliar house. Eventually, he was diagnosed with Lou Gehrig's disease, unable to walk, confined to a wheelchair. He tried to keep the flower farm going, hired a man to work for him. Dick Jr., visiting the roller-skate girl at the Red House, built ramps around the flower farm for Tracy's wheelchair. Tracy would sit in his chair in the living room of the White House and look up across the backyard to the pump house, where he watched his employee fixing machinery, carrying buckets from the fields to the barn. Even from his position inside, he could see mistakes. In 1957, Tracy fired his assistant and closed the flower farm, dismantling all the greenhouses.

Sarah Messer

Richard Warren Hatch returned often to the Red House, perhaps to be near his ailing brother. He tore down the barn where his great-grandfather Deacon Joel had breathed his last, replaced it with a blacktop driveway and a garage. He dismantled all the sheds except the bunkhouse. The renters moved out. Inside the house Richard Warren Hatch began a series of restorations—plumbing, electricity, a bathroom on the second floor. He fashioned wrought-iron hardware for the doors, and he and Ruth filled the place with rugs. "The two of them transformed a shabby old house into a home of comfort which retained the atmosphere of centuries of living," Priscilla Waldron Gladwin wrote when Richard Warren Hatch and Ruth finally moved in for good. "It was one of the oldest houses in the country to have been in one family since being built. It had become a family shrine to the ancestors."

Twelve

A death's-head gravestone carving, 1700

A seventeenth-century flying death's-head appeared on the computer screen. A mouth shaped like a heart; a mouth shaped like a house, crosshatched; a mouth with two rows of teeth cutting opposite ways. I put the clicker, a tiny magnifying glass, on the screen at the top edge of the stone and zoomed in— the screen was then consumed by the engraving: "Here Lyes the Body of . . . Here Lyes . . . Here . . . He."

In the microfilm room of the American Antiquarian Society, in Worcester, Massachusetts, the Farber Collection's "Grave Stone CD ROM" flashed blue light with each click. The twenty-CD collection of photographs of seventeenth- and eighteenth-century New England gravestones offered the option to sort by state, county, grave carver, name of deceased, or inscription on the stone. I searched for the name HATCH in SCITUATE, MASSACHUSETTS, and the craftsmen NORTH RIVER CARVERS. I thought perhaps if I could find the grave of Walter

Hatch I could somehow link him to the house and prove the house was indeed first-period. Maybe Walter was hidden somewhere in CD-ROMs and microfilm.

Outside the microfilm room, the larger Antiquarian Society was silent—rows of oak reading tables under a vaulted ceiling, a dome of glass half-moons, marble pillars, two floors of oil portraits of grim Puritans, hidden back rooms. Curved balconies on the second floor overlooked the reading room, creating a pan-optical effect, a friendly police-state of heritage presiding over the scattered book cradles and velvet book-snakes, sturdy rows of card catalogues with typed menus of subject headings: "Catchechisms–Cere Cloth," "Shipbuilding–Tailor," "Violin–War."

———

When I wasn't surfing the Grave Stone CD-ROM, I would sit at the long wooden tables next to historians ranging in age from graduate students to retired professors—all with laptops plugged into floor sockets beneath the tables, all having arrived promptly at 9 a.m., all typing. I told archivists that I was searching for anything that had to do with Scituate, Marshfield, or old houses.

In my search at AAS, I examined early-twentieth-century handwritten accounts of Scituate cemeteries, including private and common burial grounds. A walking tour of graves was compiled in 1900–1905 by W. J. Litchfield of Southbridge, Massachusetts. A pencil-scribbled precursor to CD-ROM, the notebooks were long and thin loose-leaf cemetery-plot records.

By examining other people's paper trails, I learned that Plymouth Colony had always had split agendas—the split was reflected in the CD-ROM grave carvings I clicked on and enlarged. Those of the conservative shipbuilders were scowling death's-heads; a few miles, a few clicks, away, another group of carvers produced cartoonish and giddy gravestone images. The latter style was one that seemed to mock itself, to be caught in dualistic agendas—skulls with eyelashes, hidden noses, churlish smiles, a broken collar, or a lacy neck-brace. The stones, although craved in the mid-seventeenth century, resembled alien faces—wings like spider legs, zippered teeth, hair spiraling from skulls like unbound Slinkys. These "aliens" I realized were in the "Men of Kent" cemetery—located, of course, in Scituate.

It was all leading up to this. After looking at the CD-ROM, I left Worcester and drove an hour east on the Mass. Pike to back roads through Two Mile to Scituate, looking for Meeting House Lane. I needed to stand in the graveyard, to touch the stones; it was this impulse, I realized, that millions of vacationers and children on class trips experienced when they visited Civil War battle sites, the bed where George Washington once slept, the cellar holes of Plimoth and Jamestown: as if, being in the spot where the historical bodies once were, we'd learn something about them we couldn't learn in books.

I brought a flashlight with me. The "Men of Kent" cemetery was a long, thin piece of land at the side of the road. I parked on the shoulder and walked toward the dark shape of headstones. The spot of the flashlight hit the curved top of a stone; I bent down on my knee and rubbed my hand over it. It was not Walter's grave, but these were from the same time period—his neighbors and contemporaries. A giddy three-hundred-year-old face with wings, eyelashes, and two sets of teeth looked back; perhaps three-hundred-year-old bones still remained beneath me, or they had turned to dirt; and their dirt remained, or the dirt had turned to worm food, every cell or molecule gone. But this was the final resting ground of the "Men of Kent"; they had all been here once. It was as close to Walter as I was going to get.

———·———

"What we really need," Jean told me next time I saw her, "is a portable X-ray machine. That way, we could X-ray down through the floorboards to find traces of where the beams were, or perhaps find the remains of a summer beam that had been trimmed down. Some architects use doctor's tools, like lasers and scopes, to do exploratory carpentry. They stick a tiny camera on a long wire and run it between floors, between boards."

Jean described how she would stand with her back against the east wall of the Borning Room and point the machine face-down through the floor. The summer beam would traverse either the ceiling of the dining room or my father's study, and would be extending out from the chimney itself, attached to framing members on the other side of the room.

Short of ripping out all the other walls in the house, X-raying was the best way to determine whether the house contained more first-period details. Betty Bates had mentioned core samples of the painted panels we had recently uncovered in the walls; but we would also need a three-hundred-year-old Marshfield tree for comparison. One glance out at the denuded hillside eliminated this option. Jean wanted to take the boxing off the beams in several of the bedrooms upstairs and in the corners of my father's study. She had her hunches. If we could find the summer beam, or a shadow of where it once was, we'd have our proof.

But when I mentioned X-raying the house to my father, he said no.

"Can't you do carbon dating?" he asked. I told him that, though a beam might be old, carbon dating would not necessarily prove that the beam was original to the house. "It could have been taken from an old barn or another, earlier version of the house," I said. And then added, "Jean thinks this is the best way."

But again he refused, and his refusal bore the weight of someone who thought this prospect was ridiculous. As a technician and a doctor, perhaps he was insulted. Imagine: hauling an X-ray machine up a tight and narrow staircase, placing it face-down, and passing its beam through two floors. Or maybe there was another reason he was resisting.

"Richard Warren Hatch *told* me the house was built in 1646," he said when I pushed him.

"Well, how did he know?" I asked.

"He was a very smart man," my father said. "And, besides, why would he lie?"

Betty Bates was apprised of the Jean Hall situation. She thought that Jean's adviser was rigid, that he didn't know what he was talking about, or that he was sending Jean to snoop and needlessly discredit. "What's history except a collection of what people have said? What else have you to go on?" Betty said. We were at Cynthia's house, thick with the atmosphere of a giddy historian's slumber party. The coffee table was strewn with local history books, old photo albums. Cynthia had just finished showing photos of the summer her family had spent motorboating around New England with Tracy and Betty Hatch. Cynthia had been a teenager with a broken leg, the thigh-to-ankle cast shackling her for the entire school vacation. "Everywhere we went, Tracy would carry me," Cynthia said. "Everywhere. He was such a gentleman." She pointed at photos of a blond, smiling Tracy holding her ponytailed, squinting younger self in a basket-toss before boat docks, the river, the side of a boat trailer.

Then Betty said, "You really should go to the vault. You could find out about that Stoddard fire, and perhaps some other things about Two Mile."

"What's the vault?" I asked.

"The Marshfield Historical Commission Records in Town Hall. Cynthia and I can take you there. Basically, we *are* the vault."

Marshfield Town Hall is squarish with a rising, tentlike roof and sleek, angular columns. The large glass front doors open onto a slate-floor lobby, and a large portrait of Daniel Webster hangs on a wood-paneled wall. The day I visited, it smelled of Lysol and bologna.

I took a seat on a bench beneath the portrait, facing the doors, and waited for Cynthia and Betty. To the left and right, I could see the offices of the city clerk and others. Across from me sat a diorama of the Daniel Webster House and grounds and the plans for future restoration. Blueprints and maps hung framed on the walls.

Then Cynthia and Betty entered, apologizing for being late, while Betty fiddled with a key before a shut door.

"The vault" was a windowless seven-by-ten-foot room with painted concrete block walls. An institutional gunmetal desk sat in the corner, but the rest of the room was consumed by floor-to-ceiling bookshelves filled with stacks of papers, notebooks, archival file boxes. These were the holdings of the Marshfield Historical Commission, next door to the town records.

"Everything you want to know should be here or in the town records," Betty said.

To begin, we looked in a card catalogue for vital records under the name Stoddard. I had the date for the fire, October 30, 1853, but I wasn't sure when or if the mother and daughter had died from their injuries. We found the mother first: "Sarah S. Stoddard, died November 1, 1853." The card gave a volume number for the vital record, and Betty disappeared, to return carting a large bound book, which she laid before me on a table.

We found the entry for Sarah S. Stoddard. Next to the date, the cause of death read: "lockjaw effects of burning with camphrene." Had an infection set into her burns? Had the camphor killed her?

The rest of our search involved flipping back and forth

between birth, death, and marriage records. Sarah and Alfred Stoddard had given birth to a daughter on January 25, 1852. Mary Stoddard would have been ten months old when her mother, engulfed in flames, snatched her from her bed. We searched, but there was no death record for Mary Stoddard.

"She could have died in another town," Betty said. Alfred Stoddard was a "cordwainer," or shoemaker. Soon after Sarah Stoddard's death, the marriage records showed that Alfred married a woman named Jane B. Perry.

"Maybe Mary Stoddard's death was never recorded," Betty said. "Or you could look under marriages—maybe she survived."

In the card catalogue, I found a listing. The burned child had survived; when she was eighteen, she had married William F. Henderson, a shoemaker.

I flipped back in the death records, came across Rebekah's children, the sisters who had died a few days apart. Then I found Thomas. Thomas R. Oakman, listed as a "mariner," had lived thirty-eight years, nine months, and seventeen days, before dying of typhoid fever.

———

All summer, the fire alarm at the Red House had been going off—a combination of humidity and bad wiring, too many old systems competing with each other.

One night, at 3 a.m., while I was sleeping alone in the house, a red light swept over the long ceiling beams. A pulse, the loud wonk of the alarm.

Downstairs, I found the doors of the house wide open. Firemen had been walking through the house with flashlights. I heard their boots ascending the back staircase, their voices above me and below me. One of them approached and said, "Oh, sorry, we thought no one was home. The alarm rang at the station and the door was open when we arrived."

One fireman had found the boiler room and flicked the switch that turned off the alarm. Another had turned the light on in the stairwell. Descending from the second floor, I saw three more firemen standing at the base of the stairs. One smiled at me, and I recognized him as if from a dream—familiar eyes beneath the rim of his hat. I thought at first it was Tom—my first boyfriend—not a sailor, not drowned, not dead of typhoid. Had he returned as a fireman? But as I got to the bottom of the stairs, I realized that the familiar eyes belonged not to Tom but to Mike, my friend from high school—the pool player who lived in Thomas Oakman's house up the street. I hadn't seen him in more than ten years. He looked the same, except his hair was shorter, his face clean-shaven and round. I could see his dimples when he smiled.

"Hey," I said, "how are you?"

"I knew this was your house," he said, "but I didn't think I'd find you here." He asked what I was doing, and I said that I'd been traveling; I told him that I was back to help restore the house.

"A carpenter," he said. "That's different."

"No, not a carpenter, really."

"Not really? I guess I'm not really a fireman either."

"Really?"

"No," he laughed. "I'm a fireman. What does it look like?"

The rest of the firemen gathered then, having searched every floor of the house for smoke and found nothing.

"I don't know what to say, except there's no fire here. A false alarm, maybe. You might want to check your smoke-alarm units again," the chief said as the firemen were leaving. I was so shocked to see Mike that all I could do was smile when he waved goodbye.

"See you around?" he said. And then they left.

I walked upstairs and heard the faint beep of a smoke detector. I followed the sound to the west wall of the renovated second-floor bathroom. In the wall behind the shower was a small door that led to a crawl space; when I opened the door, the beeping became louder. The crawl space had a low-slanted ceiling following the pitch of the roof—it extended to the most westerly peak of the house, and the beeping was coming from there. I walked out over the floor joists divided by rolls of pink fiberglass insulation. I placed my hand on the slanted roof for balance. The walk was tentative, my arms balancing in the dark as I edged toward the sound, and when I reached the end of the peak, I could see the moon in a tiny window at the end, and there, attached to one of the last rafters, was an ancient smoke alarm, perhaps placed there by Richard Warren Hatch.

I pulled the rim of the detector down and the beeping stopped. The detector itself remained closed, and immediately another sound began. A buzzing, the vibration of an insect trapped inside. A wasp, I realized, had been building a nest all summer within the smoke detector, and had tripped the whole system. I unlatched the plastic lid, which dropped open to reveal the tiny paper hive attached to its ceiling; the wasp itself, corset-waisted and shellacked, crawled to the edge of the rim and escaped.

———

A week later, Mike and I met for lunch at Maria's Sub Shop in Scituate Harbor. Mike ordered a large tuna sub with everything—diced pickles, onions, tomatoes, and hot peppers—heated under the broiler with a piece of provolone cheese. Above our booth hung a pastel drawing of a hippie in cutoffs and sunglasses. "That's been here for frickin-ever," he told me.

I felt sixteen again—I'd returned to the same spot, the same sub shop as high school, seeing the same people behind the counter.

"You dropped off the planet," Mike said.

"Yeah, I know," I said.

I *had* dropped off the planet, and until now had cared only about returning to the house. But the house, the land, and the town included people, included everyone.

At the same time, it also seemed that my absence hadn't changed anything—hadn't changed the *place*. It was arrogant of me to think that it could. Life went on as usual at the Red House and Maria's Sub Shop. I had the slightly sick feeling I'd had many times before at the Red House: that time was not linear but circular—patterns repeated themselves, and everything was a mirror of something that had happened before.

I had been staring too long at my sandwich.

"Off the frickin' planet!" Mike said. Then he flicked a pickle chunk at me. "Yo, Space."

"Come off it," I said.

After we had talked about nearly everything, caught up on ten years, he filled in one of the blanks by mentioning the Glades, the rambling mansion built by the Adamses (the family of former U.S. presidents John and John Quincy Adams). The land around the Glades was also the location of the first recorded interaction between the English and Native Americans in this area.

Mike said he had to go pick up our friend Kevin at the Glades. Did I want to come?

———•———

The back roads through Scituate to the Glades were a catalogue of increasing wealth. The modest homes we drove past gradually gave way to larger homes, then, at road's end, to a large gate, the entry to the Glades. The Glades sat on a rocky peninsula, originally the town's northern boundary. Beginning at the Glades, and running southwest through the Bound Brook Estuary, was the Patent Line, which, in the seventeenth century, divided Plymouth Colony from Massachusetts Bay Colony.

The landscape was scattered with large granite boulders left there by the last glacier. As we entered the gate, we passed a series of outbuildings that ended in a circular drive before a nineteenth-century mansion complete with rows of close-pressed windows, spindled porches, and a cupola. The house was built on a rocky peninsula; only a few seaweed-clumped rocks stretched farther to a lighthouse. I looked out at the white-capped waves. I remembered the story I had read about Captain Smith and his party shooting at the natives in a canoe, and the hail of arrows the men fired back. The car door pulled from my hand in the wind as I opened it.

The Glades was more like a hotel or a small hospital than a house. "A great place to film a horror movie or rock video," I said. But Mike told me that someone had beaten me to it: in the eighties, a B-movie called *Witchery* was filmed in the old part of the house. The movie starred Linda Blair.

"You can still get it on video," Mike said.

We met Kevin, who led us into the main house through banging screen doors to a stairwell he had been painting. We were in one section of the crooked tunnel of three floors of rooms, a nineteenth-century addition that connected two separate structures. The stairwell was grand and decrepit, draped with drop cloths and scraps of used sandpaper.

We climbed the stairs, Kevin chattering, picking up painting equipment, pointing out places where he had repaired plaster. The farther we explored, the smaller his work became, until it seemed symbiotic, as if the house were dependent on his being there and practicing his love of aesthetic details, his devotion to the walls.

Kevin referred to this type of devotion as "a love of the decrepit." "Some people have it, some people don't," Kevin said.

The decrepit was manifest in the sun-bleached rooms smelling of mothballs and wicker, in the faded wool rugs and cast-iron button switches, in the broken fan, cloth suitcase, wooden dresser, and rooms empty save for a child-sized iron bed, a girl's abandoned leather boot.

Sometime in the past, as many as forty-five children had visited the Glades at once, Kevin told me. And now the rooms in the Glades were divided and owned by descendants of descendants, some clusters of rooms renovated, some not, like a half-colonized hive.

Mike and Kevin, who had known each other since grade school, began to act like high-school boys again.

"Remember that anchor lamp you made in woodshop?" Kevin asked.

"Yeah, and you made one shaped like a giant tooth." Mike laughed.

"That was wicked pissa."

"Wicked."

"Pissa. Well, it was actually a molar, not just any tooth."

———

Kevin continued the tour. Mike smiled at me, whispered, "Love of the decrepit," as if this place, this house tour, was the perfect gift for me.

Kevin led us to "the babysitter's room," the cupola on top of the oldest section of the house. The room had eight-foot ceilings and rows of single beds. In the corners of the room sat embroidered iron grates where a heat shaft extended through the floors below down to the basement and the furnace. I knelt and laced my fingers down through the holes.

I realized that in my years away I'd misremembered the Red House as something more akin to the Glades—too large, too desperate. But the Red House wasn't like the Glades at all. The Glades was built to be abandoned—it had always been owned by many families, used in the summer for vacations; it was never a home, it was never "lived in."

The significance of the Red House, I realized then, was that it had been clutched too tightly, burned, reworked, written about over and over again, nearly consumed. The story that

Rebekah had written to Israel, about the burning woman who grabbed her child, was not a story of abandonment or lack of love. It was a story about too much love.

Standing in the babysitter's room at the Glades, I recognized my mistake. When thinking of old houses, it was so easy to fall into the image of the gothic, the dead, the lost.

The cupola certainly seemed this way. The walls, floors, windowsills, dresser tops, rungs of the beds all dripped with purple-and-white bird droppings. A flock of birds must have been trapped inside at some point. But now even the birds were gone.

"How did they get in here?" Mike asked. "And how did they get out?"

"Ghost birds," Kevin said.

All the beds in the cupola were empty—no one had slept there for years.

———

I returned to the Red House and found a note, "There has been an accident," in Kim's handwriting, including directions to the hospital.

I found Kim and Philippe in a small room off the hospital's emergency entrance. Philippe was sitting up on a table, his foot raised in a giant hive of towel and ice and bandages.

Philippe had nearly cut off his big toe with a skill saw. He had been making a picnic table quickly, not thinking, wearing a pair of flip-flops, and had laid the long boards he was cutting on the cement floor of the barn. Having cut one board, he had put the saw down on the ground without the guard; the whirring blade, still moving, had jumped across the floor over his foot. The tiny plastic divider in the thong of the flip-flop between his big toe and his second toe had stopped the blade, but the big toe was nearly severed—held to the foot by a thin flap of skin.

Now they were waiting for an expert, to see if the toe should be reattached or amputated.

Philippe, strangely, seemed in great spirits. "I felt no pain at all," he said, and went on to explain how Kim had thought quickly—packing the toe in ice and dragging him to the car.

But Kim didn't look well: her face was green, she was drained of blood, her body weaved in the corner of the room. I led her out to the hallway, where she leaned her head against the wall, her hair falling over her face.

"You take for granted that people are whole," she said. "To see his body cut apart like that—a part of him that was supposed to be there suddenly wasn't."

Back in the room, the on-call doctor had returned to explain that, because it was Labor Day, they would have a hard time getting hold of a specialist, an orthopedic or vascular surgeon.

"Please tell me," Philippe said, "how much this is going to cost?"

"You just relax," the doctor said. "You don't need to worry about that right now."

"Well, you see, I have no insurance," Philippe said, "and say you tell me that to replace my toe would be five thousand dollars, I would say 'Forget it, my toe is not worth that much money.'" And then he made a *pffttt* sound and shrugged, as if everything he was saying was perfectly reasonable. "So, just finish it off, but save the part so I can have a funeral for it."

"Don't worry about that," the doctor said. "Your toe may not need a funeral."

"It's gone, but I feel nothing," Philippe said aloud to the room, as if the room could answer back.

———

The day after the accident, my father stood in the kitchen of the Red House holding the X-ray of Philippe's toe up to the square ceiling light. The X-ray showed his entire foot, a glowing white rake, and the severed toe. The bone was cut through at the first metatarsal, a neat road of black where the split occurred. My father held the X-ray above his head with both hands. The toe had been reattached, but the success of the operation depended upon whether or not Philippe could keep his foot elevated and perfectly still for two months. He sat in one of the twin beds on the second floor reading *The Art of Happiness* by the Dalai Lama, his foot hoisted on a stack of pillows. The restoration project had come to a grinding halt.

Meanwhile, Cynthia and Betty had secured a small hand-painted sign to the side of the house reading, "Walter Hatch, circa 1646."

"It seemed like too much trouble to argue about one year," Betty told me. Within a month, the restoration was taken up by our sculptor neighbor Theo and Jean's brother Ed, a musician who had just moved east from Colorado and needed work. Jean, consumed with her graduate work, moved on to another project. And within the month, I received a writing fellowship in Provincetown, Massachusetts.

Kim and Philippe returned to Maine and left the chopping block in the kitchen littered with colorful notes calling Ed "the Savior" and Theo "Lord Theo." "Most talented carpenters," Philippe wrote, "and cute too." Then he drew a small heart with an arrow shooting through it.

The house was never X-rayed.

———

I had heard about the ancient highway. "It's right in the woods behind your house," Betty Bates had mentioned once. Like the yellow brick road, I thought, there beneath my feet, there all along. And, true, I was beginning to realize that beneath contemporary Marshfield was colonial Marshfield. One simply had to look for the slippage, where present eroded into past. Pylons from a North River shipyard as seen from the Route 3 bridge; the foundation of a barn in the middle of the woods; a stone wall behind a Dunkin' Donuts.

Betty had told me that the road ran past the Red House and into the woods. It followed the east side of the river to the Plymouth–Boston road in what was now Hanover, at the corner of Routes 139 and 53.

My mother had arrived for the weekend soon after Philippe's accident, and I convinced her to come walking in the woods with me to look for the road. Except for her hair's having gone completely white, my mother had aged little since I was a teenager. Even more athletic than she was when I was a child, she wore hiking boots most of the year. It was a late-summer day, and we walked over damp ground, a path of pine straw and oak leaves. We followed a few logging trails, surveying the land for a large sunken swath. Betty had said that we would know it when we saw it—the years of travel on the road had sunk it into the earth like a small canyon. We talked about nothing particular, a house that was being built a mile away, a coyote I had seen in the field the week before, and the mockingbird (perhaps the great-great-grandson of the one we had heard as children) that had learned to imitate Kim yelling *"Phi-leep!"*

"They're gone," my mother said, "but I can still hear her warning him." Then she sighed. "Everything changes."

"Except the mockingbird," I said.

"No, seriously," my mother said. "It's what happens." "The only thing you can count on," I remembered her saying during my childhood, one of many homilies, "is that nothing stays the same." I found this ironic, because it seemed that a lot of things were the same; my mother and father had spent a large part of their lives trying to keep the Red House just as it was when Richard Warren Hatch sold it to them. Of course, they had failed at this task, but at least she was admitting it.

In 1903, a few years after Roentgen discovered the X-ray, a French physicist, René-Prosper Blondlot, discovered the far more powerful N-ray. Named after the town of Nancy, where they were discovered, N-rays were invisible to the naked eye, yet when properly transmitted allowed scientists to see objects in dark or dimly lit rooms. Emitted by a wide variety of common sources, N-rays, when passed through prisms, increased the exactness of vision. In other words, the discovery of the N-ray promised to revolutionize the properties of sight.

Dozens of scientists confirmed the existence of the N-ray in their laboratories, and more than three hundred papers on the topic were published in the months following their discovery. Scientists claimed that N-rays enhanced vision and magnified sparks or flames.

But N-rays, it turns out, do not exist. In 1904, the science magazine *Nature,* skeptical of Blondlot's claims, sent American physicist Robert W. Wood to investigate the N-ray. Wood outed Blondlot as a fraud, writing that he and his associates suffered from "self-induced visual hallucinations."

It struck me as odd that two scientific contemporaries Roentgen and Blondlot had "discovered" similar rays—one of them turning out to revolutionize modern medicine, and the other to be a complete hoax. Tragically, the person who believed in the N-ray the most was Blondlot himself: soon after his exposure and discredit, Blondlot suffered from spells of madness that eventually led to his death. If Blondlot succeeded at anything, it was to believe in something that did not exist, and to convince others to follow him in his myth. Sometimes I wondered if my family had fallen under the spell of a myth as well.

We walked over a slight incline where we could see a curve in the river between the trees. "I used to tell Suzy a story," I said, "of you being a shipbuilder down by the river."

"Really?" my mother asked.

"Yeah, you were a shipbuilder, and you wore men's clothes, but everyone knew you were a woman. You were the only woman. But you were also sort of the boss. All the shipbuilders were in love with you. That's how you got them to work so hard."

"When did you tell these stories?"

"You know, at night, when we used to hold hands."

"And why did they fall in love with me?"

"Because you were so beautiful and tough."

"Oh, I am not!" she said, but she had walked right into it.

"Yes, you are—we all think you are."

"Well, I never feel very tough." And I realized then that she was right. From her perspective, she had just been trying to survive. This was the river that ran through her, underneath all the toughness, the icy exterior. "I'm not tough," she said.

Our trail wound down an incline and intersected with another, forming a cross. When we reached the middle, I looked to my left and saw the trail leading toward the river, Hanover, and the Route 3 bridge. I noticed that this path ran through the middle of a larger, submerged valley. Two soft cliffs of soil cut evenly twenty feet across from each other ran the length of the forest. This small valley was too even to have been left by a glacier. Around it and in its wake were white pine and scrub oak that I knew were more than a hundred years old. It was the ancient road, and we were standing in the middle of it. I turned and looked behind me. The remnant of the road stretched over the hill in the direction of the Red House—it was giant, vast.

"There's the road," I said, drawing my arm across the trees toward its subtle imprint.

The Land
1932–1935

Tracy Hatch, Betty Hatch, and Rosella Ames

Campers at archery class

On Monday morning, clouds started to form on the North River Day Camp, but the sky cleared for a perfect Indian Day for the Marshfield Girl Scouts. After opening circle, Capt. Day, officer of the day, led the girls to Hatch's big barn, where Mrs. Tracy Hatch had assembled some very interesting Indian relics, among them a skeleton and rare arrow heads.

While the older girls had high tide swimming, Thyra Vickery showed the younger ones how to carve Indian totem poles. After a snack of crackers and milk, morning classes met. Mrs. Hatch had charge of archery and Captains Day and Ames had camp craft.

Luncheon tasted very delicious under the pine trees and during rest hour, some very interesting Indian legends were read.

After this, each patrol dramatized what might have taken place on the hill 300 years ago. The spectators witnessed a massacre, a peace pipe ceremony, a trading post and the antics of a medicine man.

The low tide swimmers went to the river just before closing circle at which Pauline Brett sang an Indian song.

> —"Girl Scouts Had North River Day (Marshfield Maidens Presented Very Attractive Program at Their Camp Last Monday)," *Marshfield Mariner*, 1932

From 1932 to 1935, Tracy and Betty Hatch ran a summer Girl Scout camp called Wy Sibo, an Indian-sounding name they invented to mean "Peaceful River." The location—woods, marshes, hunting cabin—provided a perfect environment. The river was bottle-glass brown, the color of root beer. The tides changed every six hours: dead low and flood high.

The camp ran from 9 A.M. to 5 P.M., the beginning of July through the end of August, and included approximately thirty-five girls and five instructors or "captains." Cost: ten cents per day. Location: "The Cabin, North River Farms, Marshfield. Tel 238-2." There was a Transportation Committee, a Holly Troop, and a Pine Cone Troop. Each girl needed a health certificate to swim and a note signed by her parents. Campers were to bring a tin plate, cup, knife, fork, spoon, a notebook, a pencil, a rope, suitable camping clothes (i.e., gym suits, middy and bloomers, wrap) and, if going swimming, a bathing suit, towel, and cap.

Swimmers were divided with colored caps: Red Cap (nonswimmers—water not over head); Yellow Cap (beginners—must be able to swim twenty-five yards); Green Cap (intermediates—must be able to swim fifty yards); Blue Cap (swimmers—tread water

thirty seconds, float motionless); Advanced Caps (perform a dive
in good form, swim a hundred yards using side and one other standard stroke, witness artificial respiration, swim fifty feet on their
back, using legs only, and recover an object in six to eight feet of
water by means of surface dive); White Caps (Junior and Senior
Life Savers).

And there were other rules:

> *Hang bathing suits on line provided in the Temple of
> Trees. Clothes clips will be found in a bag at the line. Put
> all your equipment in the Treasure chests to be found in the
> Temple of Trees. Leave* NOTHING *on the porch or in the
> Cabin.*

Waterfront Rules:
1. Anyone breaking waterfront rules forfeits ALL
   swimming privileges for the rest of the season.
2. Check your tag! At beginning of swimming period
   before entering water turn red side out. At close of
   swimming period turn white side, with name on it,
   out. No scout shall turn another's tag.
3. Swim only after health certificate has been checked
   by swimming counselor.
4. Do not swim when stomach is upset.
5. Do not enter the water until at least two hours have
   elapsed after eating.
6. Swim during swimming periods only.
7. Do not enter the water until the signal is given by
   the swimming counselor.
8. Always swim with a buddy.
9. Stay in your own swimming area.
10. Dive only in water of known depth.
11. Get out of water when chilled or tired.
12. Do not swim during menstruation.

Besides swimming, daily camp activities typically included: Archery, Camp Craft, Story Hour, Dramatization, Flag Raising, Password Service, Snack, Lunch, Rest Hour, Do What You Please If Quiet Hour, Retreat, Auction in the Cathedral of Pines, First Aid, Signaling, Fire Building and Prevention, Artificial Respiration, Pyramids, Canoeing, Nature Walk, Flag Lowering. Lunch was banana-and-peanut salad or banana bobs with extra bacon; lettuce salad with mayonnaise; or rye-bread-and-butter sandwiches; milk; s'mores.

Camp began and ended with the singing of songs, written by the Hatches and others, detailing the epic of the Wy Sibo Camp:

> *There is a cabin on a little hill*
> *'Round which the pine trees murmur lovingly.*
> *At night the stars keep watch when all is still,*
> *And sleepy song birds chirrup cozily.*
> *By day one sees the sparkling river flow*
> *On which a thousand ships sailed out to sea;*
> *From morning mist to sunset afterglow*
> *It sings the song of days that used to be.*
> *Where flame of Council fires cast ruddy darts*
> *On Red Men's tepees hid among the trees*
> *There stands this cabin dear to all hearts*
> *That know it. Cabin, let the wand'ring breeze*
> *Bear you the Girl Scouts' love and hope that long*
> *Your logs may echo their laugh and song*

Photos taken the first year of the camp show ten tan-faced girls posed in baggy cargo shorts before rows of gladiolus; girls arranged by height beside a flagpole in front of a row of pines; grouped in a line at the edge of water as someone completed a dive, feet and legs a blur entering the water; girls in bloomers pulling archery bows; or sitting with their shiny knees together at the cabin porch, holding tin cups. Girls with names like

Winifred, Dorothea, Doris, Esther, Olive, Eula, Oleana, Lois, Lorraine, Thyra, Gertrude, Verna, Pansy, Pauline.

Their favorite captain was a woman named Cappy Day.

In one camp photo, Betty Hatch sits with her back against one of the log poles of the cabin porch. Her back turned to the camera, she looks indifferently over her shoulder. She has a strong, serious face with dark eyes and high cheekbones. Tracy sits to her right, his hands resting on his knees. He wears a white sleeveless shirt and trousers, the cuffs lit by the sun. His blond hair is slicked back, and he smiles. Betty has her legs turned toward him, wearing a short white dress pulled up her thigh; she holds a cup in her lap. Some distance away, as if retreating down the hill, sits a Model A Ford with a rumble seat, a spare tire strapped to its back. In all other pictures, they are separate—Betty in a canoe with a Red Cross swimming suit, Tracy instructing archery. But it was clear, through their posture, through their presence in so many photos, that the camp was their mutual endeavor, something they created out of the myths and natural resources of the land.

On July 3, 1934, the "Password Service" was recited by a Captain Mrs. McMillan: "Our password for today is a little French word 'Voila'—Behold—See—and I will give you two short Bible verses found in Psalms—'Behold and see the work of the Lord.' 'Be still and know that I am God.'"

Day camp, the next week, proceeded as follows:

PROGRAM

July 10, 1934

9:00–9:15	*Flag raising and opening ceremony*
	Password Ceremony—Cappy Day
	Announcements—Officer of the Day—Mrs. Hatch.
	Patrols in Council
9:15–10:00	*Hike Cribbage.*

10:00–10:45	Low Tide Swimming (Red and Yellow Caps)
	First aid for High Tide Swimmers (Green and Blue caps)
10:45	Snack
10:45–11:15	Fire Building—Troop Project
11:15–12:00	Archery—Mrs. Hatch.
	Camp craft—Capt. Ames, Cappy Day
12:00–1:00	Cooks prepare lunch
	Free time for patrols
1:00	Lunch
1:30–2:00	Absolute quiet
2:00–2:30	Do what you please, if quiet, Court of Honor. Shop
	Library
2:30–3:30	Dramatize what might have happened on this hill 300 yrs ago
3:30–4:00	Name Camp, Choose Camp Color and Camp Song
4:00–4:15	High Tide Swimming (Green and Blue Caps)
	First Aid for low Tide swimmers (Red and Yellow Caps)
4:45	Retreat. Change Color Guard

Break Camp

Yet, after all the expenses and the dime dues were added up, the Wy Sibo's profit for 1934 was $2.86. There were also rumors— some girls got polio swimming in the mill ponds, and all water was suddenly suspect. There were rumors townwide of strife between Hatches and Hatch relatives. "Hatches," a neighbor said, "have a history of disputes and deafness."

Yet, because of Tracy and Betty, the mill road was flanked each spring with daffodils, tulips, and stands of jonquils. The bulbs, planted randomly and out of habit by Betty, flowered into sprays of color that ran around the mill pond, the streambed, and past the mill itself, which filled the air with sawdust. The flowers returned each year, long after the Girl Scout camp closed and the flower farm business dried up; long after Tracy died and Betty remarried and moved away. It was this beautifully flow-ered road that connected the Red and White Houses to the mill, the town, the highway, the outside world; it was also the road that allowed the world to enter.

Thirteen

Israel H. Hatch, by Sears Gallagher

In January 2000, I got up the nerve to call Richard Warren Hatch's older son, Richard Warren Hatch Jr. My hesitation in part had to do with myth—the stories I had heard about Dick Jr.—and the assumptions bred out of years of living with those stories. Some describe him as a "philosopher," with a Zen-like calm; a person completely at peace with himself. Some said he was "different" or "a character," which in New Englandese could mean anything from having an offbeat sense of humor to being a full-blown nutcase. As long as I can remember, Dick Jr. was also always described as brilliant and "an inventor," a man who held more than twenty-five patents, a man with an "artistic temperament."

On the phone, Dick Jr.'s voice was low and pleasant. In his semiretirement, he lived in Maine, where he now repaired antique clocks. The background noise of that first phone call included the cacophonous bong of clocks in the background all striking the hour of four.

I introduced myself as "Sarah Messer, the daughter of Ronald Messer, who bought the Red House." He recognized me as "one of the twins."

I learned that Richard Warren Hatch Jr. was the father of seven children from two marriages. Though it was true that he had all those patents to his name, he had received a degree in English literature from Brown University. He worked in metallurgy on the U.S. nuclear attack submarines the *Nautilus* and the *Sea Wolf*, and for the Foxboro Company, inventing mechanical devices and logic systems—i.e., early computer technology. "You know, zeros and ones," he said.

I told him I was calling because I was writing a book. He asked me if this book had anything to do with a "certain will," making a pun; I said yes, quoting the Walter Hatch will regarding the house being passed down through "my heirs forever."

Even in this early conversation, Dick Jr. made it clear that he mourned the loss of the house. He believed that his father had never needed to sell the house for money. "He sold it," Dick Jr. said, "because he couldn't get along with Betty Hatch after his brother Tracy died."

"The day my father called me and told me the Red House had been sold," he continued, "I sat down and cried."

Despite his friendly and confessional tone, the conversation was still somewhat awkward. Several times, Dick Jr. said that I could certainly come up and talk to him but he wasn't sure if he had anything to say.

In a second conversation, to arrange a meeting, his tone was cautious. "You know how I feel about the Red House, right?"

"Well, not exactly," I said.

"It is true that I was very upset when the house was sold, but I never want to go back there. My family is very well settled here in Maine. The Red House is behind me, in the past."

My drive from Marshfield to Maine was seventies flashback mixed with a bad horror flick: stores selling stained glass, wooden seagulls, miniature lobster traps, moccasins, lawn ornaments of housewives' rear ends. I passed stores in the shape of giant Indians, wrecked ships, wheels of cheese. I passed busted neon bar signs, Harley-Davidson riders with braided beards, three girls in parkas jumping on a Dumpster behind a Shop 'n Save; I passed dark stretches of spruce, abandoned stoves in front of houses covered in plastic.

I turned off Route 1 onto 27, winding through Wiscasset, past a tepee on the roadside advertising "Native Arts" and, just beyond it, a placard with the block letters NEW, BIG, X-TRA beside a giant pile of dirty snow and a dented mailbox. The air smelled of melting snow, the beginning of spring, each day growing longer. Route 27 was a string of red taillights, stop-and-go, up the crest of a hill. The sky seemed gray for hours, a slow darkening, and I was reminded of falling asleep in the back of my father's old Suburban, the White Whale, on trips north when I was a child, all the houses staring out at the freeway as the whale drove past.

Coincidentally, Dick Jr. lived very close to where Kim and Philippe had settled after the restoration of the Red House. They had moved to Boothbay Harbor and bought the Mount Pisgah Lodge, a burned-out structure that was named, I assumed, for the mountain in the Bible that Moses climbed to see the Promised Land. A mysterious fire had occurred in the house, burning a hole through three floors, but many of the five bedrooms, the screened sleeping porches, the industrial kitchen, basement, dining room, and attic remained intact.

"We were able to buy it for twenty thousand, including a half acre of land," Kim had told me over the phone.

"How could you do that?" I said, thinking, *After, you know, everything.*

"It was a coup," Kim said, and I knew what she meant: if they hadn't bought the lodge, they wouldn't have been able to live in Boothbay Harbor.

Kim made most of her money now as an artist. When I arrived, I met her in town at a gallery that was opening a show of her paintings called "Just Desserts." For two months, Kim had kept French pastries frozen in a coffin freezer in the basement while she worked on the paintings—a series of tiny oils. "Philippe kept wanting to eat them," she said, "but they were my models, and by the time I was done, they were sort of freezer-burned."

Their station wagon was parked in front of the gallery with a stovepipe tied to its roof. Philippe came out to greet me.

"Hey, check this out, do you know how much these cost? I found this one on the side of the road," he said, patting the pipe. He hardly limped at all anymore—the toe surgery a seamless success, the nerves, bone, and skin completely restored. Kim and Philippe and I got in the car and we drove in and out of the Maine coves, the rocky points, trying to waste time before the opening.

At the Hidden Harbor Wharf restaurant, we ordered a fried-scallop basket and a fried-combo basket of clams, shrimps, scallops, cod, onion rings, and French fries. Each basket came with a tiny plastic cup of coleslaw and a cup of tartar sauce. Spots of grease appeared like clouds over the Maine shoreline printed on the placemats.

"How's Mount Pisgah?" I said.

"Good," Kim said. "It's almost completely finished." Philippe used a tomato garnish to scoop up the last bits of fried batter and shovel them into his mouth.

I knew what had gone into saving the lodge—that they had spent days sweeping and shoveling burned furniture, pushing wheelbarrows of charred junk off the porch into a rented Dumpster; that doors were removed and plastic was stapled over holes, the light bulbs flickering as if in a hurricane. I knew that for months all their cooking had to be done in a makeshift kitchen on a two-burner hot plate, and that Philippe had hauled water in ten-gallon plastic jugs and propped them up over the sink. I wondered if they would spend the rest of their lives restoring houses.

They had said the lodge was almost finished, but when I arrived that night, everything in the house smelled burned. Kim's show had been a success—she had sold eight small paintings. After hours of meeting and greeting, we agreed to turn in early.

That night, I slept in the attic, where the crooked chimney rose through the floor to the roof. Layers of plywood and two-by-fours skirted the chimney where the fire had eaten away through the floor. After setting my backpack down, I knelt at the side of the narrow bed and put my face into the sheets. They were drenched in the smell of mothballs, Chantilly powder, and soot. A single bulb twisted on a strand of cloth wiring above the bed.

Recently, my sister Bekah told me about her nightmare. She dreamed that Israel H. Hatch was angry and was slowly killing off every member of our family. "He was mad that you're writing the book," she said.

"Are *you* mad that I am writing the book?" I asked, but she didn't answer.

"Are you?" I pushed.

"Well," she said after a long pause, "I'm just afraid that someone is going to get hurt."

And I wondered what she meant by that. I wondered whether she thought that the book would rupture some of the myths that our family held dear. Or maybe she was thinking not of our family but of the Hatches—Dick Jr., or the ghost of his father or his great-grandfather. Israel, in her dream, was a menacing figure.

Sarah Messer

"He killed Kim," she said.

"He would never do that," I said. "Israel would never kill anyone." As if I knew him.

This had ended the discussion between us. But because I had read Israel's notebooks and diaries, I felt I did know him. I had read his personal letters—those he wrote and received—his diary and cash book, words not necessarily intended for an audience. I had read each drop in barometric pressure he had recorded, each change of wind outside the house. I had followed his handwriting, his notes on his ancestors, out the door of the Red House and into the larger world of saved historical documents and institutionalized history. It is true I had something of a crush on Israel. Whenever I found a new scrap of paper with his handwriting on it, in an archive or somewhere in the house, my heart raced.

Later, I heard a thump on the roof of Mount Pisgah, from a tree or wind, and imagined footsteps walking over me, the entire house caving in. I woke in the iron bed with its rusted springs. When I spread my arms to either side of my body, they fell over the sides of the mattress. I heard the sloshing of water, and I imagined someone sitting in a washtub on top of the roof, bathing. It sounded as if the whole house were being washed down with water, the way Kim had told me to hold the hose on the bunkhouse kerosene tank the night it burned.

———

The next morning, I called Dick Jr. from Mount Pisgah. His house was a twenty-minute drive away. He said he was leaving to deliver a clock and I should call him back at twelve-thirty, when he would give me directions to his house. When I called back at the appointed time, he gave me specific instructions— the long bridge across the river and landmarks of several antique barns, the road where I should turn. "What time should I come by?" I asked. "Two-thirty," he said, bluntly.

Dick Jr. informed me that his son Josh was going to be present at the interview. "He is very upset that the house was sold out of the family—he is very interested in hearing what you have to say." Josh would be bringing his wife and their son and new baby.

"Can I bring my sister?" I asked.

"Sure," he said.

I hung up the phone, not sure what to do with the next two hours. The conversation had felt confrontational, as if all of us were revolving around the ghost of Richard Warren Hatch.

Part of my hesitation had to do with my own shame at being involved, however tangentially, in some sort of interrupted legacy—even though the house had been bought and sold legally between competent adults.

From a young age, I had been instructed by my father in the "specialness" of the place, but it was a specialness we had bought. In this sense, my father was perhaps living out what the American dream offered—adopting a different class status, and adopting the family that had sold him that status as well.

One might imagine that this transference was because of a lack—a simple lack of traceable old family documents on either my mother's or my father's side of the family. Yet this too is untrue. I had recently spent two years near my father's relatives in the Midwest; visiting my grandmother's house, I discovered that she was a meticulous pack rat. In the basement I had found many old photographs, letters, and spelling books. My father hailed from generations of farmers, just like the Hatches. The difference was that the Messers were migrant workers who rented the land they farmed and the houses in which they lived; the Hatches were inextricably linked to a piece of soil, an owned place. Whereas owning the Red House seemed to elevate my family to a status of wealth, the Hatches, in the writings of Richard Warren and others, always refer to their ancestors as "gentleman farmers," meaning "landowner," or "gentry," which is different from "migrant farmer."

When the Pilgrims came to Plymouth, they were looking for their own version of the Promised Land. But as religious leader William Bradford says in his account, they had no Mount Pisgah, no place from which to visualize their destiny.

When I thought about Mount Pisgah, I didn't think about the Bible passage; I thought instead about what William Bradford had written: "Neither could they, as it were, go up to the top of Mount Pisgah to view from this wilderness a more goodly country to feed their hopes; for which way soever they turned their eyes (save upward to the heavens) they could have little solace or content in respect of outward objects."

For my father, the Red House might have been a metaphoric Mount Pisgah—a place from which he could view a new world. But the Hatches, descending from ancestors who arrived in Scituate at the time of Bradford's writing, were perhaps unable to view the house in the same way. Dick Jr. had said that there would be three generations of Hatches at his house that afternoon—three generations, related by blood, none of whom had owned the Red House. Dick Jr., despite all his attachment, had only spent summers there.

Kim informed me, crankily, that she had a headache.

"You're still coming with me, aren't you?" I asked in a pleading tone.

"Yeah, I'm coming." She was wearing a long kimono beneath an unzipped Polartec fleece jacket. The table was crowded with bowls of Brazil nuts, a small crate of clementines, a plate of salt, a French box of sugar, a cordless phone, and a tub of Veggie Butter. Kim and Philippe had been talking about a new diet they were starting, inspired by a book about "eating for your blood type," which listed menus and philosophies of life based on O+ or A– or AB blood.

"Philippe and I are the same blood type, which is convenient," Kim said; their strict vegetarian diet was ideal for type A's. Kim told me that my blood type, type O, was the oldest in the world, predating agrarian societies. "Your bloodline is a hunter," she said. "You should do a lot of running and sports where you throw things."

The Veggie Butter tasted like plastic, but we all spread it anyway onto pieces of spelt toast.

———•———

Richard Warren Hatch Jr.'s house was a neat Cape with a red pickup truck parked between the house and a two-car garage. The house was visible from Newcastle Road, but set back a ways, with a sweeping view of the Dyer River—a name I realized I had written as "Dire" in my phone notes. A path had been shoveled from the driveway to the entrance of the house, a porch with a very neatly stacked half-cord of wood. A small brass plaque next to the door read "Mr. and Mrs. Richard Warren Hatch Jr."

Dick Jr. appeared before me, a very tall man, more than 6'5", with dark eyes, whiskered eyebrows, and dark, slightly graying hair. He was wearing a red-plaid shirt and jeans. We were all trying to be nice. He said he remembered Kim, though the last time he had seen her she was ten years old.

"I always thought you were a cute kid," he said.

"So—you repair clocks now?" I asked. Dick Jr. explained that originally the clocks were just a side hobby. But then word got around, and as the requests started building up, he started to charge people for repairs.

We began a tour of clocks, moving into the living room. Some of them, he pointed out, were too beautiful, or valuable, to dismantle.

"This is the John Bailey," Hatch said, pointing to a grandfather clock in the corner of the room. I knew that this clock was a Hatch family relic that had been passed down with the house. The clock's case was plain blond wood, the name "John Bailey" painted in black across the face. Right below twelve o'clock was a small circle with just one hand, dangling like a spinner on a board game. It pointed to two words, one above the other at the edges of the circle: "strike," "silence." Hatch opened the door in the body of the clock, where two large weights hung on chains. Inside the door was a list of owners since the first, Israel Three, who bought it in 1785: "Israel Hatch, Deacon Joel Hatch, Israel H. Hatch, Harris B. Hatch, Richard Warren Hatch, Richard Warren Hatch Jr."

Dick Jr. pointed out other items in the room that were "from the Red House"—a painting of a ship launching, two brass candlesticks, a side table, and a bed-warmer with a partially charred wooden handle.

"This caught on fire?" I asked, trying to imagine when, what year, what season it happened, what room in the house, who held the handle, and who got burned.

"Oh yes," Hatch said, "everything caught on fire back then."

We roamed portions of the small house—select rooms, not really a tour. It seemed as if we should have been sitting down to talk, but we didn't. Dick Jr. repeated that Josh was upset that the house had been sold out of the family.

Finally, we moved past the kitchen and stepped down into a sunken dining room. One wall of the long room was all windows, offering a view of a sloping snowy lawn, the frozen marsh, and the river. Dick Jr. sat at one end of a long table set with woven maroon placemats. To his back was a bookcase filled with framed pictures of his children. He held one up and began naming all seven. Kim remarked that our family and the Hatches both had daughters named Rebekah and Sarah—that our Rebekah was actually named after a Hatch.

"We're all 'the oldest,'" claimed Kim, sitting with her back to the windows. She meant that Dick Jr. was R.W.'s older son, and that she was her mother's eldest daughter, as I was my mother's eldest. Richard Warren Hatch Sr. had married twice and had children from his first marriage; our father was married twice and had children from both, as did Dick Jr.

Dick Jr. seemed more interested in the lineage of Hatch poetry. He held two manila folders in his hands. In the center of the table, next to a vase of flowers, I noticed a typewritten manuscript titled "The Hatches and the Red House," written by his cousin Priscilla Gladwin, who seemed to have taken over for Richard Warren Hatch as the family historian. She had written another volume, "Uncle Dick," after R.W.'s death in 1985.

Dick Jr. smiled. "In her letter to me, she says it isn't a love story" (implying a love story between a woman and her uncle). "*It is*," he said.

He flipped through the pages and landed on a poem of Richard Warren Hatch's titled "Warning in November," which had been published in the *Saturday Review of Literature* and later reprinted in *The Best Poems of 1935*:

> *The uncreative soul must feed*
> *On life; the empty heart*
> *Turns from itself, its desperate need*
> *Transformed, its secret art*
>
> *Corrupt: these cannot longer bear*
> *In silence their disease,*
> *Nor face the autumn everywhere—*
> *With cold hills and stark trees. . . .*

Priscilla Gladwin included the poem to shed some insight into R.W.'s divorce from Harriet Hildreth, Dick Jr.'s mother. "He must have known anguish . . ." she wrote. "Of all the reasons I have encountered for shooting birds out of the air, this is the first expression of its being an act of hate, bitter defeat, futility and hurt." And, true, the last lines of the poem were anguished:

Beware, O wild things flying south!
Beware! I watch your flight!
Defeat is bitter in my mouth
I fear the winter night . . .

Oh, I have seen your wild hearts stilled,
And I have known your pain.
I have been empty . . . I have killed . . .
And I shall kill again.

Dick Jr. pointed to the last lines, as if indicating that the poem was a window into the emotional tornado that was Richard Warren Hatch Sr.

Dick Jr. was direct about his troubled relationship with his father, the strife before the divorce. When I asked him to tell me about his summers in the Red House, he said, "I could tell you some raunchy stories," but then didn't elaborate.

He showed me some of his own poetry, some inspired by the landscape of "the Farm," as he called the Red House. He spoke of being a child and loving the marshes and woods, the mud flats near the Union Street Bridge where his father used to take him digging for arrowheads. At this moment in the conversation, Dick Jr. seemed almost boyish, his hands lifting up off the table to grasp mine, his eyebrows rising. "We used to ride our bikes down Union Street, and at the end there, where it met Route 139, there was nothing, just the 'Standish Trading Post.'"

"Why do you think your father was so unhappy?" I asked, changing the subject. I felt off my game in the conversation. Hatch trusted Kim more, I thought—she lived in Maine; she was a craftsperson; she knew about boats. Several times, Hatch had looked at me and squirreled his eyebrows as if to imply jokingly, "Are you nuts?"

I dropped the ball a number of times, and Kim picked it up. "Well, my father was unhappy because he always had a monkey on his back." I let the lead bounce off my shoulder and roll under the table. I moved on to my next question—something that brought us back to the house.

"Wait, what was the monkey on his back?" Kim asked, and I thought, *Oh yeah, right, monkey, what was the monkey?!*

"The monkey on his back," Hatch said, "is that he always wanted to be a *doctor*." And he described his father's insecurity, that the novels never did very well, and that his father essentially considered himself a failed writer. "He always said his writing 'fell between two stools,' " Dick Jr. said.

It seemed that Dick Jr. felt this way too about the novels, preferring the poetry. "The children's books," he added, "were wonderful, and we heard those stories for years before they were written down." He was referring to *The Curious Lobster* and *The Curious Lobster's Island* books. The personalities of Mr. Lobster, Mr. Badger, and Mr. Bear might have embodied Hatch himself—self-described as rebellious, curious, unsettled with the norm. "He was never satisfied with himself," Dick Jr. said. "He was always looking outside himself for things to be different."

We had been with Dick Jr. for approximately a half-hour. Throughout the visit, Kim kept repeating threads of a conversation she seemed to be having with herself: "We are the mongrels here," or "We are the interlopers." After one such comment, Dick Jr.'s son and daughter-in-law entered with two children, a six-year-old boy and an infant girl.

Josh Hatch was in his twenties, bearded, with a friendly, open face, dark eyes, and finer, more delicate features than his father. His wife had her dark blond hair pulled back in a white scrunchie, and she held the very tiny, red-faced Anna before her; Roy stood beside them. The entire family, except Anna, wore jeans and Timberline boots.

I began to explain myself to Josh, saying that I was writing a book based in part on an article I had written for *Yankee*

Sarah Messer

Magazine a few years back. "Oh, I read that article," said Josh, adding nothing more.

Dick Hatch Jr., seconded by Josh, asked what the book would be *about*.

"It's about growing up with someone else's history," I said. "It's the story of the house. . . ." I explained, as I had earlier, that Kim and I grew up in this house with wills and documents that didn't belong to us, yet, because it was where we grew up, we had no knowledge that this might be peculiar or strange. "There were daguerreotypes of *your* great-grandfather on the fireplace mantels," I said, looking at Josh, "not our."

"We're a mongrel group," Kim repeated.

I asked Josh how he felt about the house's being sold. We were now all sitting around the long table; the sun was beginning to set beyond the marsh. Josh said that he was upset, particularly after he had read the manuscript *The Hatch Family and the Red House,* by Priscilla Gladwin. At first, he had been looking at the manuscript to get names for his new child, but then he discovered the family story of the house. "I felt disappointed," he said, "like I had been left out of something." I got the feeling he wasn't sure the sale had needed to happen.

"The house didn't need to be sold because of money," Dick Jr. said again, as he frequently did in conversations about the house.

Josh admitted that he had tried to visit the Red House the previous summer, but only made it as far as the Hatch Mill before he chickened out and turned around. "That mill was in pretty bad shape," he said.

"Well, if you had gone just a bit farther, you would have seen the house," I said. "You should come see it."

"*I'll* never go back," Dick Jr. repeated. "I have no desire to. . . . It's in the past." Then he looked down the table at Josh. "I wouldn't go if I were you," he said. "It's too upsetting."

"Well, we're different," Josh said. "I'd like to see it."

314

"Just don't expect to go there and remain unchanged," Dick Jr. said. "The place has a pull to it."

Kim turned to Dick Jr. and asked the obvious question: "How do you feel about our father?"

Dick Jr. said that he had nothing against him personally—he was just a person buying a house. Kim told the story of the first day she met Richard Warren Hatch, the day our father decided to buy the house. She explained how she always felt they had been "picked," so to speak, as the "right people" for the house. Someone turned a light on in the room. Kim leaned back in her chair with one leg crossed over the other.

"Did you spend much time with your grandfather?" she asked Josh.

"No, not really," Josh replied.

"I feel like he thought we were the right people for the house, you know, to be its 'caretakers.'" Then she told the story of finding the arrowhead in the grass. "I think he saw it as some sort of sign," she offered. "I don't know if your father told you—there are eight children in our family."

Dick Jr. smiled, saying something about karma. And then the conversation split—I began talking to Josh around a vase of flowers arranged in the middle of the table, while Kim was talking to Dick Jr. about the 1790s ell added to the house after a kitchen fire. Dick Jr. described it as a beautiful old kitchen with a chimney rising through the center of the ell. Apparently his father tore all that down in the late 1950s. "It's strange," Kim said, "that someone so obsessed with the history of the house and its restoration and preservation would rip out a Dutch oven and tear down a chimney."

"He wanted a bedroom," Hatch replied.

I asked Josh how often he'd seen his grandfather. Kim and Dick Jr. were talking about the fate of the eighteen elm trees that were on the property in the 1950s. "Now there's only one left,"

Kim was saying. The rest had succumbed to Dutch elm disease or storms.

"Nineteen eighty-six. We moved in 1986, I think," Josh was saying.

"After your grandfather died?"

"You know how he died, don't you?" Dick Jr. interrupted. "He walked into the ocean!"

"Are you sure it was a suicide?" I asked.

"Yes, I'm sure."

"How are you sure?"

Dick Jr. shuffled through the poems again and brought out the "Uncle Dick" manuscript. In it were several letters Priscilla had received at the end of Richard Warren's life. One described how Ruth had been taken away from him, and he described himself as "furious and helpless and blind." Nowhere in the letter did it say he was going to end it all, but the tone was one of desperation. I looked at the letter, which was typed with a frayed ribbon, and noticed that many words and letters of words were missing, adding to its urgent and fragmented tone. The letter was signed "Love," and then with the fat scrawled initials: R.W.H.

"I wish we had known he was that bad," Dick Jr. said. "No one knew."

I mentioned a letter my father had received from R.W.H.— he had gone from owning a house and acres to not even owning a shingle over his head, and he believed the next "compression" would be the grave.

"Why didn't you tell us?" Dick Jr. asked, but then made a swatting gesture with his hand, implying, "It's all over now."

Josh and his family were getting ready to leave, so I took a folder out of my bag and placed it on the table. Inside it were the series of letters between Deacon Joel Hatch and his son Joel Jr. and grandson Joel Henry when they moved to Michigan. Josh stood before the folder of his ancestor's letters and flipped very gently through the paper, looking at the handwriting, a small drawing, remnants of red wax. I pointed out the letter that Joel Henry wrote to his grandfather informing him that his father had died.

"There's this description of how he died," I said. "He had an infectious fever and holes in his tongue the size of a bean."

Roy stood next to his father, watching as we turned the pages. The magnitude of the moment suddenly struck me: Josh was seeing the letters of his great-great-great-grandfather for the first time. Josh had a part of Deacon Joel: the inherited high forehead and long straight nose. I had a part of Deacon Joel: these letters, the wills, and the house. I wondered who was more entitled to own the documents and the house: the person who was related by blood, or the person who had paid money for them? This, I realized, was where the twins of the American Dream—Capitalist Success and Birthright—began to butt heads.

"Look here," Josh said to Roy. "Look how they addressed this letter—it just says 'Deacon Joel Hatch, North Marshfield, Massachusetts.' They knew exactly who he was and where he lived. That was all you had to write back then in order to find somebody."

After Josh left, Dick Jr. wanted to keep talking. He led us through the kitchen and down a flight of unfinished stairs to his basement workshop. It was a typical basement—neat cement floor with small rectangular windows at ground level. Drill presses, table saws, jigsaws, and lathes sat in corners of the room. With this equipment, Hatch made the external wooden clock cases, and all of the intricate metal gears.

Shelves held large and small clocks in different stages of disrepair—some simply faces and gears, others faceless, marble or wood cases. Hand-painted parlor clocks, small mantel clocks, banjo clocks, a clock from an old train station.

"So you're a painter," Hatch said to Kim. "Do you ever do reverse-glass painting?"

"I knew you were going to ask me that," Kim replied. They were talking about a style of tiny landscape painting within a clock case. We moved farther into the workshop, away from the stairs, and stood in front of a large Plexiglas case. Inside it, an inch-wide plastic ribbon ran from a large spool through a series of wheels and pulleys, the crevices of a small machine. Copper tinsel dangle at the edges. "Christmas decoration?" Kim asked.

"No, it prevents static," Hatch said, "I invented this machine for the electronics industry." From what I gathered, the machine made tiny plastic folders that held a hair (1/1000 of an inch) of an electric circuit—all of this having something to do with tension in the wings of airplanes. A poster of the plane Dick Jr. flew during his navy service hung behind us on the wall, along with a faded blueprint of a lobster boat he had designed.

Two cats paced the room, leaping on and off a workbench and pawing at a door. The skeleton of an old grandfather clock hung between exposed two-by-four wall framing. Without its wooden outer case, the clock seemed naked and exposed, its insides made entirely of brass, ticking softly. The scrolled hands moved slowly across the face. In another corner of the room sat the charred case—the remnant, Dick told us, of a house fire. "The clock can be saved," Dick Jr. said, "but the case is hopeless." The case had an empty hole where the face used to be. The panels, the base, and the door were blackened and peeled.

Dick Jr., affectionate now, invited Kim to join him sometime on his lobster boat. He rested his hand on her shoulder. We walked back upstairs, where he continued, proudly, to show us things: an organ in the living room and some sheet music; a Christmas carol he had written. As we headed toward the door, Hatch kept pointing at the ceiling, describing how he had re-designed it in a cathedral style, and how the irregularly pitched angles of the roof made the room better, much more interesting.

On the drive back to Boothbay Harbor, we discussed the four-hour interview and how it had gone. Kim was admittedly over-whelmed. In the car, she talked about how incredible it had seemed to be standing in Dick Jr's. house after all these years.

Part of her self-confessed trauma had to do with being one of the last people—Hatches or Messers—to see Richard Warren Hatch alive. She recounted again his romance with the fishing schooner, slouched in the passenger seat as the roads curved in the dark. Maybe she could have done something.

"Maybe you're giving yourself too much credit?" I asked, thinking about the letters Dick Jr. had shown us.

It was clear to me that Kim felt it was a mistake that we'd ended up with the house. "There was a break in the chain," she said.

What was going to happen to the house? "The Hatches should have the house back. None of us want the house after Mom and Dad die. Maybe Hatches across the country should start a trust to buy it," she speculated.

For some reason, the drive back took far less time than the drive out, and suddenly we were standing in front of a mountain of shaved ice and Maine shrimp at the seafood section of the Shop 'n Save. I watched a woman on the other side of the counter, in a bright-blue cap and apron, lifting a scoop of squid onto a piece of butcher paper laid out on the scale. Their bodies were like deflated party balloons. We were trying to think about dinner, but the conversation persisted of its own volition, even here in the supermarket.

"The thing is," Kim said, "this whole situation is like a book. The Hatches are the book. I mean, they're the paper, the body of the book."

"OK," I said.

"And we're nothing. We're just the cover of the book, or the little piece of cloth on the cover, but none of the contents."

"But the cover of the book is pretty important, don't you

think? I mean, without a cover, a book isn't a book, it's just a pile of paper."

"You know what I mean."

"Well, yeah, it's their history, you're right," I said.

"I still feel like it's their house, like we have no right to it. We've just been watching it for them."

"Yeah, but maybe it took someone outside the Hatch family to see the story and make it into a book, and not just a pile of paper."

"It must be some bizarre karma," Kim said. "Let's get a pound of shrimp and a bag of lemons." And then we were passing through the automatic doors.

"Maybe it was karma, maybe it was necessary," I heard myself saying. "Maybe the house was sick. The monkey on Richard Warren Hatch's back was that he always wanted to be a doctor," I said now, on the verge of a rant. "Maybe the house needed a doctor. Maybe it needed an X-ray. Maybe we are the X-ray."

Out in the parking lot, I realized that the whole time we had been in the store Kim had been pushing a miniature shopping cart meant for children who were pretending to shop with their parents. On a pole rising from its side wobbled a pendant-shaped plastic flag; it read, "Customer of Tomorrow."

Richard Warren Hatch
1934–1965

South bedroom, Red House, during 1959 restoration

Yes, the continuity with the past, the sense of being indissolubly linked to the past not only of one's own forebears but also of all men, of being part of an ongoing current of hope and will and belief, comes only with the accumulation of years. If we really are developing a rootless society, a society of people with no homeplace, if the mania for change is to be the basic criterion for survival . . . what then? It would seem that the aged, always the custodians of the past, will have less and less to be custodians of. . . . The real question: are we as a society on a straight course or traveling in a circle?

—Richard Warren Hatch,
letter to Priscilla Waldron Gladwin, 1964

Even after Tracy fell ill, Richard Warren Hatch continued to argue with his brother and sister in-law about property lines, about access on the quarter-mile mill road. The disputes reached the point where Richard Warren refused to talk to Betty. Gradually, Tracy grew more debilitated by his disease. In 1959, Richard Warren and Ruth moved into the Red House permanently. When Tracy died in 1960, Betty tore down her father-in-law's hunting cabin, where the camp had been, and built a small ranch house. Then she sold the White House and moved up on the hill—farther, but not much farther, away from Richard Warren and Ruth.

Richard Warren set up a forge near the far stone wall and the row of elms, and turned the bunkhouse into a blacksmith shop. In it he made H&L hinges, door clates, and nails similar to the ones originally found in the Red House. Apparently, though, as soon as he had restored the house, he had become dissatisfied with it. "Take an aging crock who once tried his hand at writing, found that his writing fell between two stools, being neither facile enough to be popular nor brilliant enough to be significant, and so turned to the mechanics of art and became an editor in the field of social science; add that he is a pedagog at heart and hence loves to sound off at every opportunity; now throw in some spare time, teasing questions, a still at least partially active mind—and what do you get? Obviously a writer of long-winded letters," Richard Warren Hatch wrote to his niece Priscilla.

When asked by Priscilla, in 1964, to "put down his memoirs" of the old place, he wrote to his niece, "Family history where there is no fame, no national figure, only personal knowledge of people long gone is pure abstraction to the young of today." Her nostalgia-inspired inquiry fueled a prolonged epistolary debate. He wrote:

> An impractical, leaky, hard-to-heat, wooden house: what attraction could it have for a generation guided by modern standards? And 35 acres of what will be a dormitory backyard of the city: where would be the money for taxes? And lastly, I wonder if, with the general rootlessness of our culture, the obsessive compulsion to speed, mobility, and being anywhere but where the individual now is—I wonder if continuity of heritage in terms of a piece of land occupied by one family for 300 years will have any meaning.

He continued to project a disappointing slide-reel of future careless grandkids, none of whom (except perhaps Priscilla herself) had matched his own level of interest in the property. Priscilla would later accuse him of selling his birthright. Hatch rebutted:

> All older people, looking back on life and an era that is gone, like to think someone will be interested in their thoughts; . . . but this generation of grandchildren has not, like me, any connection to another way of life; they have no

memory, no sentiment, no concrete or even symbolic attachment to the old. It would be unreasonable of me to expect them to share my feeling, unreasonable of me to expect them to see the old place as anything except what it is materially—an old house and a piece of land.

And then the debate concluded, with Hatch, of course, having the last word:

Put simply, memoirs derive their interest and validity either from their special family or historical context or from the distinction and genius of the author. Neither our family nor the individuals in it qualify. . . . As to survival here, it is truly a toss-up; sometimes I am privately despairing about it, sometimes confident.

And here endeth my return blast.

Love, Dick

"How many people we each appear to be as we move in and out of relationships," Priscilla wrote after Richard Warren Hatch's death. "It is as if one stood in a many-sided room, every facet of the wall a mirror with a different person reflected in each. Each is oneself, but not the whole self."

Richard Warren Hatch, the ever-faceted, perhaps most enigmatic Hatch, would write, in early 1985, about interplanetary travel—according to Priscilla, it was one of his last forays into literary prose. He had left the Red House twenty years earlier, and must have written the essay half blind in the retirement home, his hearing tinny and distant.

"Report on a Recent Visit" detailed his philosophy of the nature of the universe and an ideal heavenlike "Center" that had no reference points, existing outside of time and space. Chained as he was to the weight of history, a self-confessed atheist with no belief in a concrete or timeless afterlife, "The Center" was Hatch's solution.

The piece, which Hatch called "an essay," read more like a science-fiction fantasy. In a dream or vision, Richard Warren Hatch found himself on a NASA voyage, exploring the depths of space. Separated from his crew, he landed on what he imagined to be a planet; an alien St. Peter met him at a gate. "The Center" was at once a location and nonlocation, a no-place where Hatch had arrived.

"I seem to be at the gate of heaven," Hatch wrote, confronting the man at the gate. The gatekeeper explained that the occupants of "The Center" were "aware of time without ever being slaves to it, never having to be at a certain place or complete an activity by a preordained time."

The gatekeeper continued:

> "Man is so constantly creating crises and the compulsion to cope with them that he must be aware of what he calls day-to-day developments. In short, the concept of time at the Center has for us no implications of pressure of any kind. . . . We are satisfied with our belief that the universe is ageless, timeless."

And then a dialogue ensued between them:

> "Is the Center larger than Earth?"
> "Yes."
> "From what I have been able to see in my short time here there are no signs of its inhabitants. There are no sounds of activity."
> "There are a great many inhabitants. As I have said, there are many entrances to the Center. There are no gates. . . ."

RED HOUSE

The essay ended with the following exchange:

"Is the Center a planet?"
"No."
"It is not in orbit?"
"No. It is the Center."

Fourteen

Red House today

Since 1831, the entrance of Cambridge's Mount Auburn Cemetery has represented a gateway to the River Styx, a passageway to the city of the dead. Built in the Egyptian Revival style, the wooden gate looms, an ornate doorway. It stands in contrast to the buildings on the grounds immediately behind it—a sanded brick French villa and a copy of a sixteenth-century English stone church. Just beyond the gate and the buildings wind newly blacktopped drives that loop into cul-de-sacs and disappear over ridges and fields of graves. Along the edges of the road, small white signs pop up from the immaculately trimmed grass like cartoon bubbles: "Do Not Park Here," "Do Not Park Here," "Do Not Park Here."

I arrived at Mount Auburn to meet Jean Hall, who, after completing her graduate work, had taken a job as assistant director of buildings and structures and director of operations and horticulture. "In other words," she said to me the day before on the phone, "I fix all the broken gravestones. I work in a cemetery now."

It had been four years since I had seen Jean, but in that time she'd remained close to my family. In fact, her brother Ed, who finished the Red House restorations after Philippe's accident, wound up marrying my youngest sister, Jessica. I had called inquiring about the work Jean had done on the house two summers before; she had completed a master's thesis about the house, and I wanted to clarify a few things.

Jean had told me to meet her in the French building, which was also the main office, but I missed the parking lot and got lost in the cemetery roadways. I parked by a row of cherry trees and at the edge of a bank of tombs. Jean would later tell me that these were "receiving tombs," large rooms where remains or coffins were laid out on shelves and family members could enter and visit.

I entered the office building and was greeted by two very heavy oak doors opening to a long receptionist's desk, where a gray-haired woman stood before a registry book. Behind her was a large room filled with desks where a few people milled about. The neatly printed sign on the desk read: "NEXT TOUR, 2:30 p.m." On the wall to the left hung framed maps of the building, the various floors and levels, beneath a portrait of a bearded benefactor. The *Mount Auburn News Letter* fanned out from a wooden basket nailed to the wall.

The building had the feel of a giant corporation, the receptionist a gatekeeper to unknown and hidden goings-on in the far reaches of back rooms, lower levels. I told her that I was there to see Jean, and she said that Jean was in a meeting and would be just a moment. It was a few minutes before I realized that the pamphlets I had seen upon entering concerned interment—Mount Auburn Cemetery was still an active graveyard.

"Discover One of Boston's Oldest Gardens," read one brochure, describing Mount Auburn as "an inspired concept,"

created for the "commemoration of the dead and for the conso-
lation of the living" in a rural cemetery. There was a flier from
the Friends of Mount Auburn offering a "Cremation Workshop," and a pamphlet providing general information about interment space. According to the 1999 annual report, Mount
Auburn had that year facilitated 333 casket interments, 154 cremated remains, and one removal. Total interments since 1831:
90,577. There were lots, single graves, lawn crypts, urn graves,
niches, memorial lots, and garden crypts.

I saw in an open book on the desk that a funeral was planned
for 2:00 p.m. that day, right before the cemetery tour. "Is there
something else I can help you with?" the receptionist asked.

"No," I said, "just looking." *Just browsing at the cemetery
store,* I thought to myself, feeling suddenly awkward and cold on
the polished marble floor. Then Jean appeared on a flight of
stairs, entering the desk-filled room behind the receptionist. Her
hair was long and straight, and she wore loose black slacks that
flounced as she walked.

"Where are you parked?" she asked as we walked out into the
bright parking lot. I pointed over islands of flowering shrubs.
"You can't park there," she said, and I followed her, moved my
car, and joined her in a shiny green truck. "I'll give you the
nickel tour," she said.

"This place began because of America's growing sentimentalism about death," Jean told me as the truck rolled over a hill
and I saw valleys of graves, spotted with elms and other old-
growth trees. One hundred and ninety-seven acres—now famous as an arboretum and a bird sanctuary. "The Victorians
were much more mournful and emotional about death—much
different than the Puritan belief of predestination." Also, Jean
said, in the early 1800s, the city of Boston was growing crowded,
and the old cemetery had a problem "with vapors." The city
came up with the idea of re-creating a "rural cemetery," where
mourners could walk in a beautiful setting and reflect on the

passage of their loved ones. It became, oddly enough, America's first public park, where families came and had picnics at grave sites. "It existed before the Boston Public Gardens," Jean said, and I tried to imagine the Victorian family, in corsets, lace, and muttonchops, strolling among the graves.

We were now climbing slowly up a steep hill; Jean had her arm out the window and waved at another green truck coming the other way.

"That's my crew," she said.

We hadn't talked at all about the Red House—Jean spoke only of gravestones now, driving the truck very slowly along the winding blacktop, and pointing, saying "pudding stone," "colonial revival slate," "marble," "modern slate." She pointed to stones carved with sheaves of wheat. "That person died old, they were 'harvested in late age.'" A lamb, on the other hand, might symbolize a child taken early. "Some people," Jean said, "didn't have a perpetual-care contract, and their tombstones broke, or were buried. Eventually, we had to dig them up and try to repair them, or bury them again."

The road wound around a rising hill, graves to our left and right. I wondered whether the earth might shift and slide the buried coffins downhill. We passed a row of children's graves. "See," Jean said, pointing, "a whole dead family"—sleeping child, broken lily, trapped lily, bent flower, a tiny hand pointing up. Opposite the row of children sat some willow trees and a corral of blockish rectangular stones with faded carvings of draped urns. The stones were streaked with gray and green lines, as if a heavy smoke had fallen over them. "Those used to be white," Jean said. "We're working on a solvent that will clean the stones without hurting the trees, but we haven't found anything that works very well so far."

We passed large statues and obelisks, many tiny versions of the Washington Monument. We passed Faith, Hope, and Charity, and lichen-covered angels. Sixteen white horses and a stringless lute. Jean wheeled the truck around a man-made lake ringed with large willow trees. At the far end of the lake sat the lane of family tombs and mausoleums, some as big as two-car garages, and I felt suddenly as if I had entered a strange housing development, while Jean called out the names of the families.

"In grad school, I started out in preservation carpentry. But mainly I focused on plaster—you know, plaster research, consolidation, conservation. And what I do here could be loosely called preservation of materials."

"So, if someone kicks over a tombstone, they call you?"

"Right."

"And what if a grave opens up?"

"Well, yeah, that too."

We were now perched at the highest point in the cemetery, where the road cinches itself into an eye hook, a tight circle around a giant obelisk dedicated to George Washington, called "Washington's Tower."

"Tomb with a view," Jean said as she turned off the engine and stepped out of the truck. I followed her across the road to a grassy opening between trees that looked out over the city of Boston.

"You can see the entire river valley from here on clear days," she said. In the distance I could see the Boston skyline, the John Hancock Building, and the Prudential Tower, squared off in the distance like stacked Legos. The air was hazy and humid, with a bright, misty cast. "More than sentimentalism," she said, "the cemetery founders really believed they were creating a city of the dead that would look out over all of this—the city of the living."

Two conjoined cities—dead and living. "This one," Jean said, her voice arched, "is the silent city on the hill." As we drove the truck back down the hill, we turned our back on the skyline and descended into the cemetery. I watched a group of tourists clothed in windbreakers plod up the hill, each with his or her own Walkman playing a tape of the cemetery tour. And behind them, a long row of cars topped with flickering orange funeral flags wove toward the gate, slowly making their way out.

———

Over lunch, Jean confessed that she was never happy with the Massachusetts Historical Commission's study of the Red House. We were at an Indian restaurant off Boylston Street, squashed in a two-top near the kitchen, waiters running back and forth behind me, trays clattering. Jean had to lean forward in order to be heard. "Basically, the state supported me in going from house to house and pulling the pants down on the owner's ideas of history."

According to Jean, there was a short list of first-period homes in the Marshfield and Scituate area, but she was also encouraged to include others that were not on the list. The Red House was one of these. Jean had decided to write her master's thesis on the house, but in doing so, she now said, she "opened up a can of worms.

"The academic world of historic preservation is very conservative," she said, "and the process of proving a house is first-period is very scientific.

"The footprint didn't fit," she continued, "and my adviser was narrow-minded. For him, it was either yes or no. Me, I'm not interested in yes or no, I'm interested in the process. I am a process freak."

In the end, Jean's adviser decided that there wasn't enough evidence to prove that the house was first-period. And then there was my father's refusal to X-ray the house.

"So the idea that it was built in 1647 is wrong?" I asked.

"Well, yes, the earliest I would place it is 1680s. Which would still make it first-period."

Jean had looked closely at the house—at the beams, the

framing, the cellar hole, the orientation toward the road and the pond. She admitted that she found early details in the house—the paint evidence, a part of the old chimney, and perhaps one post in what was now my father's office, the room where I had originally found the documents. But these seventeenth-century details were usually right next to eighteenth-century details, which made a diagnosis tricky and confusing. If Jean were a doctor and the Red House a patient, it would have failed major aspects of its physical exam. Not finding the summer beam was like saying that the house was missing a backbone. The house was a mishmash of styles, most of them within the range of the mid- to late eighteenth century, with the occasional seventeenth-century detail thrown in.

If the Red House was indeed the house built by Walter, it was the center of Hatchville and Two Mile, out of which the spokes of inheritance and generations expanded. This would explain why, over time, the Red House had ceased to be the most valuable piece of property: constantly rebuilt and restored for dowager residents and other family members, it couldn't compare to the elegance and privacy of newer Hatch houses in the area.

"In the end, it just got silly," Jean said, describing her battle to prove the Red House's legitimacy to the academic community. "Perhaps I was being too idealistic, but I believed in what I was doing. I thought my job was to advocate and protect without dismissing or romanticizing. Most academic thought in this area is based on the work of a few select people. I began to question the job itself. Finally, I thought, What I am doing? I found that there was not enough evidence to prove the Red House was first-period, but there also wasn't enough to prove that it wasn't. In the end, who really cares?"

"So—my father believes that the house was built in 1646. Did you tell him what you thought?"

"Yeah," Jean said, "I told him, and he didn't really want to hear it, but that's OK." There is a difference, she said, between interpreting history and preserving history—everyone fails at perfect preservation. "The history of built environments would like to be more scientific than it is."

"But according to this science," I said, "the Red House is anachronistic. Putting red-cedar shingles on the Red House is anachronistic. Using Tyvek is anachronistic."

"Right, and using beaded clapboards on that south side is also historically inaccurate," Jean said, but then she stopped herself. "I think your father sees himself as a caretaker in a relationship of stewardship with the Red House. But he also has to live there. The Hatches were anachronistic too—they'd use whatever they could to patch a hole in the wall. I think your father sees himself as someone imbued with this incredible gift, to honor and preserve this place. He's like a shepherd. And I can relate to that. I have felt, at times, like a shepherd too."

———

The night before I met Jean, I had interviewed my father about Richard Warren Hatch's death. My father was packing for a trip. I sat in my parents' bedroom, on the large canopy bed, my back against the headboard. My father moved back and forth—between the bed and the fireplace, traversing the distance between the dresser and the closet. Small piles of folded shirts and pants appeared on either side of my outstretched legs.

How, I had asked him, did the suicide happen? What did he know?

"The last time I saw Dick," my father said, "was in late August of 1985. He had invited your mom and me down to the Cape for lunch." At the time, my father reminded me, Richard Warren Hatch was living in a retirement home in Orleans, and Ruth recently had been taken away to a place where she could have more care.

"How did he seem when you saw him?" I asked.

"He seemed fine," my father said. "Well, he did seem depressed. But we had a nice lunch, crab-salad sandwiches, and everything seemed fine, until he said, 'Now for the real reason I have brought you down here.'"

And then, according to my father, Richard Warren Hatch asked my father to help him kill himself. "He said Ruth wasn't doing so well and he had thought a lot about it and he didn't want to live anymore—he didn't want to be a burden to others—and asked me if I would, you know, write him a prescription for drugs to kill himself. He wanted to commit suicide. He wanted me to give him some drugs so he would go to sleep and not wake up."

"What did you say?"

"Well, I said no. First of all, because it's illegal. And second, but more importantly, because I felt that he had a lot to live for. Your mom and I both tried to tell him that. He was a very brilliant man."

But apparently Richard Warren Hatch wouldn't listen to them. "He felt that he had nothing. Ruth no longer recognized him. And he could no longer read or listen to books on tape. He was going deaf and blind. And that was the only thing that gave him joy, to listen to books.

"He became very angry," my father continued. "He said, 'Well, what would you have me do? Shoot myself and have a big bloody mess for my family to find? Would you prefer that? What kind of doctor are you? You're supposed to help people.' And I said, 'Do what you want, but I'm not going to help you do it.'

"Then he said, 'I thought you were my friend,' and I said, 'I am your friend.'" Then, after that, Richard Warren Hatch grew silent, and my mother and father left.

"Did you ever see him again?"

"No."

"Did you talk to him?"

"Less than two weeks later, the phone rang. It was Betty

Hatch. They had found Dick. Then I told her about our last conversation."

"And how did you feel?"

"Well, of course I was devastated. I mean, I never thought he would do it. And I was angry with him. I thought he was very selfish, and I felt very bad for his family. And Betty said she wished I had told her."

"Why didn't you?"

"I don't know," he said. "I guess I never thought that he would do it. Also, I was thinking about professional courtesy, that you never betray your patient's confidence, but maybe I was wrong," he said, and quietly continued to pack the small suitcase he had set at my feet.

When I returned to the Red House after my lunch with Jean, I noticed, as I had many times that spring, the housing development growing on the hillside beyond the Red House. The view from the Red House had always been of pine hills, but the previous winter swaths of trees had been chopped down, and slowly the half-framed houses grew, with the occasional sound of a hammer or a radio echoing along the hillside. I had seen the cellar holes, the two-by-eights going up, but it wasn't until today that I realized that the Red House was now a part of "a view" from those houses on the hillside. I was overwhelmed with the desire to see the Red House from the perspective of the developers. Because, I realized, if I could see their houses, they could undoubtedly see mine.

I didn't like being part of a view. As I drove up Union Street, I remembered that Betty Bates had mentioned going up into that development and being shocked that she could see Boston. "It was as if the world had shrunk," she told me. The Boston skyline had grown, and so had Marshfield; and now the distance between the two didn't seem so great.

Ironically, the entrance to the Arrowhead Development sat directly across from the Hatch Cemetery. A small billboard included a map of partitioned "one-acre lots." "Bike paths," the sign read, "custom-designed homes." And at the bottom of the billboard: "Arrowhead Road, now selling *last phase*."

Roads in Arrowhead were all named after local Native American tribes or fallen sachems: "Pokanoket Lane," "Canochet Drive." The roads, newly blacktopped, stretched out unlined, and the air smelled of hot tar, manure, and newly laid sod. Every few yards sat another grand house, all of them "colonials"—blocky, with double-hung windows, shutters, and fat central chimneys. Each house had a perfect square of lawn, a newly planted tree or two. I felt as if I had discovered a hidden alien colony. I had had no idea how large the development was; it seemed to stretch on and on, one house after another, along roads of intertwining Native American names, green lawns, new mailboxes.

It was strange too how closely the new houses mimicked the original Hatch houses on Union Street—white with green shutters, or colonial yellow clapboards. Many houses had chimneys painted white, the top ringed with a ribbon of black. Several houses in Marshfield had this same paint pattern. Jean had told me that it was once thought that the chimney paint indicated a Tory household: when the British invaded, crown sympathizers painted this pattern on their chimneys to signal the troops not to sack their houses. But then she added that this was probably a myth, and that a painted chimney, especially white (which was a very expensive paint), indicated wealth more than anything else. So were the builders of the houses in the Arrowhead Development signaling that they were Tory? Or were they copying colonial style, oblivious of the folkloric implications? Or were they simply signaling that they were rich?

Betty had told me that most of the development's residents were first-time homeowners, young couples in their thirties who mostly "worked with computers." And as I drove, I passed young mothers with strollers who walked along hillsides half seeded and covered with hay.

The half-finished house with a view of the Red House was lot number 51 of Pokanoket Lane. Most of the houses along the ridgeline were in various stages of completion—from cement foundations, to studs and framing, to tarpaper and Tyvek siding. The acre lots were torn-up patches of dirt. When I pulled my car to the side of lot number 51, I could see several small Bobcats and bulldozers parked near the house site. As I got out of the car, I saw the valley and the leafless trees below. A yellow Komat'su backhoe bent its big head downhill.

The new house was two and a half stories. Plywood slabs posed as flooring, and framing studs sketched future walls and roof. The house was open and abandoned, and I wanted to walk into it, over the plywood where the new owners would eventually walk, to look at their view. But from where I stood I could see right through it anyway, and what I saw was the last pink of a stretched-out sunset and the distant foil edge of the North River. And there, through the frame of the construction, I could also see the Red House. It was small but unmistakably red, a dot in the landscape below. The perspective shifted and revealed itself—here was the body, the ribs, of a new house, and beyond, in the horizon, the Red House hovering in the place where the heart should be. The Red House had been like this once when Walter built it—just framing studs, just the idea of a house. I found myself walking toward it, over boards planked in the mud. But at that moment, a truck pulled up and a man walked briskly to the house. When he saw me standing at the edge, he stopped and said, "Are you looking for Ellen? Because I think she's running a little late."

"No," I said.

The man suddenly turned suspicious. "Well, can I help you?"

"No, I just came up here to look at the view."

"First-class, isn't it?" he said, smiling and walking away.

First-class. I wanted to follow him, to take his hand and point down the valley to the Red House and say, "See that? Do you know what you're looking at?" But instead I got into my car and drove back into the web of interconnected roads of the development. In my rearview mirror, the sun was setting, the sky glowing purple and orange. And I noticed other drivers along the roads with me, driving and parking before the still-unfinished houses. I saw a new silver Volvo slow down in front of a house covered in tarpaper. The driver was a young man dressed in a suit and tie. This must be the owner, I thought, returning from his job in the city, and I watched him get out of the car, the wind grabbing his tie and flinging it back around his neck. This, I realized, was the first place he drove to: the house. He had come right here—I could tell by the look on his face. He wore the expression of a man transfixed by his beloved, a man who could look at nothing else, and in that moment he was Richard Warren Hatch, and all the Hatches who came before him, and he was my father too. This man standing in the Arrowhead Development, which I had thought up until that moment was an insult and affront to all things meaningful and worth preserving, was suddenly bound by this gesture, which was the same as a whole history of gestures that I had come to know—a man looking up at his house—one-room lean to, colonial, family inheritance, legacy or imitation, tarpaper shack, future and fake colonial. They all walked together toward it, as this man did now, seeing nothing except his own dream, with a gesture that is always the same—intent upon the future, intent to create something new, a new life, his hand reaching toward the door, and the face he holds as he enters filled with joy.

Epilogue

What won't the house do in the meantime?
Compelled by our drama, it sighs through
afternoons, anxious to open its cupboards
to evening. The house wants us moving inside

it . . . Disciplined at day, at night abandoned,
the ghosts offer their devotion. The house builds

itself around us. The house burns down for us.
When we walk the lawn late at night, arms looped,
circling its structure, we are faithful. Lights lure
us inside . . .

—Cate Marvin, "Discipline, Abandon,"
from *The World's Tallest Disaster*, 2001

It took me six years to write this book.

Meanwhile, my father has become a wood-carver. He's trying to retire from X-rays, though some ghost still holds him. But carving seems a way out, an escape. In the same way he used to bend over his light box, he now bends over slabs of wood winched to the kitchen table, or a workbench out in the barn. He wears the same gray X-ray–examining mole-glasses pulled down over his nose. Sometimes he ventures out, carves animals—bears, pigs, sleeping dogs—out of downed trees, or he carves faces into the sides of trees one could happen upon on the road to the river, slightly off the path. He carved a snake around a lamppost. He carved a fourteen-foot totem pole, having determined from a book on Native American customs the totems of all of his children and grandchildren. (Counting all of us, there are now twenty.) He found that wood, not watercolor, was the best medium for his flowers. So, over the past ten years, he has taken pictures of wildflowers and transformed them on three-by-three panels into an abstraction of flowers. He carves circles and rippling petals, each one slightly different, into sixty panels that

345

cover the entire ceiling of the kitchen and long hallway in the Red House, where he and my mother still live.

Since the restoration, my parents have finally begun to claim physical ownership of the house. Three walls of the stairwell to the basement are now covered with family photos. Our family. "Why didn't you put these pictures up before?" I asked my mother.

"Oh, I never got around to it," she said.

"For thirty-eight years you never got around to it?"

And she didn't respond. While my father carved the flowers, stencils of cattails and red-winged blackbirds began to appear on the back stairwell, a wisteria vine painted in my mother's hand arched over the corn-chamber door. They have both blossomed into what had been hiding inside them all along. Wind no longer whistles through the living room and parlor; the carpeting on the stairs has finally been replaced. The whole house has settled, shifting to the south and leaving new cracks in the wall paneling upstairs.

The house can't speak for itself; it has no baby book, no personal photo album. I have chronicled here some of the changes that have occurred there over more than three hundred years— but even in the six years it's taken to write this book, the house continues to change. For example: it is no longer red. Well, some of it is: the oldest part, the north and south clapboards. The rest of the house is shingled with red cedar that will eventually turn to dark gray. But now the peaks and ells are blond.

My father used to speak with morbid nostalgia of his own demise, how he could never give up the house, how he wanted to be cremated, his ashes mixed with my mother's and buried under the old millstone. He had wanted to carve words on the millstone—their names, perhaps, or all the names of their children— and set it all up like a Two Mile monument in the old Indian burial ground. But my father has since sobered up this fantasy.

The Messers, it turns out, have their own center, their own

lineage spiraling from it. "When you start working on projects like this, stuff will just show up," Betty Bates had said to me four years ago, and she was right. What turned up was a newspaper clipping from my father's sister, Bernadyne, bearing the headline: "History of Messer Family Dates Back to Colonial Time: Carolina Paper Describes 116-year-Old 'Fed' Messer, Who Lived in Three Centuries." My ancestor Uncle Fed, who was (for lack of a better descriptor) an illiterate hillbilly who lived in the mountains west of Waynesville, North Carolina, was born in 1791 and died in 1907, having lived through the New Republic, the Civil War, the Reconstruction, the Gilded Age, women's suffrage, the invention of the telephone, the automobile, the airplane, and an inkling of World War I. He only buttoned up his shirt twice in his life; he swam across the Pigeon River at the age of 110, and was proclaimed by some papers, on his 114th birthday, to be the "South's Oldest Living Citizen."

Which bestows on me the following: "Descendant of the South's Oldest Living Citizen Grows Up in Oldest Continuously Lived-In House in New England."

If I'm labeled, my parents are still, sadly, cursed. In the summer of 2000, my parents' planned retirement home in Vermont, the 1860s bed and breakfast my mother ran each summer, was struck by lightning and burned nearly entirely to the ground. The fire's configuration was exactly the same as that of the 1971 Red House fire, leading my parents (and some of their children) to believe that perhaps Israel or Walter or Richard Warren or somebody else was mad at them and taking revenge beyond the boundaries of Two Mile. Having inhabited the house with the Hatch ghosts for so long, we wondered if maybe the ghosts now inhabited us.

My parents restored the Vermont house anyway. What else could they do? By now they were experts in the art of salvaging burned wreckage. During the writing of this book, my parents' retirement plans changed many times—they were going to spend their old age in Vermont baking scones and running the restored B&B; they were going to donate the Red House to a public land trust, or to Harvard University; they were going to sell the Red House and the B&B and move somewhere else entirely; every six months we heard a different story. But in the end it was my mother, not my father, who presented the strongest opinion—when confronted with Realtors at the door of the Red House, she broke down. After inhabiting it for thirty-eight years, my mother realized that the Red House was the center—not just for her children, or the Hatches, or all the history, but for her. The Red House was the only home she'd ever really had. So, having once thought about selling the Red House, they've now decided to keep it.

Hatch ancestors, or anyone interested in primary Hatch documents, should know that the letters and wills from the Red House will be donated to the Massachusetts Historical Society in Boston, where they will join the journals of Otis B. Oakman (Thomas R. Oakman's brother), in order to give future historians a more comprehensive record of Two Mile life. Hatch family documents are also currently housed at the New England Historic Genealogical Society and the Mayflower Society in Boston. Kettles, swing arms, and fire tools from the original Red House kitchen can be found at the Museum of Historic Deerfield in Deerfield, Massachusetts. And as of this writing, I have begun the process of placing the house on the National Historic Register. Rumor has it that the Hatch Mill, in desperate need of salvation, may at last be purchased and turned into a Living History Hands-On Museum. In short, much of the Hatch property (letters and land) that I've written about here will eventually be accessible to the public. Yet, for now and until my parents' death, the Red House remains a private home.

Kim and Philippe split their time between Maine and the EU; Kerry has moved back to California; Kate lives in Massachusetts;

Patrick lives in New Hampshire; Bekah in Vermont; Suzy in a log cabin in Wyoming; Jess in Marshfield. Jean Hall has moved to Scotland. Maryanne McGuire married a Wisconsin boy and moved to Minnesota.

Recently Kim and Philippe visited Richard Warren Hatch Jr., who was celebrating the birth of Josh's son. In his garage, Dick Jr. showed them several surfboards he had made for the town of Marshfield years ago. By the end of the visit, Philippe and Dick Jr. had made a date to go surfing together.

I live in the South now, in an old house in a neighborhood the Realtors politely call "transitional." It's a small cottage built in 1894. It has seen a race riot in 1898, sat in the lot next door as nine white men burned down the town's African American press and then forced nearly a thousand businesspeople and citizens on a train out of town. The city is still split over it, over a hundred years later. Recently a guy named Israel moved onto the block. He haunts the curbside late at night, waving at passing cars—desperately, as if he wants something. Some people say he is trafficking in drugs, but nothing has confirmed this yet.

Israel Hatch, I still think of you—whoever and wherever you are. When I pass my neighbor, I like to say his name out loud: "Hey, Israel."

"Hey," he always says.

What had the Red House needed all this time? It hadn't needed me. It went on of its own accord, and always will. Marshfield is now one of the most popular places to live on the South Shore, filling up with what our neighbors call "McMansions." The Red House hadn't needed a doctor. We didn't solve anything.

Houses, like bodies, are sometimes afflicted. Puritans saw lightning, fire, floods, as acts of Providence, and the Red House over the years was certainly afflicted. But houses can also benefit from challenge and change. Like wildflowers that bloom only after violent firestorms, perhaps heat, all the fires, was necessary to push the seeds of the future into being. One day the Red House may fall apart gently, like the unclenching layered fist of a peony. Then maybe it will reveal its whole story. The Puritans believed that they were building heavenly mansions in the wilderness. And some of them, like the Red House, are still with us.

I want to thank it, here and finally, for surviving.

Appendix

Unproved Will of Walter Hatch
Dated March 1681 When Walter Was 59

[A copy of the will is in the possession of Ronald J. Messer from Israel H. Hatch collection. See also Kaye Hooely. http://home.comcast.net/~kaeh/ Wills/Walter1.html.]

I give an bequeath to Mari my wife all that dowri or _____ mutually agreed upon before marriage out of my estate, all the rest of my lands, goods, tenements I give and bequeath to my 5 sons and my two daughters as followeth:

First I give to Samuel Hatch my sun al that lot as he livs upone that is an hundred and twenty acres of upland more or less and ten acres of meadow or marsh land more or less bounded towards the land of John Magoun westerly towards the North river northerly towards the land of Edward Wanton, Easterly towards the common lands. All this land above mentioned with whatsoever other of my lands I shall give I give it to him and to the heirs begotten of his body forever from generation to generation to the world's end never to be sold nor mortgaged from my children nor grandchildren forever.

I give and bequeath all my lands I live upon with the houses and housing "barne" or barns, upland and meadow gardens and orchard that is to say all my lot or lots lying between the lands of Thomas Lapham on the North and Edward Wanton on the south Easterly to the common lands and Westerly to the river. All this land above mentioned lands, orchards and meadows, housing and gardens I give and bequeath to Antipas Hatch my son and to the heirs begotten of his body forever from generation to generation forever never to be sold nor mortgaged from my children or grandchildren forever.

351

APPENDIX

To my three youngest sons John Hatch, Israel Hatch and Joseph Hatch I give and bequeath all my great lot at Taunton River on the easterly side of the river lying between the land of Master (Hayward?) Barri towards the south and the land of Master Line in the occupation of Master Simmons towards the North.

All my other lands or lands in Scituate undissposed of I give and bequeath to my two eldest sons Samuel Hatch and Antipas Hatch to them and the heirs of their bodies forever never to be sold nor mortgaged from my children nor grandchildren forever from generation to generation to the worlds end that is to say all such land or lands as are or hereafter shall be mine by grant gift or purchase with all the common rights and rights as belong to me and my lands in the township of Sittewate.

Furthermore I give and bequeath all my moveable estate by sea and land; money goods chattel household goods, cattle, horseflesh, swine, beeas, axes, hoes and all other tools of what sort soever with all the rest of my moveable estate by sea and land and I give and bequeath to my five sons and two daughters, Samuel Hatch, Antipas Hatch, John Hatch, Israel Hatch and Joseph Hatch, and Jane Sherman and Bethia Hatch, their sisters all this above-mentioned estate I give to be equally divided to every one an equal proportion that is to say, sons and daughters alike share of the moveable estate. Furthermore it is my will that they pay all my debts and legacies and receive all my debts and dus wheresoever and give me a decent and comely buriell. Amen.

Walter Hatch aged this present March 59 years 1681–82 March 4

APPENDIX

Proved Will of Walter Hatch
20 August 1698

[Plymouth Probate Record of Walter Hatch 1701, FHL film 550708, Volume 1, pages 335, 337–338 Also reprinted by Priscilla Waldron Gladwin from the original records of Israel H. Hatch. See also Kaye Hooely http://home. comcast.net/~kaeh/Wills/Walter2.html.]

July 9, 1698

O, God Amen. Into thy hand I commit my soul and body as into the hands of a faithful Creator and my blessed Redeemer. Amen.

I give to my son Samuel Hatch all that lot of land he now lives upon, upland 16 acres, meadow 10 acres is lying between the lands of Thomas Oldham on the North and Magoon on the South and I give him that half share of land I bought of Mr. Thomas Hinckley at Rochester divided or undivided with all the rights, titles and privileges thereunto belonging and I give to my son Samuel Hatch aforesaid the whole share of the freemans meadow I bought of John Hathaway of Taunton lying in Rochester aforesaid and I give him that lot I bought of the said Hammons 50 acres lying in Hammons Hooke and two _____ lots and 10 acres the other 3 acres _____. All the three lots lying in Scituate. And I give to him my share in the Iron Works it being a 16 part with all the rights titles and privileges thereunto belonging. All the above mentioned lands and _____ I give to my eldest son Samuel Hatch.

I give to my two sons John Hatch and Israel Hatch all my lands I live upon and the two mills the corn mill and the fulling mill with all my housing and barns, the upland by estimation 260 acres, the meadow land about 20, all these lands, mills and housing lying in Scituate on the East side of the North River between of Thomas Lapham on the North and the land of Thomas Oldham on the South. And I give to them my committee lot at Burnt Plain about 50 or 60 acres and 5 acres of swamp the committee gave to me. And my share of the sawmill pond with that share I bought of one of the Turners as appears by a deed under hand and seal with all my right and interest in the commons of Scituate belonging unto me. And the lands above mentioned to be equally divided between them, the aforesaid John Hatch and Israel Hatch and them two are to pay their mother's dowry and to have a care to provide for Antipas Hatch my son and their brother a comfortable livelyhood in meat, drink and clothing, and to bear the charges about Antipas Hatch and their mother's dowry equally between them. And if my son Joseph Hatch be not settled upon his own or elsewhere at or before my death he is to be an equal partner with John and Israel his brother in charges and profits the full space of four years, and then to be all his brothers' and settle upon his own. The charge is the maintaining his mother and brother Antipas and the housing and fences, the mills and dams. The profit is the mills and fields and meadows with their income and increase, and to have his third part of the profits of the orchard.

I Walter Hatch do give as it followeth: I give to Joseph Hatch, my youngest son, all that my great lot at Freetown will all the meadow land lying in it and belonging to it and my 4 lots at Swanzey 16 acres in a lot and two lots of meadow outlying before the fifth lot the other lying in the cover at the west side of Taunton River the meadow two acres and a half an acres in a lot, and all my part of the freemens land as it is to be divided on the West side of Taunton River. I Walter Hatch have one share of my own and one share I bought of Josiah Winslow Sen, of Marshfield, deceased. All those lots and lands above mentioned with their rights, titles, privileges, and appurtenances I give to Joseph Hatch my youngest son, to him and his heirs forever and I give to the aforesaid Joseph Hatch Twenty pound sterling in money towards the building of himself a house and a barn.

I Walter Hatch do give to my daughter Jane Sherman twenty pounds sterling in silver money and a cow.

I Walter Hatch do give to my daughter Bethiah Foord twenty pounds sterling in silver money and a cow.

I Walter Hatch do give and lend to Mary Hatch my wife as followeth. I do give to Mary Hatch my wife five pounds a year so long as she bears my name during the time of her widowhood. And it is to be paid every quarter of the year 25 shillings a quarter. And if she marry and change her name, to leave the things lent to her and to have forty shilling during the time of her natural life all of it to be paid in money or provisions at money's price.

I Walter Hatch do lend to Mary Hatch my wife to bed we lye upon and one boulster and one pillow and one pair of sheets and the least iron pot and one tray and one dish and a spoon and trencher. All those things I lend to her during the time of her widowhood.

It is my will I Walter Hatch, that if any of my sons should die and leave no heirs begotton of his own body that the lands and estates he received of me his father Walter Hatch shall be equally divided to his brothers if living or to their children if the brother be dead, and if he leave a widow she shall have a third part of the rents and profits of the land during the time of her widowhood so long as she bears my son's name. This is my will.

(Signed) Walter Hatch

July 15, 1698 The land I bought of my cousin Thomas Hatch lying at Tunk (Taunton) the foresaid Thomas Hatch sold me that my part of the land I bought of him was 3375 acres as appears by a deed under his hand and seal. All this land and lands I Walter Hatch do give to my 4 sons Samuel Hatch, John Hatch, Israel Hatch and Joseph Hatch to be equally divided between them 4 with all the rights titles privileges and appurtenances thereunto belonging with the charges and profits thereof.

I Walter Hatch do give to my son John Hatch one yoak of oxen and two cows the two cows he has received already.

And to my son Israel Hatch I give one yoak of oxen and two cows. And to my son Joseph Hatch I give one yoak of oxen and two cows. And I give to my three sons John, Israel and Joseph my carts, plows, chains, axes, saws, hoes, with all the rest of my working tools to be equally divided between them 3, John, Israel and Joseph aforesaid.

And to all my grandchildren that are borne before my death of my own sons and daughters I give to every one of them ten shillings a child to buy every one of them a Bible and to lay out the remainder of the ten shillings apiece in other good books. And the aforesaid ten shillings apiece to be paid to the sons when they are twenty one years old and to the daughters when they are eighteen years old.

All the rest of my estate that is not disposed of in this will I give to my 4 sons and two daughters, Samuel, John, Israel, Joseph Hatch and Jane Sherman and Bethiah Foord to be equally divided among them all, that is to say my money cattell, swine, bedding cloth and clothing and my books and my household stuff with all the rest of my moveables and movable estate. I Walter Hatch do make and give them power to be my executors and administrators of this my last will and testament. Two of my sons John Hatch and Israel Hatch them two to pay all my debts and legacies and to receive all my debts and dues due to me Walter hatch.

(Signed) Walter Hatch
20 August 1698

Inhabitants of the Red House

DATES OF OCCUPATION	INHABITANTS

1647–1699   **Walter Hatch**

Planter, shipbuilder, millworker. Married Elizabeth Holbrook in 1650 and Mary Stable after Elizabeth's death.

*Children of Walter and Elizabeth: Hannah (died young), Samuel, Jane, Antipas, Bethia, John, **Israel**, Joseph.*

1667–1740   **The First Israel**

Millworker, planter, son of Walter. Israel One was in his early thirties when he married his second cousin Elizabeth Hatch and inherited the Red House.

*Children of Israel and Elizabeth: Lydia, **Israel**, Elizabeth, David, Jonathan.*

1701–1767   **The Second Israel**

Millworker, son of Israel One. Married Bethia Thomas, his first cousin once removed, in 1725.

*Children of Israel and Bethia: Bethia, Elizabeth, **Israel**, Jane (died young), Anna, Thomas (died young), John, Sibyl, Rachel.*

1730–1809   **The Third Israel**
Millworker, son of Israel Two. Israel Three bought the mills from his father, and half of the Red House, in which he was living. Married Mary Doty (1775) and Jane Hatch Hall (1804).

Children of Israel and Mary: Amos, Mary, Penelope, Daniel (died young), Israel (died young), Israel (died young), Bethia, **Joel.**

1771–1849   **Deacon Joel Hatch**
Millworker, deacon in the Second Church of Scituate. On April 16, 1805, Joel Hatch purchased the house from his father, Israel Three. Deacon Joel had ten children by two wives, Huldah Trouant (1796) and Rebekah Hatch (1828).

Children of Joel and Huldah: Joel, Huldah, Samuel, William, Amos, Rhoda, Mary.
Children of Joel and Rebekah: Rebekah, Walter, **Israel H.**

1837–1921   **Israel H. Hatch**
Schoolteacher, milkman, farmer. Inherited the house from his father, Deacon Joel. Last Hatch to be born and live his entire life in the Red House. Married Caroline Blanchard Oakman in 1859.

Children of Israel H. and Caroline: Israel Ellis (died young), Alice, **Harris,** *Tracy Weston.*

1866–1934 **Harris Blanchard Hatch**
General manager of Royal Electrotype Company in Philadelphia, Pa., son of Israel H. Hatch. In 1886, he bought the Red House and land, then promptly deeded the property back to his mother, Caroline B. Hatch. Married Susanna Mabel Jones in 1888. Bought the White House next door to Red House in 1928 and retired there.

Children of Harris and Susanna: Helen, Lawrence, Esther, Richard Warren, Howard Oakman, Tracy Weston.

1928–1960 **Tracy Weston Hatch**
Farmer, son of Harris, brother of Richard Warren. Tracy moved into the White House, adjacent to the Red House, with wife Betty Sherman, soon after his parents retired in 1928, and lived there until his death in 1960.

Children of Tracy and Betty: Deborah, Anthony, Daniel, Mary.

1934–1965 **Richard Warren Hatch**
Reporter, teacher, novelist, son of Harris. In 1922, he married Harriet Hildreth; later divorced. Married Ruth Dunwoody Selser in 1938. Inherited the Red House from his father in 1934. For years it was rented or used only in the summer.

Children of Richard Warren Hatch and Harriet: Richard Warren Jr., John Christopher.

Richard Warren Hatch Jr.

Inventor, restorer of clocks. Spent his childhood summers at the Red House. Married twice, with children from each union. Currently lives in Maine.

Children of Richard and Pamela: Marcy Stewart, Jonathan Weston, Elizabeth Jackson. Children of Richard and Janet: Sarah Anne, Rebecca May, William Joshua, Joel Simmons.

John C. Hatch

Spent summers at the Red House as a child. Currently lives in western Massachusetts.

Children of John Christopher and Sherry: Christopher Howell, Mark Holbrook, Melissa Meredith.

1965–present
Ronald Messer

Physician, radiologist. Married Nina Foran in 1952; divorced. Married Patricia Ann Watrouse in 1965. Bought the Red House from Richard Warren Hatch in 1965.

Children of Ronald and Nina: Kimberly, Kerry, Kate, Patrick.
Children of Ronald and Patricia: Sarah, Susan, Rebekah, Jessica.

Notes

A Note on the Notes

This book is not a history—its project (if we can call it that) is to tell the stories surrounding the house, the Two Mile area, the Hatch family, and my own family. It does, however, use history in order to create an impression of what life was like in the Red House for more than three hundred years. A writer friend once said that he was interested in facts "as images." I hold a similar aesthetic: in earlier versions of this book, I called the history chapters "X-rays," as a metaphor for the idea of "seeing through" time. I elaborated on the process of reading X-rays—the "indication," left by a document or an artifact from the past, followed by the "impression," or diagnosis/interpretation given by a doctor. The subtitle "A *Mostly Accurate* Account" refers to this idea of interpretation or impression.

I am indebted to many historians—they are the heroes here. For this reason I want to acknowledge, before the notes, those scholars and writers who helped make this book possible. Here is a small, but by no means complete, breakdown:

If you are interested in Hatch genealogy, I recommend Perley Derby, *The Descendants of William Hatch of Scituate* (Salem, Mass.: 1874); and Elizabeth French, *New England Historic and Genealogical Register*, vol. 70, no. 279 (Boston: New England Historic Genealogical Society, 1916), 245–260. Elizabeth French got much of her source material from Israel H. Hatch, who was also a member of the society. Another good source is Priscilla Waldron Gladwin, *The Hatch Family and the Red House* (Marshfield, Mass.: Gladwin, 1981). A photocopy is available at the New England Historic Genealogical Society (NEHGS) in Boston, Mass. This is a private archive, but you can join for a fee. For on-line information, visit http://www.newenglandancestors.org. This manuscript is also in the archives of the Scituate Historical Society located at "the Little Red

Schoolhouse," 43 Cudworth Road, Scituate, MA 02066. The best and most accurate on-line source for Hatch history is a Web site by Kaye Hooley: http://home.attbi.com/~kaeh. A few years ago, Hatch descendants organized a Hatch family reunion; to read about it or get involved with the next reunion visit http://www.geocities.com/Yosemite/Gorge/5687/hatchfr.html. Or you could access Plymouth County records yourself. Record books (1686–1903) and file papers (1686–1881) in Plymouth, Mass. Or read Jeremy Bangs, *The Seventeenth Century Town Records of Scituate, Massachusetts,"* vols. I, II, and III, published by NEHGS.

If you are interested in Marshfield history, I recommend Cynthia Hagar Krusell and Betty Magoun Bates, *Marshfield: A Town of Villages, 1640–1990* (Marshfield, Mass.: Historical Research Associates, 1990). This is the best, most recent, and most comprehensive book on Marshfield history. The Marshfield Historical Commission is also a fantastic resource. More-dated yet still accurate and helpful books include Joseph C. Hagar, *Marshfield 70–40 W: 42–5 N: The Autobiography of a Pilgrim Town* (Marshfield Tercentenary Committee, Marshfield, Mass.: Rapid Service Press, 1940); and L. Vernon Briggs, *Shipbuilding on the North River* (Boston: Norwell Historical Society, Inc., Coburn Brothers, 1889).

For more information on Scituate history and Two Mile, try Harvey Hunter Pratt, *The Early Planters of Scituate* (Rockland, Mass.: Scituate Historical Society, 1929; reprint, Heritage Books, 1998). A great resource for information on Two Mile is the unpublished work of William "Gray" Curtiss at the Scituate Historical Society. Mr. Curtis has spent years collecting the history of Two Mile and has several unpublished genealogies.

If you are interested in house building, early colonial paint techniques, habits and customs of early Massachusetts, or gravestones, please consult the work of Peter Benes, Richard Candee, James Deetz, Abbott Lowell Cummings, and Jonathan Demos. If you are interested in quirky New England folklore, I would recommend any book by Alice Morse Earle. A great book on the land, wildlife, and environment of early New England is William Cronons's *Changes in the Land: Indians, Colonists and the Ecology of New England* (New York: Hill and Wang, 2003).

For more information on King Philip's War, please read the astonishing *The Name of War: King Philip's War and the Origins of American Identity* by Jill Lepore (New York: Alfred A. Knopf, 1998).

Page vii: Letter from Richard Warren Hatch to Ronald J. Messer, 1966, courtesy of John C. Hatch. Increase Mather, 1687, as quoted in St. George, 121. Theodore Roethke line from "The Waking," in *Collected Poems of*

NOTES

Theodore Roethke (New York: Doubleday, 1953). **Page 2:** Partial definition of "hatch" from *Oxford English Dictionary, 2nd Edition,* edited by John Simpson and Edmund Weiner (1989). By permission of Oxford University Press.

Chapter One

Page 3: Highway is Route 3. "Blizzard of 1978"—February 6, 1978; see Krusell and Bates, 68. For info on sea monster, see Situate Town Report, 1970. Wy Sibo Girl Scout Camp, run in the 1930s. North River Farms flower farm. Tidal wave—storm of November 1898. For a history of industry on the North River, see L. Vernon Briggs, *History of Shipbuilding on North River,* or Hagar, chapter 18, 144–160, and chapter 21, 172–181. William Vassal started an oyster bed and also ran a ferry (later called Doggett's Ferry) in 1637; see Hagar, 20. Daniel Webster died in Marshfield on October 24, 1852; see Krusell and Bates, 18. Indian raid refers to the King Philip's War, 1675–76; see Lepore. **Page 4:** Israel Hatch mill was built in 1752; it was later remodeled by Deacon Joel Hatch in 1812 and later (by others) in 1859. Deacon Joel's oldest son, Samuel, took over running the mill from his father and eventually passed it down through generations to Decker Hatch, who ran the mill until 1965. The mill was sold to the Marshfield Historical Society in 1968. A fantastic transcription of a tape-recorded interview with Decker Hatch about the history of the mill remains in the collection of the Marshfield Historical Commission, Marshfield, Mass.; see Krusell and Bates, 194–195. **Page 6:** Vertical-board construction consists of 25 feet or longer boards cut lengthwise and stacked side by side so that the length reaches up through two floors; this description thanks to Jean Hall. Football quote from *Tri-County Press,* October 29, 1948, pg. 14. **Page 15:** RWH's biography, courtesy of Gladwin, *The Hatch Family and the Red House,* 75–77. What RWH called "an Indian burial ground" is not an actual burial site; his father, Harris Hatch, did find arrowheads and other small relics there.

The Land 1614–1647

Page 21: For more information about New England in the 1600s, read William Cronon, *Changes in the Land;* Briggs, *History of Shipbuilding on North River;* Carl Brindenbaugh, "Yankee Use and Abuse of Forests in the Building of New England"; Henry F. Howe, *Salt Rivers of the Massachusetts Shore.* See also Hagar; Krusell and Bates. **Page 22:** Algonquin name for Scituate: see Gladwin, *The Hatch Family and the Red House,* 9; see also Pratt, 25. Scituate's establishment, see Benes, *Masks of Orthodoxy,* 57. References to "the Crotch," Briggs, *Shipbuilding on North River,* 6. "No-gains," see Hagar,

NOTES

145. On Captain John Smith at the Glades, see Howe, 40; see also Smith, *Works, 1608–1631* (ed. E. Arber), 719. **Page 22**: On smallpox, see Howe, 23. For an account of William Bradford's first days in Provincetown and Plymouth, see William Bradford. For an imagining of Walter's passage (age twelve), see Gladwin, *The Hatches and the Red House*, 18. **Page 23:** Two Mile, see Hagar, 24; Pratt, 28–33; Krusell and Bates, 183. Walter's birth and immigration, see Derby, French, or Gladwin, 18–19. "Horselife," etc. See Gladwin, *The Hatch Family and the Red House*, 4, quoting from the will of Thomas Hatch proved 31 December 1534, Archdeaconry of Canterbury, vol. 20. For the population of New England in 1642 see Brindenbaugh, 3; see also, Benes, *Masks of Orthodoxy*, 57. For blackbird heads and animal taxes, see Hagar, 54. Eels, gunfire, etc., see Deetz and Deetz, *The Times of Their Lives,* 4–7. Dinah Sylvester is mentioned throughout early Scituate records. A neighbor of the Hatches, her most famous accusation of witchcraft and transfiguration is cited in Pratt, 118. Dinah's later troubles are mentioned in Holliday, 248–249. Walter is old enough to bear arms, 1643, see "The 1643 Able to Bear Arms List," NEHGR 9:279, 10:42, 14:101–104. Walter's brother-in-law was James Torrey. See Derby or family histories. **Page 24:** Walter bought many pieces of land in Scituate and Two Mile over a forty-year period. Although he inherited land in Scituate, it is important to note that the supposed site of the Red House is not within that inheritance. Genealogists Perley Derby and Priscilla Gladwin both state that Walter Hatch settled on "a point of land north-east of stony cove, and south east of the Second Society Meeting House." Yet architectural historian Jean Hall writes: "Walter states that the land he is leaving his two youngest sons is, 'on the east side of the North River between the land of Thomas Lampham on the north and Thomas Oakman on the South,' signifying that it was not on the coast. Since neither of the two references to this fact specify an actual building or location the matter remains murky." Walter Hatch did purchased land in Two Mile from Thomas and Elizabeth Ensign in 1647. Although Walter makes several other purchases within the area, it is believed that this first piece of property, lot #12 of the Two Mile Grant, is where he built his original homestead. This land was "bounded on the east with common land, to the west end with the North River, to the north to land of James Torrey, to the south with land of widow Granger. Signed by Thomas Ensign and Elizabeth Ensign [mark], witnessed by John Witcomb and James Torrey. Plymouth County Deeds. III (1); 53." Also see Bangs, town records of Scituate, vol. 2, 128. Walter later bought another forty acres from Ann Vinal in 1651, followed by forty more from James Torrey in 1654. For the sake of simplicity, I have condensed several incidents of Walter marking his land into one, all from Bangs, town records of Scituate, vol. 1, 85. From Scituate town rec-

NOTES

ords: February 24, 1659/1660, 252: "Joseph Tilden's land to the northwest, beginning at the marsh by the cartway running sixty paces to a marked tree; running seventy rods south east from that tree to a heap of stones; returning northeast to the first marked tree; comprising ten acres of swamp and swampy meadow which Walter Hatch accepts in lieu of ten acres of meadow." Also, February 1, 1691/1692, 86: "Walter Hatch marks trees with 'W:H' and 'three noches.'" Josiah Wampatuck sold vast tracts of land in the areas now known as Cohasset, Scituate, Marshfield, Weymouth, Norwell, and other surrounding towns. The original transaction involved primarily a settler named Timothy Hatherly, and the grant, circa 1646, was called the "Conihasset Grant," purchased by the "Conihasset Partners," Timothy Hatherly and others. The piece of land in Two Mile where the Red House stands was originally purchased by Thomas and Elizabeth Ensign prior to 1647. Forty years later, Josiah Wampatuck's heir came before the courts and reinstated the terms of the original purchase. For more on original land grants and Josiah Wampatuck, see Pratt, 61, 157.

At the American Antiquarian Society I saw a copy of the Conihasset grant where Josiah Wampatuck marked his "X." Chickotaubut meaning "House-on-fire" is mentioned in Pratt, 155.

Chapter Two

Page 27: I'm speculating that the whale's teeth were a gift from the whaler Thomas R. Oakman to Israel H. Hatch, since they are from that time period. Here is a comprehensive list of what was left at the Red House: receipt for a church pew for Israel Hatch, March 10, 1760; receipt for six cords of wood, twenty-one bushels of salt, fifteen bushels of Indian corn, July 12, 1780; receipts for medicine from Dr. Isaac Winslow, 1785–1787; receipt for eight doctor's visits, bleeding, and medicine, 1781–1785; written notice of care for the elderly—Deacon Joel takes financial responsibility for his mother-in-law, Rhoda Trouant (widow), 1824; letter from Joel Hatch Jr. to Deacon Joel Hatch, Newbury, Mass., 1818, reporting his health being "sober" and noting his attendance at meetings; letter to Deacon Joel Hatch requesting money for a meetinghouse in Boston, 1841; a 1856 petition to the Massachusetts State Senate to build a bridge across the North River from the land of Deacon Joel Hatch to Scituate, signed by sixty men; an 1826 receipt for renting a pew in church; an 1859 note in which Israel H. Hatch witnesses a division of property between his brother Samuel and sister Rebekah—an exchange of "one old cow" for "two church pews"; tax receipts for Deacon Joel Hatch, 1814–1817 and 1833–1848; tax receipts for Israel Hatch, 1790 and 1796; receipts for doctor's bills, Israel Hatch, 1758, 1765, 1767, and 1806; versions of

NOTES

Deacon Joel's wills, 1771–1849; bill of sale for one-fourth interest in the "good sloupe" *Sally Bord*, "about 25 tons," for 120 pounds, November 4, 1745; copies of Walter Hatch's will, 1681; copy and original of original division of estate of William Hatch by his sons Walter and William Jr., November 4, 1651; Deacon Joel's account of his father's estate; seven family trees by Israel H. Hatch, 1837–1921; receipt for the boarding of a schoolteacher, $18.00; fan letters to Richard Warren Hatch after he published several short stories in *Field and Stream* magazine, 1946 and 1955; a document dated 1701 with a Winslow signature; Hatch will and inventory, 1730–1809; a contract to build a church, 1825; receipts from two gravestones, eight lines of verse, coffin, and trimmings "for your father's grave," Israel Hatch, 1809; the cost of digging a grave, 1809; the estate of Israel Hatch born in 1701 and settled in 1783–85; tax on the carriage of Israel Hatch, "farmer," 1800; tax on the carriages of Deacon Joel, 1814, 1815; an 1854 letter from a sailor in Peru; sermon preached at Marshfield, February 20, 1753, at the ordination of Mr. Joseph Green to pastoral office over the first church in said town (by his father); *The Catechism of Nature for the Uses of Children*, by Dr. Martinet, 1819; *Juvenile Poems* (J. H. Butler, 1836); *Daily Food for Christians* (H. A. Young & Co.), miniature; *The Wedding Dress* (gift book) (Boston: Thomas O. Walker, 1854); *Christian Minister's Affectionate Advice to the Married Couple* (gift book) (New York: American Tract Society, 1855), included the inscription: "for Israel H. Hatch and Caroline B. Oakman on the date of their marriage, August 1, 1859;" *Select Remains of the Reverend John Mason* (Bridgeport, 1809) *Pretty Primer* (1832, Dean & Son), *Willie's Western Visit*, miniature; *The History of King Philip's War*, Samuel G. Drake Boston: Howe & Norton Printers, 1825); children's books from Dean & Son, London: *One, Two Buckle My Shoe, The House That Jack Built, The Cherry Orchard, Dean's Steamboat Alphabet, Whittington and His Cat, The Little Doc Trusty*; Stiegel glass; two dolls; a broken wooden plate, a pewter plate and fork; a rope bed tightner; a carved wooden plover; a bookcase; an alphabet sampler circa 1750; four old bottles; half-model of a ship; a canopy bed; twin beds; a camelback couch; two Sheraton chairs; an etching of Israel H. Hatch and a medal received in the Civil War; a Queen Anne drop-leaf table; one black Windsor chair; one 20-gauge double-barrel shotgun; one 1914 Fox Sterling rifle; a series of ten hand-made linen "bride's towels" embroidered with the names of Hatch women who left the house, dating back to 1690.

Walter 1647–1699

Page 40: Walter Hatch wills and inventory in Gladwin, *The Hatch Family and the Red House*, 20, and also on Kaye Hooley's Web site:

NOTES

http://home.comcast.net/~kaeh/Wills/Walter2.html. **Page 41:** In 1916 the *New England Historic and Genealogical Register* states that Walter Hatch "settled in the part of Scituate called 'The Two Miles.'" In *Old Time Anecdotes of the North River and the South Shore*, Joseph Foster Merritt describes a gundalow as a "long flat-bottomed boat from 30–40 feet long and about 10 or 12 foot beam, sometimes square ended like a scow, and sometimes sharp at the bow like a boat"; see his chapter titled "Gundalow Days on North River," 21–27. See also Earle, *Home Life in Colonial Days*, 328. The date of the original deed between Walter and Thomas and Elizabeth Ensign is 1647. Richard Warren Hatch, Israel H. Hatch, Priscilla Waldron Gladwin, and Elizabeth French, among others, have recorded 1647 as the earliest date for the Red House. Yet, in book-jacket copy for *The Curious Lobster*, RWH mentions his love of "his ancestral home built in 1651 on Atlantic Tidewater." My book in many ways is about this inability to secure dates. For the purposes of narrative, I speculate that the house took four years to build. Funeral customs are taken from Earle, *Customs and Fashions of Old New England*, 368–380. William Hatch died on November 6, 1651. His proved will and inventory was eventually copied in the *Mayflower Descendant*, vol. X, 38. Walter's chest marked "W.H." is mentioned in an inventory left by his son Israel to Israel Jr. in 1733. I don't know if Walter actually had a sea-monster earpick but they were popular at the time. Speculation on how Walter got his loot upriver comes from Gladwin, *The Hatch Family and the Red House*, 18, quoting RWH. Of Elizabeth Holbrook's mother and grandmother, see Gladwin, *The Hatch Family and the Red House*, 33, quoting Israel H. Hatch's reference to *Holten's List of Emigrants*. Gladwin also references Davis (1883), which places a Holbrook in Weymouth and married to Experience Leland. **Page 43:** The description of how Walter built the Red House was culled from many sources, namely: Brindenbaugh, 5, 8. Candee, "A Documentary History of Plymouth Colony Architecture 1620–1700"; Cummings, *The Framed Houses of Massachusetts Bay, 1625–1725*; Benes, *New England Historical Archaeology*; Demos. *A Little Commonwealth*, 24–35, 49. I also used Cynthia Krusell's "Notes on Two Mile Houses," courtesy Marshfield Historical Commission. See also Earle, *Home Life in Colonial Days*, 14–16. **Page 47:** For general information on animal taxes in Marshfield, see Hagar, 54. See also Bangs, or Scituate town records. **Pages 44–46:** For description of Colonial hearth, see Pratt, 187–188. Earliest fork: end of seventeenth century, see Deetz and Deetz, 9. Meat eaten with hands, see Richards, 124. On clamshell spoons, snails, osprey bones, etc., see Earle, *Customs and Fashions of Old New England*, 3–6, and *Home Life in Colonial Days*, 308–309. On infants "dying of baptism," see *Customs*, 2–3. **Page 47:** For more on Bell House neck, see Briggs, *Shipbuilding*, 283–286. See also Hagar, 148. Colonial accent, see Deetz and Deetz, 12. Duties of town constables, see Earle, *Home Life*, 362–363. **Page 48:** For Walter's earmark, see Litchfield's manuscript on Scituate records and "The Animal Book" manuscript collection, AAS. See also Earle on earmarks, generally *Home Life*, 400. **Page 50:** On William and Elizabeth Randall, see Bangs, vol. 1. For more on wolves, see Cronon, 132–134. On early responses to wolves (as cited by Cronon), see Shurtleff, "Massachusetts Records III," 10, 17; Wood, *Prospect*, 15–16. For the list of "don'ts," see town records as cited in Pratt, 110–111. **Page 51:** The scene at the end of this chapter is imagined. I take inspiration from the practice of posting engagement announcements, and the knowledge that Walter's son Israel and his second cousin Elizabeth Hatch were pregnant before wedlock. For descriptions of meeting houses and wolves, see Earle, *Home Life*, 366–367, 368–378.

Chapter Three

Page 58: The Borning Room was a name given to my room by Richard Warren Hatch and passed on to our family. It is a colloquial/family name for the room where babies were born, where bodies were "laid out," and, perhaps, where the sick were quarantined. At other times it was used as storage.

The First Israel 1667–1740

Page 64: Janeway's *A Token for Children* was originally published in England. On October 24, 1700, Cotton Mather published an American edition, *A Token for the Children of New-England*. Later still, Janeway published *A Token for Children; being an exact account of the conversion, holy and exemplary lives and joyful deaths, of several young children. To which is added, A token for the children of New England. Or, some examples of children in whom the fear of God was remarkably budding before they died; in several parts of New England* (Worcester, Mass., 1795). In reprint editions in the nineteenth century, an introduction was added for "parents, schoolmasters, and schoolmistresses—or any that are concerned in the education of children," indicating a shift in ideas of education from a personal relationship of the child with God to a civic duty of a community. **Page 65:** The courting tube is described in B. A. Bodkin, *Treasury of New England Folklore* (New York, 1947), 725. My speculation on Israel and Elizabeth's bundling comes from two sources: (1) Israel H. Hatch records that indicate they conceived a child before wedlock, and (2) Gladwin, *The Hatch Family and the Red House*, (speaking of Israel waiting to inherit the house), "they must have bundled for years waiting . . ." **Page 67:** For weather descriptions, see

NOTES

Shurtleff, *Thunder and Lightning; and deaths in Marshfield in 1658 and 1666.* The best, most comprehensive book I've found on the history and practice of bundling (a courting ritual that went out of practice in the late 1700s) remains Stiles. Walter died on May 24, 1699. L. Vernon Briggs in *History and Genealogy of the Briggs Family* (670) cites that Walter was "struck by lightning" but claims the date to be 1701. French, Israel H. Hatch, and Gladwin stick with 1699. For more information on lightning, see *The Old Farmer's Almanac Book of Weather Lore* by Edward F. Dolan (Dublin, N.H.: Yankee Books, 1988); *Acts of God: The Old Farmer's Almanac Unpredictable Guide to Weather and Natural Disasters*, by Benjamin A. Watson and the editors of the *Old Farmer's Almanac* (Francestown, N.H.: Random House, 1993); and also *New England's Disastrous Weather: Hurricanes, Tornados, Blizzards, Dark Days, Heat Waves, Cold Snaps, and the Human Stories Behind Them*, edited by Ben Watson (Camden, Maine: Yankee Books, 1990) **Pages 67–68:** Marriage customs: see Earle, *Customs and Fashions in Old New England*, 75. **Page 69:** For more information on the Puritan church, pews, deacon's box, etc., see Earle, *Home Life*, 368–378. **Page 70:** W. J. Litchfield, whose private handwritten records I followed around cemeteries in Scituate, also compiled records from approximately 1718 to 1738 of the Second Church of Scituate (which later became the Unitarian church in Norwell, Mass). Litchfield published these records in 1905 in the NEHGR in a series of volumes, apparently taking over the task begun by George C. Turner, who transcribed records beginning in 1645. The Hatch family and others in Two Mile for the most part were all members of the Second Church of Scituate until the mid-1700s. The Hatch family (under Israel Two) switched to the Second Church in Marshfield, which later was called the Chapel of Ease at North River. Reading the church records reveals much about the area and the tenor of the inhabitants' lives. Many children and infants who were on the verge of death were baptized "in their home(s)." The inscription usually bore the child's name and those of its parents and ended with a brief description of the child being "very sick" and "not expected to live long." Whether the children did live is never mentioned in the se volumes. There are many entries of baptisms—the parents apparently are in a hurry to save the child's soul. Over a period of forty-five years (1711–1757), the ministers of the Second Congregational Church of Scituate (now Norwell) baptized more than ninety infants in their parents' homes. Litchfield's church records also include lists of persons of color who were baptized in Two Mile and Scituate. For hazards of childbearing, see Demos, *A Little Commonwealth*, 66. *The New England Primer*, a predominantly Congregationalist-based text, is replaced in 1821 by Joseph Emerson's *The Evangelical Primer*, which includes three primers in one.

NOTES

Chapter Four

Page 73: "Harvest Home Tour of Old Two Mile, Marshfield, November 23, 1968," pamphlet courtesy of the Marshfield Historical Commission. Information on the historical society's efforts to save the Hatch Mill is collected in the holdings of the Marshfield Historical Commission. The poem "Old Two Mile" is reprinted with permission of the author, Cynthia Hagar Krusell. First published in *South Shore Mirror,* November 21, 1968. **Page 76:** For information on spontaneous combustion, I am indebted to firemen Warren Alexander and Michael Trovato of the Provincetown Fire Department (interview, February 2000); see also "Fire Safety Institute" at http://www.middlebury.org/firesafe. **Page 77:** In addition to the Provincetown firemen, I interviewed my mother, my father, Kate, and Patrick about their memories of the fire.

The Second Israel 1701–1767

Page 86: Will, courtesy of R. J. Messer. See also Gladwin, 39–40. **Page 88:** Information on early colonial paint recipes and red paint can be found in the American Antiquarian Society's reprint of the 1812 edition of Hezekiah Reynold's *Directions for House and Ship Painting.* **Pages 88–89:** For shipbuilding on North River, see *Shipbuilding* or Hagar, chapter 18, 144–160. For information on the Hatch Mills, see Decker and Hatch interview (mentioned earlier) and Krusell and Bates, 194–195. **Pages 90–92:** For more information on flax retting or linen making in colonial times, see Coons and Koob, 31–32. Earle, *Home Life in Colonial Days,* 166–185. The recipe for the bleach yard comes from Coons and Koob quoting John Wiley. "A Treatise on the Propagation of Sheep, the Manufacture of Wool and the Cultivations and Manufacture of Flax," cited in Koob and Coons. For Israel Two's disappearance, see Gladwin, 41–43.

Chapter Five

Page 100: Selection from *Ann Likes Red* by Dorothy Z. Seymour. Copyright © 1964 by Dorothy Z. Seymour. Copyright renewed 1992 by Dorothy Z. Seymour. Reprinted by permission of Purple House Press. **Page 102–103:** RWH letters used with permission, John C. Hatch. **Page 105:** Thanks to Jessica for reminding me about the Toy Dump. My best friend's name was changed to "Maryanne" to protect her privacy.

NOTES

The Third Israel 1730–1809

Page 108: Richards, 124. **Page 109:** The name of the 1768 comet was Stardust P5. Two Mile split from Scituate to Pembroke and Marshfield in 1788. For more information on Israel Three, see Gladwin, 44–45. For more information on banking houses for winter, see Nylander, 97–98. **Page 110:** For colonial flower gardens, see Earle, *Home Life in Colonial Days*, 421–451. For cleaning houses, see Nylander, 103–105. For more on the Hatches and the Revolutionary War, see Gladwin, *The Hatch Family and the Red House*, 42–43. Marshfield during the Revolutionary War: see Krusell, *Of Tea and Tories*, and Krusell and Bates, 14–15. A great primary source can be found in the James family letters, holdings of the Massachusetts Historical Society. **Page 112:** James family letters. The John Bailey clock purchased by Israel Three is now in the possession of RWH Jr. Excerpts from letters left at Red House. **Page 113:** Speculation on doctor's visits is based on receipts for blood-letting in documents left at Red House, embellished information found in Pratt, 182–183. Family history tells of a 1790 fire, but evidence of a chimney fire was found by Koopman; see her unpublished paper. **Page 114:** For a great description of the documents that Israel Three, his son Deacon Joel, and eventually RWH left behind at the Red House, see chapter 19 in Hagar, 161–166.

Chapter Six

Page 127: Horse skeletons were discovered by Frank Lachima on the ridge above Devil's Hollow on Gotham Hill, 1979. See Krusell and Bates, 18. For more information on the Rolling Thunder Review, see Deetz and Deetz. *The Times of Their Lives*, 26–27. For more on Plimoth Plantation and "Living History" see "Plimoth-on-Web," www.plimoth.org/Library/living.htm. **Page 132:** WATD is still operating! See its Web site: www.959watd.com.

Deacon Joel 1771–1849

Page 134: The Hand text is located in the holdings of the American Antiquarian Society. **Page 136:** Library books: see Hagar, 161–166, and Gladwin, 49–57. *The Duty and Advantage of Early Rising*, 1826, frontispiece; see also Hagar, 166–167. **Page 137:** Colloquial Two Mile speech is taken from George Leonard and is often quoted in various local history books, including Hagar; a copy of original manuscript available at the American Antiquarian Society. **Page 138:** William Shaw's sermons are available on microfiche, Early American imprints, second series, no.

NOTES

26725. Samuel Bartlett Parris, Diary, 1817, American Antiquarian Society manuscript collection. Information about the accident at the mill is from interview with Decker Hatch, 1968, Marshfield Historical Commission. **Pages 140–144:** Letters from collection left at Red House by RWH; see also Hagar, 161–164.

Chapter Seven

Page 145: Kim's boat was a Bud McIntosh (forty-foot schooner). **Page 150:** Hatch profile by Peggy Beals in *Marshfield Mariner*, June 1, 1983, 29–39. Kim and Richard: Formal interview with Kim Messer Villard. **Page 157:** "Marshfield Has Double-Header Thunderstorms," *Marshfield Mariner*, August 31, 1983, 18. "Linda" and "Frank" are not the real names of our current, most excellent neighbors. Some other names—of boyfriends, teachers, and students—have been changed too.

Israel H. 1837–1921

Page 162: The image of ice-fishing on the North River comes from family history, *Into the Wind* by RWH, and Lysander S. Richards's 1901 *History of Marshfield*. Richards also describes the 1843 attempt to cut a new mouth in the North River, *History of Marshfield*, 213–218. Deacon Joel's death: see Gladwin, *The Hatch Family and the Red House*, 51. **Page 163:** For RWH's quote about Israel, see Gladwin, *The Hatch Family and the Red House*, 60. **Pages 163–165:** Information in these pages is culled from Israel H. Hatch letters and journal left at Red House. See also Gladwin, *The Hatch Family and the Red House*, 58–62. **Page 166:** To get a sense of what Israel may have read, I looked at AAS's newspaper collections, including the *Pembroke Union*, January 1, 1856, and July 4, 1856. I also looked at old lithographed fair posters from 1854 to 1855 and 1884 (AAS archives). **Page 168–169:** List of Two Mile improvements, see Leonard.

Chapter Eight

Page 171: The *Spirit* is now an ocean classroom. Call 1-800-724-Sail. Parts of this chapter were originally published as the short story "The Fare," in the literary journal *Story*, fall 1999. **Page 178:** Mammogram courtesy of RJM and PWM. The phone number is not our real phone number, so don't call it. Thanks. **Page 180:** "Bring On the Boats," *Cape Codder*, September 10, 1985, 11. In this chapter I have also changed the

NOTES

physical description and characteristics of my boyfriend in order to protect him and his family.

Chapter Nine

Page 192: Found poem collage taken from various parts of the entry. *Dictionary of Anonymous and Pseudonymous English Literature*, 1921 (ed. Samuel Halkett and John Laing) (Edinburgh: Oliver and Boyd, 1926–1962. **Page 195:** For more information on Marshfield from 1950 to the present, see "Marshfield Then and Now—1950–1990." www.marshfield.net/History/pastpsnt.html. **Pages 206–207:** Roland Barthes quoted in Sanchez-Eppler, collected in Hendler and Chapman.

Israel H. 1837–1921

Page 210: I got this *Ladies World* excerpt from Loretta Britten and Paul Mathless, *Prelude to the Century 1870–1900*, Our American Century series (Alexandria, Va: Time-Life Books, 1970, 1999), 84. **Page 211:** I gathered information on typhoid from the *Merck Manual*, 17th edition/centennial edition, Mark H. Beers, M.D., and Robert Berkow, M.D., editors (Whitehouse Station, N.J.: Merck Research Laboratories, 1999), 1161–1163. **Page 214:** I originally wrote an entire chapter devoted to Thomas R. Oakman's brother, Otis B. Oakman, a simple farmer who happened to keep a journal while living in Two Mile for more than fifteen years. Many events Israel H. writes about in his 1857 journal are corroborated in Otis's. For anyone interested in pre–Civil War Two Mile I highly recommend this journal, located in holdings of the Massachusetts Historical Society. **Page 214:** For more information on Hall and Weatherby's general stores and Marshfield Hills, see Krusell and Bates, 190. **Pages 214–215:** Israel H. Hatch poem originally published in Hagar, 146–147, reprinted with permission from Marshfield Historical Commission. **Page 215:** Quote from Israel Hatch's notebooks is found at Mayflower Society holdings, donated by RWH in 1959. **Page 217–218:** Rebekah Oakman Woodman's poem written on the occasion of Israel and Carrie's fiftieth wedding anniversary is printed in a booklet by the family entitled "Golden Anniversary," courtesy of the Marshfield Historical Commission. **Page 218:** This newspaper article was found with the Hatch documents but with no source. I estimate it's from the *Marshfield Mail*, mid-June 1920. For information about Israel's death, see Gladwin, *The Hatch Family and the Red House*, 59.

NOTES

Harris 1866–1934

Pages 242–246: The information in these pages is from Gladwin, *The Hatch Family and the Red House*, 68–72, and an interview with Mary Henderson Hatch, 1999.

Chapter Eleven

Pages 248–251: Writings of RWH are printed with permission by John C. Hatch. **Pages 256–257:** Notes are used with permission, Jean Hall Muir (formerly Koopman). **Page 261:** Abbot Lowell Cummings's new book on the Fairbanks House, *The Fairbanks House: A History of the Oldest Timber-Frame Building in New England*, was published by NEHGS in 2003. Available through NewEnglandAncestors.org.

Richard Warren Hatch 1934–1965

Page 265: Jess found this newspaper photo in a copy of *In to the Wind* in the Ventress Library's rare book room, Marshfield. **Page 266:** Printed with permission, John C. Hatch. **Pages 267–268:** For more information about the 1898 storm and the wreck of the *Portland*, see Krusell and Bates, 50. My description of the flood is lifted from Otis Oakman's journals, where he is actually describing the flooding resulting from an earlier hurricane entry April 18, 1851, when he writes, "water 6 ft. deep over the meadows." The 1898 storm, however, was more severe. Also see old newspaper reports on the wreck of the *Portland* and other writings collected at Cape Cod Community College Library, W. B. Nickerson Memorial Reference Room. See Richards, 213–218, for information about the 1898 storm and the subsequent flooding of Two Mile. **Pages 268–274:** See Gladwin, *The Hatch Family and the Red House* and "Uncle Dick." **Page 272:** *Marshfield Mail*, July 19, 1940, souvenir edition. **Page 273:** William Gould Vinal, *The Legacy of Folklore, Scituate* (Scituate: South Shore Mirror, 1955).

Chapter Twelve

Page 276: These subject headings are not the actual titles on the outside of the card catalogues at the American Antiquarian Society but they're close. **Pages 284:** Manuscript on the Glades is located in the Adams Family papers at the Marshfield Historical Society holdings. **Page 291:** For more information on hoaxes and the N-ray, see http://www.spectrometer.org/path/nrays.html.

NOTES

The Land 1932–1935

Pages 295–300: This entire chapter is inspired by and uses text from a scrapbook compiled by Betty Hatch and donated to the Marshfield Historical Commission. Material printed courtesy of the Marshfield Historical Commission. Thanks to Betty Magoun Bates and Cynthia Hagar Krusell for the great support and enthusiasm, particularly in this part of the project.

Chapter Thirteen

Page 308: See Bradford, 70. **Page 311:** RWH poem reprinted with permission, John C. Hatch.

Richard Warren Hatch 1934–1965

Pages 322–327: RWH letters and unpublished writing reprinted with permission, John C. Hatch. See also Gladwin, *The Hatch Family and the Red House*, 75–77.

Chapter Fourteen

Page 329: For more on Mount Auburn, see http://www.mountauburn.org.

Epilogue

Page 344: "Discipline, Abandon" from *The World's Tallest Disaster* by Cate Marvin, published by Sarabande Books, Inc. © 2001 by Cate Marvin. Reprinted by permission of Sarabande Books and the author. **Page 347:** An interview with Uncle "Fed" Messer by H. E. C. Bryant published in the (*Charlotte, N.C.*) *Observer*, February 20, 1907; available on microfilm at the Gaston County Library, Gaston, N.C. Thanks to Brenda Messer for her genealogical help via Bernadyne Snook.

Inhabitants of the Red House

Pages 357–360: Hatch genealogy courtesy of Jean Hall Muir (formerly Koopman) in her unpublished paper, "The Red House/Walter Hatch Homestead," Boston University, Preservation Studies, 1997. Also, the private writings of Israel H. Hatch, and Priscilla Waldron Gladwin's *The Hatch Family and the Red House*, available at NEHGS.

Selected Bibliography

Bachelard, Gaston. *The Poetics of Space: The Classic Look at How We Experience Intimate Places*. Trans. Maria Jolas. Boston: Beacon Press, 1994.

Bangs, Jeremy Dupertuis. *The Seventeenth Century Town Records of Scituate, Massachusetts*, vols. I, II, and III. Boston: New England Historic Genealogical Society, 1997.

Barnes, David. "Sermons, 1782–1804." 2 vols. Worcester, Mass.: American Antiquarian Society.

———. *Thoughts on the love of Life and Fear of death; delivered in a sermon*. Boston: Samuel Hall, 1795.

Barthes, Roland. *Camera Lucida: Reflections on Photography*. Trans. Richard Howard. New York: Hill and Wang, 1981.

Beals, Peggy. "Marshfield Is the Favorite Subject of Richard Hatch," *Marshfield Mariner*, 1 June 1983: 29–30.

Benes, Peter. *Masks of Orthodoxy: Folk Gravestone Carving in Plymouth County, Massachusetts, 1689–1805*. Amherst: University of Massachusetts Press, 1977.

———. *New England Historical Archaeology*. Boston: Boston University, 1978.

———. *Wonders of the Invisible World: 1600–1900*. Boston: Boston University, 1995.

Blackwelder, Eva. "Blackwelder Papers/Journals, Photos, Postcards 1938–1939." Scituate, Mass.: Massachusetts Historical Society Archives.

Bodkin, B. A. *Treasury of New England Folklore*. New York: Crown, 1947.

Bradford, William. *Of Plymouth Plantation 1620–1647*. Ed. Samuel Eliot Morison. 1952. New York: Modern Library, 1981.

Briggs, L. Vernon. *History and Genealogy of the Briggs Family, 1245–1937*. Boston: priv. print., C. E. Goodspeed & Co., 1938.

————. *History of Shipbuilding on North River, Plymouth County, Massachusetts*. Boston: Coburn Brothers, 1889.

Brindenbaugh, Carl. "Yankee Use and Abuse of Forests in the Building of New England, 1620–1660." *Proceedings of the Massachusetts Historical Society* 89 (1977): 3–35.

"Bring On the Boats." *Cape Codder*, 10 September 1985: 11.

Brown, John Hull. *Early American Beverages*. Rutland, Mass.: Charles E. Tuttle, 1966.

Cadet de Vaux, A. *A new and cheap composition for printing: Memoir on a Method for painting with Milk*. New London, Conn.: James Springer, 1802.

Candee, Richard. "A Documentary History of Plymouth Colony Architecture 1620–1700." *Old Time New England* 59.3 and 4, 60.2 (1969): 59–111, 37–53.

————. "Housepaints in Colonial America: Their Materials, Manufacture and Application." *Color Engineering* 4.5 (1966): 26–29.

————. *Housepaints in Colonial America: Their Materials, Manufacture and Application*. New York: Chromatic Pub. Co., 1967.

————. "The Rediscovery of Milk-based House Paints and the Myth of 'Brickdust and Buttermilk' Paints." *Old Time New England* (winter 1968): 79–81.

Canfield, Catherine. *Multiple Exposures*. New York: Harper and Row, 1989.

————. "Uses and Abuses of Roentgen's Rays." *San Francisco Chronicle*, 23 July 1989, This World sec.: 9–12.

Cohen, Bruce. "Wellfleet Has the Spirit." *Cape Codder*, 24 September 1985: 4.

Coons, Martha, and Katherine Koob. *Linen-making in New England, 1640–1860: All Sorts of Good Sufficient Cloth*. North Andover, Mass.: Merrimack Valley Textile Museum, 1980.

Cott, Nancy. *The Bonds of Womanhood: Woman's Sphere in New England 1780–1835*. New Haven, Conn.: New York Press, 1977.

Cronon, William. *Changes in the Land: Indians, Colonists, and Ecology of New England*. New York: Hill and Wang, 2003.

Cummings, Abbott Lowell. *Architecture in Early New England*. Sturbridge, Mass.: Old Sturbridge Village, 1958.

————. *The Framed Houses of Massachusetts Bay, 1625–1725*. Cambridge, Mass.: Harvard University Press, 1979.

Curtiss, William. "Two Mile Land Grant and Records." Unpublished collection. Rockland, Mass.: Scituate Historical Society.

Deane, Samuel. *History of Scituate, Massachusetts, from its first settlement to 1831*. Boston: James Loring, 1831.

SELECTED BIBLIOGRAPHY

————. *A sermon delivered before the Scituate Auxiliary society for the Suppression of intemperance: at their first annual meeting 26 May, 1817.* Boston: John Eliot, 1817.

"Death of Famous Woman Radiographer." *San Francisco Chronicle*, 5 August 1905: 10.

Deetz, James. *In Small Things Forgotten: An Archeology of Early American Life.* New York: Anchor Books, 1977, 1996.

————. "Plymouth Colony Architecture: Archaeological Evidence from the Seventeenth Century," in *Architecture in Colonial Massachusetts.* Ed. Abbott Lowell Cummings. Boston: Colonial Society of Massachusetts, 1979.

Deetz, James, and Patricia Scott Deetz. *The Times of Their Lives: Life, Love, and Death in Plymouth Colony.* New York: W. H. Freeman, 2000.

Demos, Jonathan. *A Little Commonwealth: Family Life in Plymouth Colony.* Cambridge: Oxford University Press, 1970.

DeNoma, Jeanine. *Benign Hoaxes Wake-up Calls to the Gullible.* Oregonians for Rationality, 2001. http://www.o4r.org/pfv5n1/Hoaxes.htm.

Derby, Perley. *The Descendants of William Hatch of Scituate, Massachusetts.* Salem, Mass.: Observer Steam Book and Job Printing Rooms, 1874.

The Duty and Advantage of Early Rising, As It Is Favorable to Health, Business, and Devotion. London: Basil Stewart, 1826.

Earle, Alice Morse. *Child Life in Colonial Days.* New York: The Macmillan Co., 1899.

————. *Customs and Fashions in Old New England.* New York: Charles Scribner's Sons, 1893.

————. *Home Life in Colonial Days.* 1895. Williamstown, Mass.: Corner House Publishers, 1975.

————. *Two Centuries of Costume in America, 1620–1820.* 2 vols. 1903. New York: Dover Publications, 1970.

Emerson, Joseph. *The Evangelical Primer.* Boston: printed for Samuel T. Armstrong, by Crocker & Brewster, 1821.

Farber, Daniel, et al. *The Farber Gravestone Collection.* CD-ROM. Denver: Virtual Information Inc., 1997–98.

Fire Safety Institute. 1997. Middlebury Community Network. 31 December 2002. http://www.middlebury.org/firesafe.

Fischer, Sidney Geo. *Men, Women & Manners in Colonial Times.* New York and London: J. B. Lippincott Company, 1898.

French, Elizabeth. "Genealogical Research in England—Hatch," *New England Genealogical and Historical Register* 70.279:245–60. Boston: NEHGS, 1916.

SELECTED BIBLIOGRAPHY

French-Bartlett, Elizabeth. "Two Early Passenger Lists: Additions and Corrections," *New England Genealogical and Historical Register* 74:108. Boston: NEHGS, 1921.

Gladwin, Pricilla Waldron. *The Hatch Family and the Red House*. Marshfield, Mass.: Gladwin, 1981.

————. "Uncle Dick." 1989. Unpublished manuscript. Courtesy of Richard Warren Hatch Jr.

Hagar, Joseph C. *Marshfield 70-40 W: 42-5 N: The Autobiography of a Pilgrim Town*. Marshfield, Mass.: Marshfield Tercentenary Committee, 1940.

Hand, William. *House Surgeon and Physician*. Hartford, Conn.: Peter B. Gleason and Co., 1818.

"Harvest Home Tour of Old Two Mile, Marshfield, November 23, 1968." Unpublished brochure. Marshfield, Mass.: Marshfield Historical Commission.

Hatch Family Papers. Private collection of Ronald J. Messer.

Hatch, Richard Warren. Private letters to Ronald J. Messer. 1965–1982. Courtesy of John C. Hatch.

Hatch, Richard Warren. *All Aboard the Whale*. New York: Dodd and Mead, 1942.

————. *The Curious Lobster*. New York: Harcourt, 1937.

————. *The Curious Lobster's Island*. New York: Dodd and Mead, 1939.

————. *Delayed Action*. London and New York: Rich and Cowan, 1951.

————. *The Fugitive*. New York: Dodd and Mead, 1938.

————. *Into the Wind*. New York: The Macmillan Co., 1929.

————. *Leave the Salt Earth*. New York: Covici, Friede, 1933.

————. *Lift Up the Glory*. New York: Covici, Friede, 1934.

————. *This Bright Summer*. New York: Covici, Friede, 1933.

Hay, D. R. *The Interior Decorator, Being the laws of harmonious Color with Observations on the Practice of Housepainting*. Philadelphia: Henry Carey Baird, 1867.

Hingham Journal South Shore Advertiser. Hingham, Mass., 1857.

Holliday, Carl. *Woman's Life in Colonial Days*. Boston: Cornhill Pub. Co., 1922.

Hooker, Richard J. *Food and Drink in America: A History*. Indianapolis: Bobbs-Merrill Co., 1981.

Hooley, Kaye. "Thomas and William Hatch of Scituate, Plymouth Colony ca. 1634–1700." October 17, 1998; 2002. http://home.attbi.com/~kaeh/Histories/tho-wm.html.

House carpenter's book of prices and rules. Philadelphia: R. Folwell, 1801.

SELECTED BIBLIOGRAPHY

Howe, Henry F. *Salt Rivers of the Massachusetts Shore.* New York and Toronto: Rinehart & Company, 1951.

Hurd, D. Hamilton. *History of Plymouth County, Massachusetts.* Philadelphia: J. W. Lewis & Co., 1884.

Isham, Norman Morrison. *Early American Houses and Glossary of Colonial Terms.* 1928, 1939. New York: Da Capo Press, 1967.

Jacques, D. H. *Pocket Manual of Rural Architecture.* New York: Fowler and Wells Publishers, 1859.

James Family Letters. April–October 1777. Scituate, Mass.: Massachusetts Historical Society Archives.

James, Elisha. *An address delivered before the Scituate Auxiliary society for the Supression of intemperance: at their annual meeting, Jan 15, 1833.* Hingham, Mass.: J. Farmer, 1833.

Janeway, James. *A Token for Children; being an exact account of the conversion, holy and exemplary lives and joyful deaths, of several young children. To which is added, A token for the children of New England. Or, some examples of children in whom the fear of God was remarkably budding before they died; in several parts of New England.* Worcester, Mass.: James R. Hutchins, 1795.

Joyce, David Pane. *Scituate Genealogy, 1998, 2003.* http://aleph0.clarku. edu/~djoyce/gen/scituate.

Koopman, Jean Hall. "The Red House/Walter Hatch Homestead." Unpublished paper. Available in Two Mile folder at Scituate Historical Society. Boston University, Preservation Studies, 1997.

Krusell, Cynthia. "Old Two Mile." *South Shore Mirror,* 21 November 1968: 13.

Krusell, Cynthia Hagar. *Of Tea and Tories.* Marshfield, Mass.: Marshfield Bicentennial Committee, 1976.

Krusell, Cynthia Hagar, and Betty Magoun Bates. *Marshfield: A Town of Villages, 1640–1990.* Marshfield, Mass.: Historical Research Associates, 1990.

Langdon, William Chauncy. *Everyday Things in American Life 1607–1776.* New York and London: Charles Scribner's Sons, 1949.

Leland, Charles. *The Algonquin Legends of New England.* London: Sampson, Low, Marston, Searle and Rivington, 1884.

Leonard, George. *Marshfield Sixty Years Ago: a Lecture delivered in Marshfield April 23, 1872.* Boston: printed by J. Frank Farmer, 1872.

Lepore, Jill. *The Name of War: King Philip's War and the Origins of American Identity.* New York: Vintage Books, 1999.

Litchfield, W. J. "Second Church of Scituate, 1718–1738." *New England Historic and Genealogical Register* 59 (1905): 135.

"Live Music for Wellfleet's Spirit Weekend." *Cape Codder*, 13 September 1985: 14.

Ludwig, Allan I. *Graven Images: New England Stonecarving and Its Symbols, 1650–1815*. 1966. Hanover, N.H.: Wesleyan University Press pub. by University Press of New England, 1999.

Magadieu, John. "Restoration of Hatch Mill Nears Completion." *Marshfield Mariner*, 29 July 1987: 25–26.

"Marshfield Has Double-header Thunderstorms." *Marshfield Mariner*, 31 August 1983: 18.

Marshfield: Plymouth Colony. http://www.magnet.state.ma.us/dhcd/iprofile/171.htm.

"Marshfield Then and Now—1950–1990." In Marshfield Community History as Told through the Lives of Its People, Past & Present. Dallas: Curtis Media Corp, 1993. http://www.marshfield.net/History/pastpsnt.html.

Mather, Cotton. *A Token for the Children of New England*. 1700. In *A Token for Children*. Worcester, Mass.: James R. Hutchins, 1795.

"Memoirs for Israel H. Hatch, member." *New England Historic and Genealogical Register* 76: lxvi, lxvii.

Merritt, Joseph Foster. *Old Time Anecdotes of the North River and the South Shore*. Rockland, Mass.: Rockland Standard Publishing Company, 1928.

Morison, Samuel Eliot. *Maritime History of Massachusetts: 1783–1860*. Boston: Houghton Mifflin, 1941.

———. *The Puritan Pronaos: Studies in the Intellectual Life of New England in the Seventeenth Century*. New York: New York University Press, 1936.

———. *The Story of the "Old Colony" of New Plymouth, 1620–1692*. New York: Knopf, 1956.

Masury, John W. *How Shall we paint our House? A popular treatise on the art of Housepainting*. New York: D. Appleton & Co., 1868.

New England Primer, improved; or, an easy and pleasant guide to the art of reading. Boston: James Loring's Sabbath School Bookstore, 1820s.

Norton, Mary Beth. *Founding Mothers and Fathers: Gendered Power and the Forming of American Society*. New York: Knopf, 1996.

———. *Liberty's Daughters: The Revolutionary Experience of American Women, 1750–1800*. Ithaca, N.Y.: Cornell University Press, 1980.

Nylander, Jane C. *Our Own Snug Fireside: Images of the New England Home, 1760–1860*. New York: Knopf, 1994.

Oakman, Otis Briggs. "Diary, 1849–1862." Property of Massachusetts Historical Society.

SELECTED BIBLIOGRAPHY

Old Scituate. Chief Justice Cushing Chapter, Daughters of the American Revolution, 1921.

Palmquist, Peter. *Elizabeth Fleischmann: Pioneer X-ray Photographer, San Francisco, California, 1896–1905.* Berkeley: Judah L. Magnes Museum, 1990.

Parris, Samuel Bartlett. Diary, 1817. Worcester, Mass.: American Antiquarian Society.

Phillips, Morgan W., and Norman Weiss. "Some Notes on Paint Research and Reproduction." *Bulletin of the Association for Preservation Technology* 7 (1975): 14–19.

Plimoth Plantation: Living Breathing History. Plimoth Plantation. http// www.plimoth.org.

Pratt, Harvey Hunter. *The Early Planters of Scituate.* Scituate, Mass.: Scituate Historical Society, 1929. Reprinted, Rockland, Mass.: Heritage Books, 1998.

Reynolds, Hezekiah. *Directions for House and Ship Painting.* 1812. Worcester, Mass.: American Antiquarian Society, 1978.

Richards, Lysander S. *History of Marshfield.* Plymouth, Mass.: Memorial Press, 1901.

The Rise and Fall of N-rays. 1999. Mount Saint Mary's College and Seminary. http://www.spectrometer.org/path/nrays.html.

St. George, Robert Blair. *Conversing by Signs: Poetics of Implication in Colonial New England Culture.* Chapel Hill: University of North Carolina Press, 1998.

Sanchez-Eppler, Karen. "When We Clutch Hardest: On the Death of a Child and the Replication of an Image." In Glenn Hendler and Mary Chapman, eds., *Sentimental Men: Masculinity and the Politics of Affect in American Culture.* Berkeley: University of California Press, 1999.

Scolponeti, Joan. "The Hatch Mill Story." *Marshfield Mariner,* 24 March 1982: 25, 32.

———. "The Oldest Fair in Mass. About to Begin." *Marshfield Mariner,* 17 August 1983: 33.

Shannon, Fred Albert. *The Organization and Administration of the Union Army: 1861–1865.* Cleveland: A. H. Clark, 1928.

Shaw, William. *The Folly and danger of presuming on time to come: illustrated in a discourse delivered at Marshfield Nov. 24, 1811, at the funeral of six men, who on the preceding Wednesday evening were fatally shipwrecked.* Salem, Mass.: Printed by Thomas C. Cushing, 1812. (New Canaan: Early American imprints, second series, no. 26725, microfiche.)

Shurtleff, Nathaniel B. "List of Those Able to Bear Arms in the Colony of

SELECTED BIBLIOGRAPHY

New Plymouth, 1643." *New England Historic and Genealogical Register* 4 (1850): 255.

—. *Thunder and Lightning; and deaths in Marshfield in 1658 and 1666.* Boston: Priv. Print., 1850.

Simpson, J. A., and E.S.C. Weiner. *Oxford English Dictionary.* Oxford: Oxford University Press, 1989.

Smith, John. *Works, 1608–1631.* English Scholar's Library of Old and Modern Works 16. Ed. E. Arber. Birmingham, England: English Scholar's Library, 1884.

Stannard, David E. *The Puritan Way of Death.* New York: Oxford University Press, 1977.

Stiles, Henry Reed. *Bundling: Its Origin, Progress and Decline in America.* 1871. Cambridge, Mass.: Applewood Books, 1985.

Stratton, Eugene Aubrey. *Plymouth Colony: Its History and People 1620–1691.* Salt Lake City: Ancestry Publishing, 1986.

Tale of Camp Wysibo. Published pamphlet. Marshfield Historical Commission, 1933.

Taylor, Dale. *The Writer's Guide to Everyday Life in Colonial America from 1607–1783.* Cincinnati: Writer's Digest Books, 1997.

Taylor, Jane. *Physiology for Children.* New York: Saxton and Miles, 1846.

Thomas, Marcia Ahiah. *Memorials of Marshfield and guide book to its localities at Green Harbor.* Boston: Dutton and Wentworth, 1854.

Time-Life Books. *Prelude to the Century, 1870–1900.* Alexandria, Va.: Time-Life Books, 1999.

Towers, W., and T. J. Towers. *Every Man his own Painter: or a complete guide to painting and graining.* Utica, N.Y.: J. Colwell, 1830.

Trevert, Edward. *Something About X-rays for Everybody.* Lynn, Mass.: Bubier Publishing Co., 1896.

Turner, George C. "Little Journeys." *Marshfield Souvenir Edition,* 19 July 1940: 6+.

Ulrich, Laurel Thatcher. *Goodwives: Image and Reality in the Lives of Women in Northern New England, 1650–1750.* New York: Knopf, 1987.

The Union (Pembroke, Mass.). 1856: 1:1, 2:5, 7:4.

United States. House. Committee on Commerce. 1828. *Memorial of inhabitants of Scituate, Pembroke, Hancock, &c. in the state of Massachusetts, praying for the improvement of North river Channel; May 5, 1828.* Washington, D.C.: Gales & Seaton. 20th Cong., 1st sess. Doc. no. 266.

Vinal, William Gould. *The Legacy of Folklore, Scituate.* Scituate: South Shore Mirror, 1955.

SELECTED BIBLIOGRAPHY

Volz, John. "Paint Bibliography." *Newsletter of the Association for Preservation Technology*, February (1975): 1–25.

Watson, Ben, ed. *New England's Disastrous Weather: Hurricanes, Tornados, Blizzards, Dark Days, Heat Waves, Cold Snaps . . . and the Human Stories Behind Them*. Camden, Maine: Yankee Books, 1990.

Wemple, Jerry. "Union Street Reflects Town's Past." *Patriot Ledger*, 14 December 1990: R2–R13.

Winiarski, Douglas L. " 'Pale Blewish Lights' and a Dead Man's Groan: Tales of the Supernatural from Eighteenth-Century Plymouth, Massachusetts." *William and Mary Quarterly*. 3d ser. 55.4 (1998): 497–531.

Whitney, George. *Some Account of the early history and present state of the town of Quincy in the Commonwealth of Massachusetts*. [Boston] Christian Register Office: S. B. Manning, 1827.

Wiley, John. "A Treatise on the Propagation of Sheep, the Manufacture of Wool and the Cultivations and Manufacture of Flax." In Martha Coons and Katherine Koob, *All Sorts of Good Sufficient Cloth: Linen-making in New England, 1640–1860*, 31–32. North Andover, Mass.: Merrimack Valley Textile Museum, 1980.

Acknowledgments

I am so very grateful.

This project came into being because of three people: Mel Allen, my editor at *Yankee* Magazine, who commissioned the first article (published in 1997); my visionary agent, Amy Rennert; and finally, and most importantly, my editor Jane von Mehren, who loved and believed in the story, whose patience and guidance have carried me through all these years.

Thanks to William "Gray" Curtiss of the Scituate Historical Society, to the New England Historic Genealogical Society, to the Mayflower Society, and especially to the Marshfield Historical Commission.

Thanks to Jean Hall Muir, Betty Magoun Bates, and Cynthia Hagar Krusell for their wisdom and scholarship.

Thanks to the Ralph David Samuels Fellowship at Dartmouth, the American Antiquarian Society, and the Massachusetts Historical Society. Thanks to the amazing staff of both the AAS and the MHS.

Thanks to the McDowell Colony.

Thanks to all the students, staff, and colleagues at the University of North Carolina–Wilmington Creative Writing Department. Special thanks to Lorrie Smith and, most recently, David Gessner. Thanks to Dean Joanne Seiple for giving me my first year of teaching off, and for a summer research grant. Thanks to Deborah of the late night shift.

All these people gave me a place to stay, or helped me find one: Susan Wolf, Nancy Frazee, Bill Ibbs (and Red Fred, R.I.P.), the Millhouse, Mount Pisgah, Bekah and Jake Caldwell, Stacy Scott, Pat De Groot, Chuck and Julie Barbieri, Tsogyelgar, Todd Berliner and Dana Sachs, Naomi Swinton and Rick Mobbs, and Joy Morgan.

I also want to thank Jim Collins, Cleopatra Mathis, Jesse Lee Kercheval, Ronald Wallace, Renee Sentilles, Sarah Walker, Travis Drageset, Maria-Elena Cabellero-Robb, Karen Krahulik, Paul Laemmle, Mark Greer, and

ACKNOWLEDGMENTS

James Woodbridge. Thanks to Ann Noyes McGuire and the entire Noyes family, and Stan at the North Marshfield post office.

Thanks to Jessica Messer, Scout Messer, Kate Reilly, and Jason Frye who stepped in at the eleventh hour and were my robot arms.

Kim Villard is the world's best big sister and (along with Philippe) a crazy genius. You are my muse.

Thanks to Radiohead, Beck, the Magnetic Fields, bellafea, Vic Chestnutt, and the Flaming Lips.

Thanks to my friends who read all or parts or just inspired: Nick Flynn, Mick Fox, Suzanne Wise, Mark Wunderlich, Brad Land, Dana Sachs, Rebecca Lee, Wendy Brenner, Brian Lillie, Sebastian Matthews, Heather McEntire, Denise Gess, Thisbe Nissen, Ray MacDaniel, John D'Agata, Daniel Wallace, and Haven Kimmel. Bruce Burgett and Brenda Majercin were there at the beginning and always. Taylor Sisk read every word over fifty times and always with care—thanks for your belief. Thanks to Pip.

Three hundred and fifty years of continuously felt thanks to editor Jennifer Ehmann, who came late to the project but yet meant everything to it—the best companion/complement to Jane von Mehren I could have asked for. I am doubly blessed.

My love and joy to Allan Gurganus who arrived with wings. Thank you for everything and more.

To my teachers Charles Baxter, Alice Fulton, Syd Lea. To Lama A'dzom Rinpoche and Lama Traktung Rinpoche and the entire sangha—lifetimes and my heart, always.

To Richard Warren Hatch Jr. and family, John C. Hatch and family, Mary Hatch Henderson, thank you for this legacy, to be in some small way a part of your amazing family.

And to my own family—Kim and Philippe, Kerry and Bill, Kate and Craig, Patrick and Diane, Stacy, Suzy and Dave, Bekah and Jim, Jess and Ed, all ancestors, relatives, children—a giant love and so many thanks. To my parents—everything.

Illustration Credits

ILLUSTRATION CREDITS